You are respectfully invited
to return this book to
Gordon C. Fowler

# HISTORY OF THE FIRST LOCOMOTIVES IN AMERICA

## BY W. H. BROWN.

## NOTICES OF THE PRESS.—First Edition.

" There has been on our table for some weeks a book which we were reluctant to notice in the usual brief space we can generally allot to new publications. We have read this book with an interest and enjoyment that we are sure it will give to every intelligent mind. . . . We would gladly extend our rambles through this pleasant and instructive book, but our limits forbid. We have shown the reader some of its attractions, of which copious extracts from autograph letters are the chief, as they bring the reader into close contact with the individuality of a class of men which is rarely found in other works. The book is plainly but neatly bound, is published for the author by the Appletons, and is sure to meet with an extensive sale."—*Scientific American.*

" The fact that a large portion of our readers are directly interested in and connected with the railroad service, must be our apology for calling particular attention to a work which might ordinarily be supposed to be somewhat outside our province as telegraphic journalists. But the author of this work, 'The History of the First Locomotives in America,' has done a real service to the intelligent and thinking class of American railroad men, by the care and thoughtfulness which he has shown in the preparation of an authentic history of early locomotive engineering and practice in this country.

" We have not the space to enter into an extended review of this deeply interesting work, and can only mention some of its most prominent points. . . . The work is fully illustrated with engravings from authentic sources of all the early locomotives, all of which are curious and interesting in the highest degree. We can assure all our readers interested in railroad matters that they will find Mr. Brown's book well worth its cost."—*New York Telegrapher.*

" It is difficult for those who are familiar with the extent of the present railroad system in this country to realize that it was inaugurated by persons who are still living, that the present president of the American Society of Civil Engineers, Horatio Allen, Esq., ran the first locomotive which was ever put in operation in this country, and that the builder of the first experimental locomotive tried in America can be seen daily in the streets of New York. Nevertheless, such is the fact. The book whose title we have made the heading of this article, gives what has never been written before—an authentic history of early locomotive engineering on this side of the Atlantic. In this work are gathered and put in form some ' bits of history ' scattered over the country, some resting only in the memories of men still living, while others are to be found in documents scattered here and there, all of which were liable to loss or destruction had they not been preserved in some record like the book before us. This book will therefore be read by engineers, by railroad men, and indeed by every one, with great interest, especially as many of the facts contained in it have never before been clearly or authentically presented to the public.

" Scattered all through the book many very curious incidents and facts are recited, which seem as though they must have occurred in the lives of the Pharaohs instead of within the memory of men now living. We commend this work to the reading public."—*Railroad Gazette (New York).*

" An excellently written work, giving, as its title indicates, a complete history of the first efforts in the manufacture of locomotives in this country. Copiously and admirably illustrated, it contains information on this important subject, collected from every available source. We can cordially recommend this volume to all of our readers interested in the progress of the mechanical arts, as both instructive and entertaining. It is handsomely bound, both paper and press-work being fully up to the standard of the well-known publishing house by which it is issued."—*Manufacturer and Builder.*

"A very interesting book has been prepared by Mr. W. H. Brown, giving a history, from reliable sources of information, of the first locomotives used and constructed in this country.

"The author has for several years been engaged in collecting the materials for this work ; and the result is a volume of some 250 pages, containing a great number of facts, incidents, and reminiscences, connected with the early attempts to apply steam as a motive-power for land locomotion.

"Hardly any one who has a realizing sense of the magnitude of the railway system as it exists to-day in our own country, and who also takes into account the comparative brief period which has elapsed since its beginning, can fail to be interested in the contents of Mr. Brown's book. Not only is it especially attractive to engineers and railroad men generally, but it is no less adapted to popular appreciation, describing as it does the first rude and feeble attempts to bridle and break into harness the power which had for centuries lain dormant, or only now and then giving a hint of its capacities by lifting the lid of a tea-kettle. It is no less instructive than amusing to go back to these pioneer attempts, as they are graphically described and illustrated in this volume, and trace the progress which has been made in half an ordinary lifetime.

"The author of this deeply-interesting book is deserving of the thanks of the railway public for the service he has rendered in collecting and preserving, in a permanent form, the facts and materials it contains, and which would otherwise have been irrecoverably lost."—*The National Car-Builder.*

"This volume belongs to a class which has too few representatives in our technical literature—those which gather up from threatened oblivion the records of what was done in the infancy of American industrial and engineering enterprise, and provide in permanent form the material from which the historian in after-times will cull his choicest data.

"The writer of the volume before us has traced in a most satisfactory manner the history of the locomotive, as concerns its introduction and use in this country, and his book should find a place on the library-shelves of all who take an interest either in the practical workings and management of railroads, or of those who delight in studying the development of the industrial agencies to which all lands, and our own in particular, owe so much of their progress in all that pertains to civilized life.

"So much for the topic indicated on the title-page of the book before us, and to which we do but inadequate justice in this brief review. The writer has sought to verify his statements by original documents, which are frequently quoted entire, and help to make the book full of quaint, out-of-the-way, and interesting information. Read it, everybody ; it will richly repay the cost."—*American Artisan.*

"Few subjects of such recent origin have been more involved in uncertainty than the inauguration of steam transportation by locomotives in this country. Millions of persons are now living whose lives antedate the time that the first locomotive was run in America ; but the advent of this great power of modern times was so gently effected, that hardly any record was made of the event ; and, though the author of the present volume has finally settled the question, he was only able to do so after the most searching investigation. This work contains a very comprehensive account of the various inventions in locomotives, cars, and railroads, which the desire for rapid transit first brought into existence, and the principal incidents connected with the different first trial-trips. One picture, a *silhouette*, of the first locomotive and train of cars in the State of New York, from Albany to Schenectady, sketched at the very time by the author of this work, has already been widely circulated. The book will prove deeply interesting to every class, and should be found in every library."—*New York Times.*

"This is a valuable and deeply-interesting work for the scientific railroad man, and the reading public generally. It is a graphic embodiment of the early history and incidents of the locomotive, and has the merit of being a profound treatise, yet not prosy, sparkling with readable matter for the most superficial. It should be found in the library or bookcase of every house. Mr. W. H. Brown is the author."—*Harrisburg Evening Mercury.*

# THE HISTORY

OF THE

# FIRST LOCOMOTIVES IN AMERICA.

*FROM ORIGINAL DOCUMENTS, AND THE TESTIMONY
OF LIVING WITNESSES.*

BY

WILLIAM H. BROWN.

*REVISED EDITION.*

THE ASTRAGAL PRESS
Mendham, New Jersey 07945-0239

Entered according to Act of Congress,
in the year 1871,
By RUFUS A. HORRELL,
In the Office of the Librarian of Congress,
at Washington.


Copyright 2003 by the Astragal Press

This is a reprint of the original edition
published by D. Appleton and Company
in New York City in 1874.

Library of Congress Control Number 2003101675
International Standard Book Number 1-931626-12-x


*Published by*
THE ASTRAGAL PRESS
5 Cold Hill Road
PO Box 239
Mendham, New Jersey 07945-0239


Cover design by Donald Kahn
*Printed in the United States of America*

# DEDICATION.

To PETER COOPER, ESQ., NEW YORK—

MY DEAR SIR: It is my belief that your early and most successful experiments upon the Baltimore and Ohio Railroad in 1829–1830 proved that the locomotive could be used as a power upon the short-curved railroads in this country. The practicability of this was doubted at the time mentioned even by the most eminent engineers in Europe. I cannot, therefore, refrain from bestowing upon you the praise of having given the first impulse to the adoption of the locomotive in the United States, a fact which justly entitles you to the honor of being regarded as the "Father of the Locomotive System in America."

This, sir, is not the only benefit your energy, your wealth, and your liberality, have conferred upon your countrymen. The expenditure in acts of benevolence of large sums from your private fortune, acquired by your own industry and frugality, is an example to the youths of America; and in your "Institute" you will (after a long life of usefulness) leave an imperishable monument for future generations to dwell upon and admire.

Will you permit me now, my dear sir, as a slight tribute to the respect and veneration I have ever felt for your many good deeds to your countrymen, to dedicate to you this humble effort on my part to record the history of the early locomotives in America, in which you took such an active and prominent part—a system which has resulted eventually in the development of the vast resources of our country, and given employment to many thousands of the mechanical and industrial classes of this community? With the hope, sir, that my wish upon this subject may meet with your cordial approbation, and that my work may be favorably received and prove instructive and interesting to the public,

I remain, dear sir,

Respectfully yours,

WILLIAM H. BROWN.

# PREFACE.

THE author of this work, being familiar with railroads from their first construction, has, at much labor and expense, collected all the important facts in relation to their commencement and to the development of the locomotive-machine in this country. These facts have been obtained from the living witnesses who were the actors in those early events, and are presented in their own language in these pages. While making no pretensions to literary merit, he claims to have embodied in this volume all the facts of the early history of locomotives, in such a complete form as to satisfy the most skeptical. He therefore presents his work to the public with full confidence that his efforts to rescue from oblivion the names of some of the most distinguished pioneers in promoting the industrial progress of this nation will be kindly appreciated.

NEW YORK, *August*, 1873.

# CONTENTS.

CHAP.

I.—DEDICATION:           PAGE
Misrepresentations—Errors—John B. Jervis, Esq.—Horatio Allen,
Esq.—B. H. Latrobe, Esq.—David Matthew, . . . . 9

II.—EARLY RAILROADS:
The Egyptians—The Romans—Railroads in Scotland and England—First Iron Rails cast, . . . . . . 19

III.—FIRST HEAD OF STEAM:
Hero—Champollion—Cardan—Solomon de Cause—Marquis of
Worcester—First Steam-Engine—Pepin, . . . . 24

IV.—FIRST STEAMBOATS:
Savary—Blasco de Garay—Genevois—Count d'Auxiron—Perrier
—Marquis de Jouffroy—Rumsey—Fitch—Miller—John Stevens
—Stanhope—Livingston—Fulton—First Ocean-Steamer, . . 29

V.—FIRST STEAM-CARRIAGE:
Cugnot—Symington—Murdoch—Thomas Allen—Oliver Evans—
First Proposition for Railroad—Mr. Thomas's Proposal—Dr.
Anderson's, . . . . . . . . . . 34

VI.—TREVITHICK'S ENGINE:
Blankensop—Chapman—Brunton's Engine—Blackett, . . 38

VII.—GEORGE STEPHENSON:
Early Education—Experiments at the Mines, . . . . 45

VIII.—STEPHENSON'S ENGINE:
Blucher—Second Locomotive—Railways for General Use—Mr.
Thomas—Mr. Gray, . . . . . . . . 49

IX.—FIRST TRAINS:
Hatton Colliery Road—Locomotive used—Stockton and Darlington Railroad, 1825—Stephenson's Works—The Active—Experiments—First Passenger-Coach—Manner of running Passenger-
Coaches, . . . . . . . . . . . 54

X.—FIRST DELIBERATIONS ON RAILROADS:
Comparisons between Locomotive and Stationary Engines—Committee appointed—Report—Prize offered for the Best Locomotive, 60

CHAP.

XI.—COMPETITION FOR THE PRIZE:                                    PAGE
        Engines entered—Trials—The "Rocket"—"Novelty"—"Sans-
        pareil,"        .       .       .       .       .       .       .       .       .       65

XII.—RAILROADS IN AMERICA:
        First Railroad—Second Railroad—De Witt Clinton and the
        Canal—Colonel Stevens's Proposition—Chancellor Livingston's
        Opinion—Dearborn's Proposal,      .       .       .       .       .       .       70

XIII.—FIRST ENGLISH LOCOMOTIVE BROUGHT TO AMERICA:
        David Matthew's First Letter—Certificates, etc.—John B. Jer-
        vis's Letters—Horatio Allen's Letters to John B. Jervis, fixing
        Date of Arrival of the "Stourbridge Lion,"      .       .       .       .       74

XIV.—DATE OF ITS RUNNING:
        President Dickson's Letter—Superintendent Young's Letter—
        Miss Blackman's Letter—Extract from the Dundaff Republican, .   79

XV.—LANDING IN AMERICA:
        Its Performances in New York—Arrival at Honesdale—Hon.
        John Torry's Description—Mr. Matthew's Description—A Sketch
        of the English Locomotive,      .       .       .       .       .       .       83

XVI.—MORE FACTS OF THE "STOURBRIDGE LION:"
        First Stephenson Engine—Mr. Allen's Description—What be-
        came of the "Stourbridge Lion"—Mr. Allen's Account of his First
        Ride—The Last of the "Lion,"      .       .       .       .       .       .       88

XVII.—FIRST MEETING OF THE BALTIMORE AND OHIO RAIL-
        ROAD CO.:
        Road commenced—Charles Carroll, of Carrollton—Road com-
        pleted—How built—Mr. Swann's Remarks,      .       .       .       .       93

XVIII.—FIRST BRIGADE OF CARS:
        First Experiment—Charles Carroll—Railroad Notice, etc.—Travel-
        ling Memoranda—Early Passenger-Cars,      .       .       .       .       97

XIX.—ROSS WINANS'S IMPROVEMENTS:
        Passenger-Cars—First Trains—First Car with Centre Gangway—
        Horatio Allen on Springs,      .       .       .       .       .       .       103

XX.—EXPERIMENTAL LOCOMOTIVES:
        Peter Cooper's Locomotive—When and where built—Mr.
        Cooper's Letter—Why it was built—Mr. Latrobe's Letter—De-
        scription of the Experiment,      .       .       .       .       .       .       108

XXI.—PETER COOPER'S LOCOMOTIVE:
        Mr. Latrobe's Letter—Description of the Machine—Mr. Ross
        Winans's Description of the Experiment,      .       .       .       .       113

XXII.—THE TOM THUMB LOCOMOTIVE:
        First Experimental Trip—Race with Horse-Car—Ross Winans's
        Comparisons,      .       .       .       .       .       .       .       .       116

XXIII.—SKETCH OF HORSE-LOCOMOTIVE:
        Sketch of the "Meteor" or Sailing-Car—Contest for Right of
        Way—Railroad and Canal Company,      .       .       .       .       .       123

CHAP.

XXIV.—PETER COOPER:                                                    PAGE

Early History—Education and Beginning of Life—Subsequent
Career—Founding the Institute—Last Act of Liberality, .    . 127

XXV.—PRIZE FOR THE BEST LOCOMOTIVE:

Conditions—Phineas Davis's York Engine,      .    .    .    . 131

XXVI.—FIRST AMERICAN LOCOMOTIVE:

Commencement—South Carolina Railroad—Horatio Allen's Report—A Prize offered for best Horse-power Locomotive—The
Sailing - Car Experiment — Extract from Charleston Courier—
First Locomotive ordered to be built in America — What it
was to perform,      .    .    .    .    .    .    .    .    . 135

XXVII.—FURTHER TRIALS:

Letter from Mr. Matthew—Letter from Prof. Dickson—West
Point Order - book — Extract from Charleston Courier — Mr.
Petsch—Accident to Wheels—"Jockey of York"—Excursion-
Trip,    .    .    .    .    .    .    .    .    .    .    . 140

XXVIII.—EXPLOSION OF "BEST FRIEND:"

When repaired — The Cause explained—Letter from Mr. Darrell—Mr. J. M. Eason's Letter, describing the Locomotive "Native," and its First Trial-Trip,    .    .    .    .    .    . 147

XXIX.—SECOND AMERICAN LOCOMOTIVE:

Excursion of "West Point"—Extract from the Courier, 1831—
Letter from Mr. Darrell—President Tupper's Report,    .    . 153

XXX.—FIRST LOCOMOTIVE-ENGINEERS:

Necrology of Mr. Darrell—His Death—Henry E. Raworth and
his old Negro Foreman, Adam Perry,      .    .    .    .    . 158

XXXI.—FIRST RAILROAD FOR LOCOMOTIVES:

First Eight-wheeled Locomotive,      .    .    .    .    .    . 162

XXXII.—CLAIMS TO FIRST LOCOMOTIVES:

Extract from Philadelphia Ledger—Lithograph by Sage & Son—
Lithograph by Antique Publishing Company of Boston, .    . 165

XXXIII.—FIRST LOCOMOTIVE IN NEW YORK:

Description of the Ride—Sketch of the Train—Letter from Mr.
Matthew—Excursion,      .    .    .    .    .    .    .    . 170

XXXIV.—FURTHER EVIDENCES:

Letter from Mr. Matthew—Freight-bill of "John Bull"—Extracts from the Albany Argus—Last of "John Bull"—Second
Excursion to Schenectady,      .    .    .    .    .    .    . 176

XXXV.—THE JUDGE'S FIRST RIDE:

The Author's Art—Letter from Judge Gillis—Author receives
the Lithograph of the "De Witt Clinton"—Letter from J. L.
Howard & Co.,    .    .    .    .    .    .    .    .    .    . 182

XXXVI.—LETTERS FROM OFFICIALS:

First Letter from Erastus Corning—Letter from John T. Clark—
Letter from John B. Jervis,    .    .    .    .    .    .    . 188

X                          CONTENTS.

CHAP.

XXXVII.—ADDITIONAL LETTERS :                                   PAGE
    Second Letter from Mr. Corning—Letter from Thurlow Weed—
    Letter from John B. Jervis—Letter from Mr. Kemble,   .   . 192

XXXVIII.—THE AUTHOR'S ART :
    Extract from the Natchez Courier—Extract from the Albany
    Argus—Extract from the Albany Evening Journal—Extract
    from the St. Louis Bulletin—Letter from Henry A. Wise—Let-
    ter from Martin Van Buren—Letter from John C. Calhoun—
    Letter from Daniel Webster—Letter from Henry Clay,   .   . 196

XXXIX.—RECAPITULATION :
    Phineas Davis's Machine—William Kemble's Letter,   .   . 201

XL.—FIRST TRUCK-LOCOMOTIVE :
    Mr. Matthew's Letter—Mr. Jervis's Letter—The Great Changes
    of the Past—Mr: Latrobe's Remarks—Remarks of Mr. Briggs,
    of Cleveland—Excursion to Europe and the East—From the
    Knickerbocker, 1837—Remarks of Thomas H. Benton,   .   . 207

XLI.—LOCOMOTIVE WORKS :
    Schenectady Shops,   .   .   .   .   .   .   .   . 223

XLII.—CAR-WORKS :
    Gilbert Bush & Co.'s Shops, Troy, New York,   .   .   . 230

XLIII.—STREET-CAR WORKS :
    John Stephenson & Co., 47 Twenty-seventh Street, New York,   236

XLIV.—GRAND CENTRAL DEPOT, NEW YORK,   .   .   . 243

# THE FIRST LOCOMOTIVES IN AMERICA.

## CHAPTER I.

### INTRODUCTION.

THERE is, perhaps, at the present day, no subject upon which the community at large is so poorly informed as the history of the first locomotives in America—in what year they were built, where they were constructed, and upon what railroad they were first introduced and employed in actual service.

Especially less informed upon this subject are the very men who, above all others, should be thoroughly conversant with all the particulars in the history of that wonderful machine—the actual means which now contribute so much toward the maintenance and employment of a large class of the industrial portion of our community; we mean the officers, engineers, firemen, machinists, mechanics, laborers, and, in short, all employés connected with railroad service. This melancholy lack of information can only be attributed to a want of an opportunity to obtain the requisite facts from some reliable source, where they are in such a form as would bring them within the reach of the masses of the community. True it is, volumes have been published, giving accurate accounts of the early experiments and subsequent improvements in self-propelling machines, or locomotives, in England; but these works are too rare, voluminous, and expensive, to be in general circulation, and entirely beyond the reach of a large class who are interested in the subject; and even then, they bring the history down only to a period anterior to the date of railroad enterprise in this country; while all the information upon the subject since that time (a period of a little over twoscore years in duration) seems to be wrapped in impenetrable mystery. To obviate, therefore, this difficulty for the future, and to give to the public all the information upon the subject from the most reliable sources, and also to place it in such a form as to bring it within the reach of every one, are the objects of the author of the present work, now offered to the public.

Another reason which influences the author in publishing his present work, arises from the fact that, within the short period of ten or fifteen years, and especially within the last few years, under a variety of forms, he has seen and read in our public journals nearly as many different accounts of the early locomotives in America, as the number of years which have elapsed since their first introduction, all of them purporting to be "true histories of the first engine ever built and run in America." But not one of these accounts, claiming priority for its different engines and roads, produces the slightest evidence to sustain their claim of being the pioneers in this great mechanical achievement, which within the last half-century has revolutionized the trade and commerce of the civilized world. One claim to the credit of having introduced the first American locomotive, we saw in an article published in the Philadelphia *Public Ledger*, of the 18th January, 1869. Another claim to the same honor, we saw in an article in the columns of the *Boston Advertiser*, January 28, 1869. These articles we will copy in full in our work, when we come in its pages to the proper place to describe early locomotives in America, when they were built, where constructed, and upon what railroad put into practical service.

Again, some seven or eight years ago, a lithograph picture representing a locomotive, and two cars filled with passengers, was issued from the lithographic establishment of Messrs. Sage & Sons, of Buffalo, and copyrighted by Thomas Jarmy. This lithograph (a copy of which is now before the author) purports to have been copied from an original picture in the possession of the Connecticut Historical Society. It has been widely circulated throughout the country, and is said to represent "the first locomotive train in America." The engine is said to be the "John Bull, an English machine; and the engineer, who is represented at his post upon the platform of the engine," John Hampson, an Englishman, etc.

Again, in 1870, this same original picture in the rooms of the Connecticut Historical Society was lithographed by a concern in Boston, styled the "Antique Publishing Company of Boston." In this lithograph the locomotive and train are represented precisely like the one executed in Buffalo, and are here for the second time said to be a sketch of the first locomotive and train in America, and the engine named the "John Bull," an English engine, and the engineer "John Hampson."

The original picture, now in the Connecticut Historical Society, was executed by the author of this work, and presented to the Society forty years ago.

The full particulars respecting this original picture will be given hereafter; and the author, for the present, will only state that the original of the picture was not the English locomotive "John Bull," nor was the engineer on the occasion, John Hampson, an Englishman; but an American-built locomotive and an American engineer.

Such blunders and misstatements as we have just alluded to are calculated to mislead the public, and involve the early history of the locomotive in America in a cloud of obscurity; and the author unhesitatingly believes that, if the true history of this now indispensable machine is left unestablished for another half-century, we may find the great Union and Central Pacific Railroads credited by some (without a shadow of evidence, like others) with the introduction of the first locomotive upon a railroad in America, and with as much chance of establishing that claim as they no doubt have to sustain the credit of being the first in uniting the East with the far Western boundaries of our great continent by their interminable belt of railroad-iron, annihilating distance, just as the lightning-telegraph annihilates time.

The deep and intense interest always manifested, by railroad men in particular, when on frequent occasions the author has explained his knowledge of the facts connected with the early history of the locomotive in America, and the reliable sources from which his information was derived, often induced him to determine that, when a favorable opportunity presented itself, he would write out and publish a work like the present, but he has hitherto been prevented from carrying out his desire, from his isolated position, far away from the facilities requisite for such a task.

These difficulties are now removed, and, the opportunity being presented, his long-cherished determination will no further be delayed. In compiling this history, all the authorities upon which his information is based will be set forth in such a manner that it must put at rest forever the oft-disputed question, "When and where was the first locomotive built and run in America, in the actual service of a company?"

These are questions oftentimes heard, when groups of engineers and other railroad-men are congregated together and discoursing upon their universal topic, the merits and achievements of their favorite machines; and how often is there one in the group who will pretend to answer the questions, and, if answered at all, how often are they answered correctly? There is scarcely a State in the Union (especially where railroads existed at an early day) which has not enjoyed the credit on these occasions of being the pioneer in the introduction of this most wonderful auxiliary to successful railroad transportation. Sometimes we have heard the credit awarded to the State of New York, sometimes to Pennsylvania, and as a matter of course oftentimes to the States of Massachusetts and Connecticut. Some, who profess to be well posted upon this point, claim the honor for the old Portage Railroad of Pennsylvania; while others, equally certain and conversant upon the subject, in their opinion, give the credit to the Germantown and Norristown Railroad; and so on, through the catalogue of railroads (not very voluminous at that early day): but none of these are correct. True it is, that several companies, even at an early day, had locomotives constructed for their use, and put them in practical service upon their several roads, those very roads just alluded to, but not, however, until the experi-

2

ment had been tried and successfully inaugurated and reduced to a fixed fact in another quarter. Therefore, the honor of being the pioneer in having the first American locomotive constructed and put in actual service in the United States belongs elsewhere, as we are prepared to substantiate as we progress in our present work. If, however, in doing this, we should be compelled to descend too much into minutiæ, so as to bring upon us the charge of egotism from our readers, we will claim their forbearance in our anxiety to leave no stone unturned, to withhold no facts, and to bring to our aid every item, however trifling it may appear, to establish the truth. In recording the facts contained in this history, therefore, the author will accompany each position he may assume with all the evidence upon which his information is based. These authorities are from the statements of living witnesses, who are at this day (though far advanced in years) endowed with all the vigor of mind which characterized them in the early period of their lives, and are now enjoying an enviable share of the confidence and esteem of their fellow-citizens.

The names of John B. Jervis, Esq., Horatio Allen, Esq., Benjamin H. Latrobe, Esq., Ross Winans, Esq., and Peter Cooper, Esq., are well known and familiar to our railroad communities, as identified in the early days with railroad enterprise in America. To those of our readers, however, who may not be acquainted with the character and reputation of these accomplished engineers and gentlemen, we will briefly state that John B. Jervis, Esq., for many years a resident of Rome, in the State of New York, is one of the oldest (being now nearly seventy-five years of age) and most skilful engineers of the period of which we write. He was the chief engineer of the railroad that imported from England the first locomotive which turned a driving-wheel upon the American Continent. He has been engaged upon some of the most important works of improvement in our country, and his reputation as an accomplished engineer is widely known, not only in this country, but in Europe. Among the most important public works upon which Mr. Jervis was employed as chief engineer, we enumerate the Delaware and Hudson Canal and Railroad; the Mohawk and Hudson Railroad; the Saratoga and Schenectady Railroad; the Chenango Canal of New York; the Eastern Division of the Erie-Canal enlargement; the Croton Aqueduct; the Hudson River Railroad; the Michigan Southern and Northern Indiana Railroad; and the Pittsburg and Chicago Railroad. He was president of the Chicago and Rock Island Railroad, and consulting engineer of the Boston Water-works, and other important improvements. Mr. Jervis was also the inventor of the plan of having the truck under the front part of the locomotive, to assist in sustaining the weight of the boiler, and in giving direction to the machine in running upon curves, a plan now universally adopted, and found to be indispensably necessary in engines of eight or more wheels, and especially upon the short-curved railroads of America. Mr. Jervis is still living at Rome, New York, in the full possession of his vigor of mind, and we trust he may live for many years, to enjoy the reputation he has so richly earned by his valuable services to the railroad enterprise of America.

Horatio Allen, Esq., is another eminent engineer of America, and his evidence contributes much valuable information to our history, which our readers will see from his various communications to the author.

Mr. Allen graduated at Columbia College, in the State of New York, in 1823, commenced his professional life in 1824, as civil engineer with Benjamin Wright on the Chesapeake and Delaware Canal.   In 1825 he was engaged on the Delaware and Hudson Canal as resident engineer under John B. Jervis, Esq., chief engineer, in 1827 resigned his connection with the Delaware and Hudson Canal, in order to visit England in search of professional information on railroad matters, that new era in intercommunication and transportation being then in process of development.   During his visit to England, he was requested to take charge of the contract for the iron for the Delaware and Hudson Canal Company's coal-road, and also for three locomotives, being the first ever ordered and brought to this country.   On his return, in 1829, Mr. Allen had charge of the fitting up and putting in operation the first locomotive, " the Stourbridge Lion," ever put on a railroad in this country, and alone he stood upon its platform on the first experimental trip, and his hand opened the throttle-valve upon the engine that turned the first driving-wheel in America.

In 1829 Mr. Allen was engaged as chief engineer on the South Carolina Railroad, running from Charleston to Augusta, Georgia, 136 miles.   On this road was put the first one hundred miles of iron in one continuous line in the world.   Another fact in connection with this road, and to the credit of Mr. Allen, is of interest: the road was built within the estimate of its cost.

In 1834 Mr. Allen went abroad, and was in Egypt nearly three years.   On returning, in 1837, he was engaged as principal assistant engineer on the Croton Aqueduct, under John B. Jervis, the chief engineer.   On completion of the aqueduct, Mr. Allen was one of the

Croton Aqueduct commissioners, and its engineer for the introduction and distribution of the water. In 1842 Mr. Allen became one of the proprietors of the Novelty Iron Works in New York. In this establishment he continued as one of its managers and president until 1870, when the works were closed. Prior to Mr. Allen's connection with the Novelty Works, he was president of the New York and Erie Railroad, and was consulting engineer of the road at the period of its opening in 1845. In 1870 Mr. Allen became consulting engineer of the East River Bridge, now in course of construction, and which when completed will be looked upon as a wonder of the age. Of this great work Washington A. Roebling, Esq., is chief engineer.

To Benjamin H. Latrobe, Esq., we are also largely indebted for the early history of the locomotive enterprise upon the Baltimore and Ohio Railroad; for the drawing and full description of the sailing-car, invented by Mr. Thomas; and for the drawing of the little experimental machine, built to demonstrate the principle of the practicability of locomotives upon short curves, and the subsequent results from them.

Mr. Latrobe has constantly been in active employment upon some important public work in its engineer department. Among which we name the Baltimore and Ohio Railroad. In the service of this company he entered in 1830 as a member of the corps of engineers. In 1842 he was appointed chief engineer, and continued in that position until 1857. Since that time he has rendered the road much valuable assistance as consulting engineer. As chief engineer, Mr. Latrobe located and built the railroad from Baltimore to Havre de Grace, as a part of the Philadelphia, Wilmington and Baltimore Railroad, in 1835–'37, and the Northwestern

Virginia Railroad from Grafton to Parkersburg (103 miles), from 1853–'57. He has been consulting engineer on several or on special occasions to a number of railway works; the most important were: the Hoosac Tunnel, Massachusetts; the Philadelphia, Wilmington and Baltimore Railroad (which office he now holds); the North Missouri Railroad; the Blue Ridge Railroad, in South Carolina; the East River Bridge; the Portland and Ogdensburg Railroad; the Hillsborough and Parkersburg Railroad; and the Columbus and Hocking Valley Railroad.

Mr. Latrobe is the chief engineer of the Jones Falls Improvement in the city of Baltimore; and is now completing the Pittsburg and Connellsville Railroad, from Pittsburg to Cumberland.

We will also quote freely from the letters of Mr. David Matthew to the author in 1859, and we will give in our work several certificates in reference to Mr. Matthew's character and ability as an engineer, and a reliable man. Mr. Matthew superintended the men fitting up the first English locomotive imported into this country, and he also had charge of the workmen fitting up the first, second, and third locomotives built in America—the last of which, after placing it upon the road, he continued to run as the regular engineer for a long time; and his testimony is entitled to all credit.

To Julius D. Petsch, Esq., who was for many years the chief of the mechanical department upon the railroad upon which the first American-built locomotive for actual service was run, we are indebted for many valuable particulars concerning that event.

To several other prominent and well-known gentlemen, whose letters and testimony will be found in the course of our narrative, we are indebted, and under great and lasting obligations.

Prominent among those private citizens is Mr. Peter Cooper, of New-York City, a gentleman well known throughout our country as one of the warmest friends and advocates for the intellectual improvement of the mechanical and laboring classes of our community. Mr. Cooper, as we will show in the progress of our work, was the pioneer, the very first to experiment upon the practicability of the locomotive system in this country. We will show that he stepped out from the desk of his mercantile office to become the first locomotive-builder in this country, and his success and efforts will be fully recorded as we progress in our work.

The original letters from these sources (in reply to the author's numerous inquiries for information) will prove deeply interesting to the reader, and richly repay the labor of their perusal, while, at the same time, they will fill up the chain of evidence, as it were, and point out the sources from which the author has gained the desired information for his work, and will be given in their proper places, word for word, as they were received.

## CHAPTER II.

### EARLY RAILROADS.

MANY persons, otherwise well-informed upon general topics, believe that railroads were constructed especially for locomotives, as the best-adapted road for the accommodation of that peculiar machine and its train of cars.

They never call to mind that a locomotive is a modern invention, and, for want of access to works such as we have referred to, they are not informed that a railroad is an ancient institution (if we may apply such a term to such a subject). They never have dreamed nor ever imagined that this peculiar kind of road was invented and in use several centuries ago, but, like the great auxiliary, the locomotive, was very defective and simple in its primitive state, and since that time, like the latter, has been subject to vast and continued improvements.

Before, however, we enter upon the subject for which these pages were designed—"the history of the first locomotives in America"—it will not, we trust, be deemed inappropriate here to devote a small space in our work in describing the peculiar kind of road upon which the locomotive travels, now known universally as the railroad; and to such information as we have gathered of its origin and early progress.

Various devices have been employed, from the period when wheel-carriages were first used, for facilitating the movement over the ground in transportation. These devices, however, were mostly limited to the smoothing, levelling, and hardening the surface of the way. The early Egyptians, in transporting the immense stones they used in the erection of the vast pyramids from the quarries, learned the advantage of hard, smooth, and solid track-ways, and the remains of such, formed of large blocks of stone, are said to have been found on the line of the great road they constructed for this purpose.

The ancient Romans made also some approach to the invention of railroads, in the celebrated Appian Way. This was constructed of blocks of stone fitted closely together, the surface presenting a smooth and hard track for the wheels. In modern times such tracks or roadways were constructed in several European cities—London, Pisa, Milan, and many others.

The first instance on record of rails being used on highways was as early as the year 1630, over two and a quarter centuries ago. They were invented by a person named Beaumont, and built and used for the transportation of coal from the mines near New-castle, in England.

Old Roger North alludes to railways as being in use in the neighborhood of the river Tyne in the year 1676, and he thus describes them: The rails of timber were placed end to end and exactly straight, and in two lines parallel to each other. On these bulky carts were made to run on four rollers fitting these rails, whereby the carriage was made so easy that one horse would draw four or five chaldrons of coal at a load.

We read of railways existing in Scotland in 1745, at the time of the Scotch rebellion. These railways were laid down between the Tranent coal-mines and the harbor of Cockenzie, in East Lothian. Improvements were made on these roads and continued until 1765, when they began to assume the forms of our present roads, even to the use of flanges upon the wheels; but up to this period no iron surface was ever heard of. The mode of constructing a railroad at that period was as follows: After the surface was brought to as perfect a level as possible—or incline, as the case might be —square blocks of wood, called sleepers, about six feet long, were laid two or three feet apart across the track; upon these two long strips of wood, six or seven inches wide and about five inches deep, were fastened by pins to the sleepers, and parallel to each other, but about four feet apart.    Upon this wooden rail was spiked a projecting round moulding of wood, and the wheels were hollowed out like a pulley to fit upon the round surface of the wooden moulding upon the rails.

The first iron rails that we find any written account of were used at Whitehaven.    They were cast-iron mouldings, similar in shape to the wooden moulding just described, and, like them, they were spiked down upon the wooden rail to receive the weight and pressure of the hollowed-out wheel, which, pressing entirely upon the moulding of wood, soon rendered it unfit for use. This iron substitute was a wonderful saving in this respect.

Thirty years after, in 1767, five or six tons of the same description of rails were cast at the Coalbrook Dale Ironworks, at Shropshire.    St. Froud, a French traveller, describes these roads as being far superior to all other kinds of roads; that one horse, with perfect ease, could draw a wagon loaded with five or six hundred bushels of coal.

In 1776, the first iron rails we have any written account of were cast with a perpendicular ledge upon the outer side, in order to keep the wheels from running off the track, and after a while the ledge was changed to the inner side of the rail.

A railway of this kind was laid down at the Duke of Norfolk's colliery, near Sheffield.    The road was torn up and destroyed by the laboring men of the colliery in a riot, and Mr. Curr, its builder and projector, had to save his life by flight, and concealed himself in a wood three days and nights to escape the fury of the excited rioters.

Objections were soon discovered in rails with flanges either on the outside or inside, from their liability to obstruction by stones or dirt, which would impede the progress and endanger the safety of the carriages.

A great step in advance was made in 1789, by William Jessop, in the construction of a railway in Loughborough, in Leicestershire, with the first cast-iron edge rail, with flanges cast upon the wheels, instead of upon the rail, as had been done a short time before.

In 1800, Mr. Benjamin Outram, of Little Eaton, in Derbyshire, introduced stone props, instead of timber, for supporting the ends or joinings of the rails. Taking the name from the projector, this kind of road was distinguished as the Outram road, and since that time, for brevity, all roads of this kind are called Tramroads; as this plan was afterward applied to wooden roads, where long stringers were used, with the iron moulding as before described, and in our time the flat iron bar nailed upon the stringers, these roads are all familiarly known as Tram-roads.

Edge rails, as made by Jessop, were laid down in 1801, at the slate-quarry of Lord Penrhyn. The tire of the wheel was hollowed out to fit the projecting curve of the edged rail, but as the fit became soon too tight by wear, it was afterwards changed to a flat surface and rim of the wheel, and a flange around each edge of it. So great was this last improvement, that it was found that ten horses would do the work that had employed four hundred to do upon common roads.

Edge rails were soon after introduced at the collieries in England. They were made thin at the base and spread in thickness at the top. These rails, introduced in 1808, continued in use until 1820, when the machinery was invented for rolling iron into suitable shapes for rails. This was a great improvement, for, as cast-iron rails could only be made three or four feet long, requiring frequent joints, the material was more liable and subject to break, especially with heavy weights passing over it.

Up to this time the motive power was the horse. Many projects and schemes were talked of and proposed for propelling the wagons. Sails were suggested, and various other means were experimented upon, and speedily abandoned, but steam was the most favored, yet how to apply it was to be found out.

* * *

## CHAPTER III.

### FIRST HEAD OF STEAM.

It is recorded, 130 years before the Christian era, that the elder Hero of Alexandria is the first author who gives an account of the application of the vapor of boiling water as a power. Hero expressly ascribes the sounds produced by the statue of Memnon to steam generated in the pedestal and issuing from its mouth. Champollion, who is the highest authority on this point, declares that the Memnon of the Greeks is identical with Prince Amenophis II., one of the Egyptians who reigned at Thebes, 1,600 years before Christ. Therefore, if Hero's surmises of the Statue of Memnon are correct, we have an application of steam before the date of the exodus of the Israelites. Hero himself constructed a toy, one that would raise water like a fountain, keep a ball in equilibrium, and another giving a rotary motion to a ball; but he does not give the slightest hint that his invention or discovery could be made capable of any useful application, nor did he imagine that he possessed a knowledge of a power that was in future ages to produce such important results.

A knowledge of some of the properties of steam seems to have been understood during the flourishing periods and even to the decline of the Roman empire. In the reign of Justinian, the architect Artemius, of that empire, gave some experiments to demonstrate the power of steam or vapor of boiling water. He arranged several vessels containing water, each covered with the wide bottom of a tube, which rose to a narrower top, with pipes extending to the rafters of an adjoining house. When fire was kindled beneath the vessels, the rafters were raised from their positions, and the house shaken by the force of the steam ascending the tubes.

Cardan is the earliest modern author in whom we detect any hint of a knowledge of the mechanical power of steam. He gives a description of the eolipile, in a work dated 1571. The instrument showed how a current of air was made to follow the course of the steam that issued from the neck of the eolipile. Modern writers speak of various others who seemed to have ideas of the mechanical power of steam. The most worthy of notice are Baptista Porta, a Neapolitan, Brancas, a Frenchman, and De Coss. Brancas proposed to direct the current of air issuing from an eolipile upon the leaves of a wheel which, being set in motion, might serve to move machinery. This method was imperfect and wasteful, yet its attempt is deserving of praise, inasmuch as he is the first person who entertained a hope of realizing the vast benefits that steam has since conferred upon the world.

One Marion de Lorme, in a letter to the Marquis de-cinq Mars, in 1641, describes his visit to the mad-house, called the Bicêtre, at Paris, in which he saw, confined in a cell, a poor creature named Solomon de Cause, who seemed to be one of the first to conceive the idea, in 1615, of employing the steam or vapor of boiling water as a power by which both carriages on land and ships at sea could be propelled. Accompanying De Lorme in this visit to the mad-house, was the Marquis of Worcester. After relating many curious cases of madness, De Lorme writes that they saw a man named Solomon de Cause, looking through the bars of his cell. On seeing that he was noticed, Solomon exclaimed in a hoarse and melancholy voice: "I am not mad! I am not mad! But I have made a discovery that would enrich the country which would adopt it; but I am not mad! I am not mad!" "What has he discovered?" asked De Lorme of the guide. "Oh," replied the keeper, "something trifling enough, of course. The poor creature says that he has discovered a wonderful power in the use of steam from boiling water. He came from Normandy, about four years ago, to present to the king a statement of the wonderful effects that might be produced from his invention. The cardinal sent him away without listening to him. Solomon persisted, and followed the cardinal wherever he went, and finally so annoyed him with his discovery, that he had him shut up in the Bicêtre, as a madman."

Of all those who attempted to apply steam to useful purposes, the Marquis of Worcester fills the greatest space. His ideas of steam, and its applications, are to be found in a work called the "Century of Inventions," originally published in London, in 1663. The marquis, it is said, employed a mechanic thirty-five years to make models of machines for the power of steam. Many of these ideas appeared at the time absolutely impossible, yet they have been realized by modern inventors. In all his projects, the expansive power of steam alone was used.

That the steam-engine was not a mere theory in the conception of Worcester, but was actually put into operation, a recent discovery has settled upon positive testimony. The Grand-duke of Tuscany, Cosmo de Medicis, travelled in England in 1656. The manuscript of his travels remained unpublished until 1818. The following is an extract: "His highness," that he might not lose the day uselessly, "went again, after dinner, to the other side of the city, as far as Vauxhall, to see a machine, invented by my Lord Somerset, Marquis of Worcester. It raises water more than forty geometrical feet, by the power of one man only." Here, then, is a description of an engine in actual operation.

In all these projects the expansive power of steam was alone used; the steam was made to act directly upon the surface of the water; in this way the use of high steam is essential to success, and upon a large scale was attended with danger in the low state of the mechanic arts in those days, and various contrivances and improvements were introduced as in modern times. Consequently their necessity became visible, and as early as in 1680 the safety-valve, which has since been of such importance in the construction of steam-engines, was invented by Denys Pepin, a French Protestant. It was made in the following manner: A conical aperture was made in the lid or top of the boiler, and to this was fitted a conical stopper, pressed into the aperture by a weight suspended at the end of a lever. It was identical with the most usual form of safety-valves at the present day.

It has often been written that the power of steam

was first discovered by the Marquis of Worcester, from observing the motion of the lid of a tea-kettle of boiling water. It may be so, but we are more inclined to believe that the marquis got his first idea of the power of steam at the time of his visit to the Bicêtre with Marion de Lorme, when he saw poor Solomon, and heard from his keeper the cause of his malady; then experimented and improved upon the hint. It does seem far more likely that this poor madman, as he was considered, and who it must appear had neither means nor friends to get him released from this thraldom, would be the one to observe the effects of the steam upon the lid of a tea-kettle than a proud English marquis. This, however, we will leave for some one else to determine, and resume our subject, although we cannot doubt our readers will excuse this digression.

The motion of a piston in a cylinder suggested itself to Pepin, first of all, as a method of adapting the expansive power of steam to produce mechanical effects.

The history of steam, applied to purposes of acknowledged utility, commences with one Savary, a Cornish miner, who in 1718 proposed the use of it to free the mines from water; for as early as 1710 Newcomen and Cawley had completed the first steam-engine in England, a patent for which had been issued in 1705.

Pepin constructed an engine for the Elector of Hesse in 1707. Savary's engine was confined to a single object, that of raising the water from the mines; and even this was done at a great disadvantage, from the imperfection of the principle, and the make-up of the machine; yet it was important as a step to the construction of more perfect machines, and even it was itself of some value when compared with the methods of freeing the mines from water which were at that period in use.

In 1759, over a century ago, the subject of steam was first introduced to the mind of James Watt, and his first engine was made soon after, or in 1769. He was assisted by Dr. Robinson.

At a very early period the same Savary, before mentioned, proposed steam as a means of propelling carriages, but made no practical experiments.

The same James Watt in 1784 describes an engine for propelling carriages on common roads, but, being too much occupied in perfecting his condensing engine, nothing further was done by him toward constructing this locomotive.

Steam-engines, imperfect as they were at that early period, appear to have been directed first to the propelling of boats upon the water rather than carriages upon the land.

## CHAPTER IV.

### FIRST STEAMBOATS.

WORCESTER, in his " Century of Inventions," speaks of the capacity for rowing of his engine, used in raising water.

Savary proposed to make the water raised by his engine turn a water-wheel within his vessel, which should carry paddle-wheels acting on the outside; and Watt, as we are well assured, stated in conversation that, had he not been prevented by the pressure of other business, he would have made a steamboat.

In truth, before the time of Watt's improvement in his steam-engine, no modification by which steam was

3

applied to useful purposes, as raising water, would have been able to propel vessels successfully. This is exemplified by evidences found recently in an ancient record, in which we have a description of a vessel propelled by steam. Blasco de Garay, an officer in the service of the Emperor Charles V., made, at Barcelona, in Spain, in the year 1543, an experiment in a vessel, which he forced through the water by apparatus, of which a large kettle with boiling water formed a conspicuous part.

De Garay was, therefore, not only the first inventor of a steamboat, but the first (not even excepting Savary) who was successful in applying steam to useful purposes. De Garay, however, was too far in advance of the spirit of the age to be able to introduce his invention into practice. His machinery was imperfect, and the recollection of his experiment would have been lost had not the record been accidentally found among the ancient archives of the province of Catalonia.

This experiment was, therefore, without any practical result, and may be looked upon as a piece of curious antiquarian research rather than as an event filling a space in the history of steamboats.

Among the early prime movers in seeking for the means of applying steam to vessels, we will name Genevois and the Comte d'Auxiron. The first of these, whose attempts date as early as 1759, is chiefly remarkable for the peculiarity of his apparatus, which resembled the feet of a duck, opening when moved through the water in the act of propulsion, and closing on its return.

The latter, D'Auxiron, also made an experiment in 1774, but his boat moved so slowly and irregularly that it was at once abandoned.

In 1775 the elder Perrier, who afterward introduced the manufacturing of steam-engines into France,
made an attempt in a steamboat, but was unsuc-
cessful.

The Marquis de Jouffroy continued the pursuit of
the same object. His first attempt was made in 1778,
at Baume les Dames, and in 1781 he built upon the
Saone a steam-vessel one hundred and fifty feet long
and fifteen feet wide. The report of his experiment
was made to the French Academy of Sciences, and was
said to be favorable.

No successful experiment could be looked for until
Watt made public his double-acting engine, and the
improvements made in 1784 to keep up a continuous
and regular rotary motion. To America, then, we are
now to look for the first successful steamboat.

Conspicuous in the list of early experimenters in
steamboats are the names of Rumsey and Fitch. Both
constructed boats propelled by steam as early as 1783,
and models were exhibited to General Washington.

Fitch was the first to try his plan, and in 1785 he
succeeded in moving a boat upon the Delaware; and it
was not until 1786 that Rumsey got his boat in motion
on the Potomac. Fitch's plan was a system of paddles.
Rumsey at first used a kind of pump, which drew in
water at the bow and forced it out at the stern of his
boat. He soon abandoned this plan of the pump, and
employed poles set in motion by cranks on the axis of
the fly-wheel of his engine, and intended to press against
the bottom of the river. Fitch's boat was propelled
through the water at the rate of four miles an hour.
Rumsey's invention never came to any valuable results.

Next, after Fitch and Rumsey, came an ingenious
gentleman named Miller, of Dolswinton, in Scotland,

who, in 1787, made a substitute for oars, and applied wheels worked by men upon a crank; afterward steam was substituted by an engineer named Symington.

This boat was a double pleasure-boat upon a lake in his grounds at Dolswinton. The trial was so successful that Miller built a boat sixty feet long, and it is said that it moved upon the Forth and Clyde Canal at the rate of seven miles an hour; but the vessel suffered so much by the strain of the machinery that it soon became unsafe and in danger of sinking, and was set aside, and Mr. Miller's experiments were never resumed.

John Stevens, of Hoboken, next experimented in steam-vessels, in 1791. His first attempt was made in a boat with a rotary engine, but he soon substituted one of Watt's machines, and navigated his vessel five or six miles an hour. These experiments were continued up to 1807, much to the detriment of his fortune.

The project of Gerrevois was revived in England about this time by the Earl of Stanhope. An apparatus like the feet of a duck was placed in a boat, and with a powerful machine, but never gained a velocity over three miles an hour.

In 1797, Chancellor Livingston, of New York, built a steamboat on the Hudson River. He obtained from the Legislature the right and exclusive privilege, on condition that he would provide, within a year, a boat impelled by steam that would go three miles an hour. This he did not effect. In the year 1800 Stevens and Livingston united and built a boat to be propelled by a system of paddles, resembling a horizontal chain-pump, and with one of the engines of Watt, but, in consequence of the weakness of the vessel, the engine would get out of line, and the experiment did not succeed.

We have often heard and seen it written that steam-boats were invented and first run by Fulton. Such was not the case, as we have shown in the foregoing pages; but Fulton made the first successful experiment with a steamboat with side-wheels, which is the plan adopted ever since, excepting in propellers.

Fulton commenced his experiments in Paris, in 1803, upon the Seine, with a small vessel with side-wheels, driven by one of Watt's engines, adjusted for the purpose, and the experiment was a success. He soon after determined to construct a boat of a larger size, to be tried in the United States. This vessel was built in America; but as the workshops could not at that time construct the engine, one from Watt & Bolton was procured, and Fulton proceeded to England to superintend its construction. The engine arrived in New York early in 1806, and the vessel was set in motion in the summer of 1807. The success of this experiment is well known, and from that period steam-vessels have continued to increase in size and speed, from the humble efforts of these early experimenters, until they now assume the magnitude and magnificence of the floating palaces of the present day.

The first steam-vessel that traversed the ocean was the steamship Savannah, in 1817, and this early effort demonstrated the principle that steamships could be used upon the sea. The Savannah may be looked upon as the pioneer, whose path has since been followed by some of the largest and most magnificent specimens of naval architecture in the world.

Though steam, in its application to navigation, had been progressing rapidly, and even as early as 1807 attained such a degree of usefulness as to cause it to be looked upon as a fixed fact, yet its application in facilitating intercommunication upon the land had not been developed during a quarter of a century afterward.

—————◆•◆—————

## CHAPTER V.

### FIRST STEAM-CARRIAGE.

THE first actual model of a steam-carriage, of which we have a written account, was constructed by a Frenchman, named Cugnot, who exhibited it before the Marquis de Saxe, in 1763. He afterward, in 1769, built an engine to run on common roads, at the expense of the French monarch. As it is the first steam-carriage of which we have any written account, and believing that it would prove interesting to our readers, we copy this description of it from APPLETONS' JOURNAL OF POPULAR LITERATURE, SCIENCE, AND ART, August 17, 1869, as follows: "One of the earliest efforts in the way of steam locomotion was the engine of Cugnot, of France, designed to run on common roads. His first carriage was put in motion by the impulsion of two single-acting cylinders, the piston of which acted alternately on the single front wheels. It travelled about three or four miles an hour, and carried four persons; but, from the smallness of the boiler, it would not continue to work more than twelve or fifteen minutes without stopping to get up steam. Cugnot's locomotive presented a simple and ingenious form of a high-pressure engine, and, though of rude construction, was a creditable piece of work, considering the time. He made a second engine, with which several successful trials were made in the streets of Paris, which excited much interest. An accident, however, put an end to his experiments. Turning the corner of the street one day, near the Madeleine, when the machine was running at a speed of about three miles an hour, it upset with a crash, and, being considered dangerous, was locked up in the Arsenal. Cugnot's locomotive is still to be seen in the Museum of the Conservatoire des Arts et Metiers, at Paris, and is a most interesting relic of early locomotion."

FIG. 1.

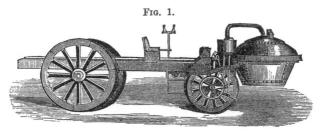

CUGNOT'S LOCOMOTIVE, 1769.

In 1784 William Symington conceived the idea of steam being applied to propelling carriages, and in 1786 made a working model, but soon gave it up, and nothing was ever after heard of the project.

The first English model of a steam-carriage was made in 1784, by William Murdoch; this model was upon the principle of the high pressure, and ran on three wheels (for common roads, of course). It worked to admiration, but nothing further was ever done to bring the idea into a more practical form.

A few years after, Thomas Allen, of London, published the plan of a newly invented machine for carrying goods, without the use of horses, and by the use of steam alone for the motive power. His plan was to have cogged wheels to run upon cogged rails. The plan was all that was ever brought out.

In 1801 Oliver Evans, of Philadelphia, a mill-wright, who had entertained the idea, as early as 1772, of propelling wagons by the action of high steam, was employed by the corporation of that city to construct a dredging-machine. The experiment was of a most remarkable character. The machine was, as you may term it, an amphibious affair. He built both the vessel and the machine at his works, a mile and a half from the water. The whole weighing 42,000 lbs., it was mounted upon wheels, to which motion was given by the engine, and moved without any further aid from the shop to the river. After the machine was in its proper element, a wheel was then fixed to the stern of the vessel, and the engine being again set in motion, she was conveyed to her designed position. Here is the first propeller. As late as the year 1800, wooden or tram roads were general in all the coal and mining districts in England, using horse-power for the means of transportation of their coal or ore from the mines to the point of shipment.

The first idea and proposition to introduce the rail-road, imperfect as it then was, for the transportation of goods and for commercial purposes generally, and to be used as a highway between one city and another, as at the present day, was made before the Literary and Philosophical Society of Newcastle, England, by Mr. Thomas, of Denton, on the 11th February, 1800. The same idea was taken hold of in 1802, by a Mr. Edge-worth, who urged the same plan for the transit of passengers. He urges that stage-coaches might be made to go at six miles an hour, and post-coaches and gentlemen's travelling-carriages at eight miles an hour, with one horse alone. He also suggested that small stationary engines placed from distance to dis-

tance might be made, and by the use of endless
chains draw the carriages, at a great diminution of
horse-power.

These ideas of Mr. Thomas were followed by a
recommendation from a Dr. Anderson, of Edinburgh, a
friend and co-laborer with Watt in his experiments
upon the improvements in steam-engines. The doctor
dilated upon the subject with great warmth and enthusiasm. So apparently extravagant were his views
upon this his favorite topic considered, that many of
his friends thought his mind had become affected.
"If," said he, "we can diminish only one single farthing
in the cost of transportation and personal intercommunication, and you at once widen the circle of intercourse,
you form, as it were, a new creation—not only of stone
and earth, of trees and plants, but of men also; and,
what is of far greater consequence, you promote industry, happiness, and joy. The cost of all human consumption would be reduced, the facilities of agriculture
promoted, time and distance would be almost annihi-
lated; the country would be brought nearer to the
town; the number of horses to carry on traffic would
be diminished; mines and manufactories would appear
in neighborhoods hitherto considered almost isolated
by distance; villages, towns, and even cities, would
spring up all through the country; and spots now
silent as the grave would be enlivened with the busy
hum of human voices, the sound of the hammer, and the
clatter of machinery; the whole country would be, as
it were, revolutionized with life and activity, and a
general prosperity would be the result of this mighty
auxiliary to trade and commerce throughout the land."

How perfectly true were these arguments of Anderson, and how his predictions have been verified even in

our own State! What else could have developed the boundless wealth of our mountain-regions but the introduction of the railroad system and its powerful auxiliary the locomotive, by which means their hitherto inaccessible fastnesses have been penetrated, and access thereto made comparatively easy; while their vast resources of wealth in lumber, coal, minerals, and oil, have been brought nearer to a market, and, but for this system of transportation, they would to this day have been locked up in impenetrable mystery in the deep recesses of the mountains?

## CHAPTER VI.

### TREVITHICK'S ENGINE.

WHILE these propositions were developing, one Richard Trevithick, a foreman in a Cornish tin-mine, prompted, no doubt, by seeing the model engine which Murdoch had constructed, determined to build a carriage to run on common roads, and a Mr. Vivian joined him in the enterprise. They took out a patent in 1802. A description of this machine will not be uninteresting to our readers:

This steam-carriage resembled a stage-coach, and was upon four wheels. It had one horizontal cylinder, which, together with the boiler and furnace-box, was placed in the rear of the hind axle. The motion of the piston was transmitted to a separate crank-axle, from which, through the medium of spur-gear, the axle of the driving-wheel derived its motion. It is worthy of note that the steam-racks and force-pumps, as also the bellows used in generating combustion, were worked off the same crank-axle.

This was the first successful high-pressure engine constructed on the principle of moving a piston, by the elasticity of steam, against the pressure of the atmosphere, and without a vacuum. Such an engine had been described by Leopold, though in his apparatus the pressure acted only on one side of the piston, while in Trevithick's and Vivian's engine the piston was not only raised but likewise depressed by the steam. This was original with them, and of great merit.

This kind of carriage on common roads was tolerably successful. It was exhibited at the city of London, and attracted great crowds to witness its performance; and it drew behind it a carriage filled with passengers. But it soon became obvious that the roads in England were too rough and uneven for the successful use of such machines, and it was soon after abandoned by Trevithick as a practical failure.

Trevithick next turned his attention to the invention of a steam-carriage or locomotive, to run upon the tram-roads then in general use in England; and in 1804 he commenced his machine; in the same year it was completed and tried upon the Merthyr-Tydvil Railway, in South Wales. On this occasion it succeeded in drawing after it several wagons containing ten tons of bar-iron, at the rate of five miles an hour. The boiler of this machine was cylindrical in form, flat at the ends, and constructed of cast-iron. The furnace and flues were inside the boiler, in which a single cylinder of eight inches in diameter and four feet six inch stroke was immersed upright. Although this locomotive, when tried upon the railroad as above stated, succeeded in drawing a considerable weight, and travelling at a fair speed, from other causes it proved like his first steam-carriage, a practical failure, and was soon abandoned. This experiment, however, may be considered as the first attempt to adapt the locomotive to service upon a railroad of which we have any written account.

The great difficulty and obstacle which at that early day did more than any thing else to retard the successful progress of the locomotive for railroad purposes, was the idea that, upon the smooth surface of a rail or iron plate then in use, the smooth surface of the driving-wheel would not have adhesive power to cause the engine to move forward, much less have a sufficient friction to enable the machine, not only to go ahead itself, but to draw a weight of carriages behind it. To remedy this evil, Trevithick recommended, and caused to be placed upon the surface of the driving-wheels of his machine, heads of bolts and numerous grooves, to produce the required adhesion. It proved successful, but produced a succession of jolts very trying upon the cast-iron plates upon the roads upon which the experiments were tried, as well as upon the machine.

In 1811 a Mr. Blankensop, of Leeds, took out a patent for a machine and rail adapted to each other: a rack or toothed rail was to be laid down along one side of the track, into which a tooth-wheel of his locomotive worked. The boiler of his engine was supported by a carriage upon four wheels without teeth, and resting immediately on the axles. These were entirely independent of the working-parts of the engine, and merely supported its weight, the progress being effected by the motion of the cogged wheels working on the cogged rail. This engine began running on the railroad from the Middleton collieries to the town of Leeds, about three and a quarter miles, on the 12th of August, 1812. For a number of years it was a permanent object of curiosity, and was visited by crowds of strangers from all parts. These engines (for several were afterward constructed) drew after them thirty coal-cars, loaded, at a speed of three and a quarter miles per hour, and were in use for many years, and may justly be considered as the first instance of the employment of locomotive power for commercial purposes.

Another curious experiment was tried in 1812, to overcome the want of friction upon the road and increase the power of the engine. A Mr. Chapman, of Newcastle, took out a patent for this invention. The plan was a chain stretched from one end of the road to the other. The chain was passed once round a grooved barrel-wheel under the centre of the engine, so that, when the wheels turned, the locomotive would, as it were, drag itself along the railway. The experiment was tried with an engine constructed for the purpose on the Heaton Railway, near Newcastle, but it was so clumsy in its action that it was soon abandoned.

But the most remarkable, extravagant, and amusing experiment of all, and one which must bring to the countenance of our readers at the present day a smile, was the one adopted by a Mr. Brunton, of the Butterby Works, Derbyshire, in 1813, who took out a patent for a machine which was to go upon legs like a horse. This contrivance had two legs attached to the back part, which, being alternately moved by the engine, pushed it before them. These legs, or propellers, imitated the legs of a man or the fore-legs of a horse, with joints, and when worked by the machine alternately lifted and pressed against the ground or road, propelling the engine forward, as a man shoves a boat ahead by pressing with a pole against the bottom of a river.

FIG. 2.

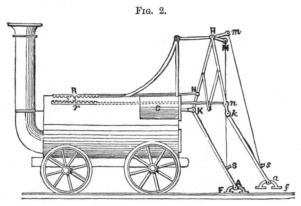

WILLIAM BRUNTON LOCOMOTIVE.

This contrivance was so singular and ingenious that we cannot refrain from giving a description of it, taken from a very interesting work upon road-making, by W. M. Gillespie, A. M., C. E.

The legs are indicated by H K F and H *k f*. H represents the hip-joint, K and *k* the knee-joints, A and *a* the ankle-joints, and F and *f* the feet. We will first examine the action of the front leg. The knee, K, is attached to the end of a piston-rod, which the steam drives backward and forward in the horizontal cylinder, C. When the piston is driven outward, it presses the leg K F against the ground, and thus propels the engine forward, as a man shoves a boat ahead by pressing with a pole against the bottom of a river. As the engine advances, the leg straightens, the point H is carried forward, and the extremity, M, of the bent lever H M, is raised. A cord, M S, being attached to S, the shin of the leg, the motion of the lever tightens the cord, and finally raises the foot from the ground, and prepares it to take a fresh step where the reversed action of the piston has lowered it again. The action of the other leg is precisely similar, but motion communicated to it from the first one. Just above the knee of the front leg, at N, is attached a rod, on which is a toothed rack, R. Working in it is a cog-wheel, which enters also a second rack, r, below it, which is connected by a second rod with point n of the other leg. When the piston is driven out and pushes the engine from the knee, the rack R is drawn backward, and turns the cog-wheel, which then draws the lower rack r forward, and operates on the hind leg precisely as the piston-rod does on the front one, and thus the legs take alternate steps, and walk on with the engine.

This locomotive or " mechanical traveller," as it was termed by its inventor, moved on a railway at the rate of two and a half miles per hour, with the tractive force of four horses. Mr. Brunton's machine, however, never got beyond the experimental state, for, on one of its trials, it unhappily blew up, killing and wounding several of the by-standers, was never repaired, but laid aside as one of the failures of the times.

These experiments, though failures in their results, were followed up by a Mr. Blackett, of Wylam, whose persevering efforts paved the way for the future labors of George Stephenson.

To make his experiments Mr. Blackett ordered one of the locomotives of the Trevithick patent, and also employed rack - rails and tooth driving - wheels like Blankensop's, and had his road altered for the occasion. This engine was the most awkwardly-constructed machine imaginable. It had a single cylinder six inches in diameter, and a fly-wheel working on one side to carry the cranks over the dead-points. The boiler was of cast-iron, and the weight of the whole was about six tons; a wooden frame was supported by four pairs of wheels, and a barrel of water placed upon another frame sustained by two pairs of wheels served as a tender. When all was ready, the word was given to go ahead, but the engine would not move an inch; when it was finally set in motion, it flew to pieces, and the workmen and spectators, with Mr. Blackett at their head, scattered and fled in every direction! The machine, or what was left of it, was taken off the road, and afterward a portion of it was used as a pump at one of the mines.

Mr. Blackett was not, however, discouraged. His next experiment was an engine with a single eight-inch cylinder, which was fitted with a fly-wheel, the driving-wheel on one side being cogged in order to enable it to travel on the rack-rail. This engine proved more successful than its predecessors, and, although it was clumsy and unsightly, it was capable of drawing eight or nine wagons loaded with coal to the shipping-point at Lemington; its weight, however, was too great for the road, and the cast-iron rails were continually breaking. Its work was by no means successful. It crept along at a snail's pace, sometimes taking six hours to go five miles to the landing-place. It was continually getting off the track, and there it would stick. Horses would then have to be sent out to pull it on the track. The engine often broke down; its pumps, plugs, and cranks would get wrong, then the horses again would be needed to drag the machine back to the shop. In fact, it at last got so cranky that the horses were frequently sent out to follow the engine to be in readiness to draw it along when it gave out. At last it was abandoned.

Notwithstanding the repeated failures, and the amount of money expended on these experiments, Mr.

Blackett persevered. In 1813 he made an experiment with a frame upon four wheels, to determine the much-disputed point, the adhesive power of a smooth-surfaced driving-wheel upon a smooth-surfaced rail. Six men were placed upon this frame, which was fitted up with a windlass attached by gearing to the several wheels. When the men worked the windlass, the adhesion was found sufficient to enable them to propel the machine without slipping. This experiment settled the difficulty which was always thought to be in the way of the successful use of the locomotive upon the smooth surface of a railroad with smooth-surfaced driving-wheels, proving that rack-rails, tooth-wheels, endless chains, and legs, were useless requisites to the successful use of a locomotive with smooth-surfaced driving-wheels upon a smooth-surfaced railroad-track, and drawing loaded wagons behind it.

## CHAPTER VII.

### GEORGE STEPHENSON.

WHILE Mr. Blackett was building locomotives and experimenting with them, George Stephenson, then enjoying a high reputation for his ingenuity and skill as a machinist, was deliberating in his mind on the possibility of locomotives being made and improved so as eventually to supersede the use of horse-power upon tram-roads; but the want of means, and the difficulty of obtaining skilful mechanics at that early day to do the requisite work, retarded him in his long-cherished idea of making a machine that would answer

4

effectually the purpose for which the locomotive was intended. True it was that Blankensop's engine, built in 1813, had been in use upon the tram-way at Wylam, and improvements were subsequently made so that a machine had been constructed and run upon the tram-way between Kenton and Cox Lodge, which was enabled to draw after it sixteen loaded cars, of about seventy tons, at the rate of three miles an hour. Yet this engine, and others like it, were far from being perfect, or adapted to the purpose for which they were intended, being clumsy, cumbrous, and awkward, in all their movements. Mr. Stephenson saw one of these at work, and when asked by one of his companions what he thought of it, he replied that he "could make a better one than that;" and, to accomplish this, he devoted his whole mind and energies, the result of which we will show hereafter.

It will not, we trust, be deemed out of place to devote a small space in our pages to give, as briefly as possible, some of the early history of this afterward most distinguished engineer and machinist, who may be justly looked upon as the father of the locomotive system in England, now so successful and essential to its commerce and manufactures. His history may tend to impress upon the mind of any youthful reader and mechanic who may be now, as he once was, a poor boy, how a young man, by industry and perseverance in a good cause, may ultimately build up for himself a position which would lead eventually to eminence and fame.

GEORGE STEPHENSON was born on June 9, 1781, in a small colliery village called Wylam, on the north bank of the river Tyne. The tram-road between Newcastle and Carlisle runs along the opposite bank of the river from the coal-pits to the shipping-point. Robert

Stephenson, the father of George, was a poor, hard-working man, and supported his family entirely from his own wages of less at first than, but afterward raised to, twelve shillings a week.

The wagons loaded with coal passed by Wylam several times a day. These wagons were drawn by horses; for locomotives had not been dreamed of by the most visionary of that early period. George's first wages were twopence per day, to herd some cows owned by a neighbor which were allowed to feed along the road; to watch and keep them off the tram-road, and out of the way of the coal-wagons; also, to close the gates after the day's work of the wagons was over.

The old mine being worked out, the Stephenson family removed to the new opening at Dudley Burn, where Robert, the father, worked as fireman. George's first work about these mines was at what is known as a picker. His duty was to clean the coal of stone, slate, and other impurities, at wages advanced to sixpence per day, and, after promotion, raised to eighteen-pence per day.

After several removals to new openings, as the coal would be worked out in the old, George, who had always lived at home, and was now about fifteen years of age, found himself at the new opening, at Jolly's Close, where he was promoted to the position of fireman, at the opening called " Mid Mill Winnin." There he remained two years, and was then again removed to a new pit near Throckly Bridge, where he worked, and his wages were raised to twelve shillings per week. He next worked at a new opening called Water Row, where a pumping machine was erected, and George, who was then seventeen years of age, was placed in charge as plugman and engineer, while his father worked under him as the fireman.  At that time he never suffered an opportunity to pass without improving himself in the knowledge of his engine.  When not at work, and while others, employed in and about the mines, would be spending their time and earnings in drinking and idle sports, George employed himself in taking to pieces his engine, to possess himself of knowledge and of every peculiarity about it.  By these means he became thoroughly acquainted with his engine, and, if at any time it got wrong, he was able to adjust and even repair it, without calling in the aid of the chief engineer of the colliery.  At this time (for want of an opportunity), George Stephenson, now entering upon the very threshold of manhood, could not read, nor did he even know his letters.  The first rudiments of his education were derived from one Robert Cowen, who had a night-school in the village of Wallbottle ; with him he took lessons in spelling and reading, three nights in the week, paying threepence per week for his tuition. Notwithstanding these obstacles in his way, George labored, studied, and persevered, and at eighteen he was able to write his own name.

In 1799 he attended another night school, at Newburn.  His teacher was one Andrew Robinson, from whom he learned his arithmetic.  During his leisure hours he employed himself in working out the sums set him by Robinson, and in the evening handed in his slate to the master for examination and a fresh supply of sums for his study.  George's wages now amounted to £1 15s. 6d. to £2, per fortnight.  To this he added his earnings for shoe-mending and shoe-making, which he had taken up.

In 1804 he walked on foot to Scotland, to take charge of one of Bolton & Watt's engines.  He returned, after a year's absence, to Killingworth, on foot, as he had gone, and was soon at work as brakesman at the lifting engine on the West Moore pit.

In 1807 George Stephenson meditated upon emigrating to America; but found himself too poor to pay his passage, and was compelled to abandon the project. To his earnings then he added the repairing of clocks and watches, and the cutting out of clothes for the wives of the workmen to make up. Thus did this energetic and untiring man persevere and labor for advancement in knowledge, until he was promoted as head engineer or plugman, as the engineer was called, at the colliery.

## CHAPTER VIII.

### STEPHENSON'S ENGINE.

IT was now that Mr. Stephenson, about twenty-six years of age, set about the construction of his first locomotive. As we before stated, the want of good and skilful workmen was a great drawback. None of the magnificent and ingenious machinery of the present day to be seen in our machine-shops had been invented. At that early period every part of the engine had to be made by hand, and hammered into shape as a horse-shoe was; and John Thorswall, the colliery blacksmith, was his chief workman; and with all these disadvantages and difficulties to contend with, Mr. Stephenson persevered and finally completed his first locomotive.

It will no doubt be interesting to our mechanical readers to have a full description of Mr. Stephenson's

first effort. The boiler was cylindrical, eight feet long
and thirty-four inches in diameter, with an internal flue-
tube twenty inches wide passing through the boiler.
The engine had two vertical cylinders of eight inches
in diameter and two feet stroke, let into the boiler,
working the propelling gear, with cross-heads and connecting rods; the power of the two cylinders was continued by means of spur-wheels, which communicated
the motive power to the wheels supporting the engine
upon the rails. The adoption of the spur-gear was the
chief peculiarity of this new engine; it worked upon
what is termed the second motion. The chimney was of
wrought-iron, around which was a chamber extending
back to the feed-pumps, for the purpose of heating the
water previous to its injection into the boiler. The
engine had no springs, was mounted on a wooden
frame upon four wheels. In order, however, to equalize
the jolts and shocks which such an engine would encounter, the water-barrel, which served as a tender,
was fixed at the end of a lever and weighted, the other
end being connected with the frame of the carriage.
The wheels of this locomotive were all smooth, and it
was the first engine so constructed. After ten months'
labor, this locomotive was completed and put upon the
Killingwood Railway on the 25th July, 1814, and tried.
On an ascending grade of one in four hundred and fifty
feet, this engine succeeded in drawing after it eight
loaded wagons of thirty tons' weight, at about four
miles an hour, and was the most successful working-
engine that had ever been constructed up to this period.
It was called "Blucher." Although successful, this
improvement over horse-power was not sufficient to
justify the abandonment of the latter. The great trouble with this new machine was the inability of keeping

up steam sufficient to answer its demands; and this experiment, like all its predecessors, might have been set
aside as a practical failure, had not Mr. Stephenson hit
upon (accidentally) the invention or discovery of the
steam-blast. The puffing and noise occasioned by the
escapement of the steam from the steam-pipe into the
open air, after it had performed its duty in the cylinder,
frightened the horses upon the common roads hard by
and near the vicinity of the crossings, and occasioned
much complaint to the authorities. Mr. Stephenson
was warned by the police to abate the nuisance, or be
subject to a prosecution. To remedy the evil he hit
upon the plan of discharging the surplus steam into
the smoke-stack, which produced a vacuum, and the
draught in his furnace became so perfect, that double the
quantity of steam was generated, and the power of his
engine increased to double its former capacity. This
was a triumph, and encouraged the inventor to further
experiments. Seeing all the defects of his first engine,
and the wonderful effects of the steam-blast in facilitating the combustion of the fuel used in generating steam,
Mr. Stephenson set about constructing his second engine, the patent dated February 28, 1815.

This second locomotive we will describe, as we think
it will prove interesting to our readers, especially so to
our engine-drivers or engineers and our locomotive-ma-
chinists.

Like the first, this engine had two vertical cylinders,
communicating directly with each pair of the fore-wheels
which supported the engine, by means of a cross-head
and a pair of connecting-rods. It was soon seen that
the direct action from the cylinder to the wheels upon
such uneven roads would not answer with the rigidity
of the machinery, particularly the stiff connecting-rods

communicating from the wheels to the piston-heads. To obviate this difficulty, Mr. Stephenson invented and applied the ball-and-socket joint upon his connecting-rods, where they were attached to the pistons, and crank-pins upon the crank-axles.

Many other experiments were tried and as quickly abandoned in England by this accomplished engineer, whose name and reputation were as well known in America as they were in England. These experiments tended in a great measure to prevent our own country-men subsequently from falling into the same errors and mistakes that would be found in the pathway of the early developments of this wonder of science and me-chanics, the locomotive.

We will not believe but that a description, step by step — from the first experiments by Trevithick, in 1804, on the Merthyr-Tydvil Railway, in South Wales, when his machine drew after it several wagons contain-ing ten tons of bar-iron at the rate of five miles an hour, to the experiments of Stephenson, with his far-famed Rocket—will prove interesting to the machinists and engineers among our readers, and we will continue our accounts until we come to the date of our own experi-ments in America.

It will be remembered by our readers that in the Blucher the motion was continued by the spur-wheel system, and its place was supplied by inserting into the axle two cranks at right angles to each other, and this method answered extremely well; but even here Mr. Stephenson found obstacles, in the difficulty, at that early day, of forging cranks of sufficient strength and accuracy to answer the purpose, and stand the jars and jolts occasioned by the rough roads, and he tried a sub-stitute for the requisite object. This new arrangement was a chain which rolled over indented wheels on the centre of each axle, and so arranged that the two pair of wheels were effectually coupled and made to keep pace with each other. This did well for a while, but the chains soon proved troublesome, and were abandoned for the new plan of connecting the front and hind wheels together by rods outside of the wheels, instead of rods and cranks inside, as at first. This method completely answered the purpose, and is in use at the present day.

Although many other improvements were afterward suggested to the fertile mind of Mr. Stephenson, and introduced in the machinery of the locomotive Blucher, yet, as a mechanical construction, it may be considered as the type of the present successful locomotive system.

Mr. Stephenson was now left alone in locomotive experiments and improvements: all the other experimentalists before him quitted the field of that kind of enterprise, and all their works in the shape of machines were thrown away and entirely abandoned.

Railways, as we have before stated, had been in successful operation for many years, in the transportation of coal and mineral ores from the mines to the places of shipment. The idea had never been suggested to the mind of any one, or had never, at least, been advocated, to use them for general purposes of traffic, or, as at the present time, for the transportation of goods, wares, merchandise, produce, or for the transportation of passengers from one city to another, until about the year 1800, as we before stated, by a Mr. Thomas, who introduced the subject before the Literary and Philosophical Society of Newcastle, and a few years after by a Mr. Edgeworth, and even then no other power was thought or dreamed of but the horse-power then in use upon all the tram-roads (as the railroads were called in all the mining regions throughout England and wherever else they were used), and which had by this time become general, and was looked upon as one of the essential necessaries for such enterprises. But the use of steam-power had not entered the minds of the warmest advocates of railroads for general purposes, as at the present day.

It was not until 1820 that the first suggestion of using the locomotive (imperfect as it then was) in the place of horse-power, was advocated by one Thomas Gray, who devoted much of his time and money in publishing articles and pamphlets upon the subject. He pointed out the importance of such a road between Liverpool and Manchester and other important points, all of which have since been carried out. He was so energetic and pertinacious in his efforts to impress it upon the minds of the people, and so untiring in his labors, that many pronounced him a bore, and those who knew him declared that he was cracked or deranged —just as, nearly two hundred years before, poor Solomon de Cause was shut up in a mad-house for advocating his discovery of a great power in the steam of boiling water.

While Mr. Gray was advocating the adoption of railways for general transportation purposes, George Stephenson was planning locomotives to run upon them.

## CHAPTER IX.

### FIRST TRAINS.

IN 1819 the Hatton Colliery, in Durham, was altered into a locomotive railroad, and Mr. Stephenson appointed its chief engineer. He soon began his labors, and on the 18th of November, 1822, the road was opened for the first time for locomotives. Crowds came from all directions to witness the experiment. Five of Mr. Stephenson's engines were upon the road that day, each engine drawing after it seventeen wagons loaded, averaging sixty-four tons, at the rate of four miles an hour.

Mr. Stephenson next became chief engineer of the Stockton and Darlington Railway, another coal-road about being constructed. On account of the nature of the ground over which this road would pass, and the limited means put into Mr. Stephenson's hands for its construction, he was compelled to adopt the incline-plane system in those places where too much labor and money would be required. Other parts of the road were made for horse or steam power, which of the two had not as yet been determined upon. The success of Mr. Stephenson's locomotives had been tried and proved practical, although as yet not a saving in the expense of transportation. But Mr. Stephenson's views prevailed, and when the road was finished, on the 27th of September, 1825, he had three engines ready for its use, They were built at his works, the first ever established for locomotive manufacture. The Active, No. 1, was the first built at this establishment. A great deal of excitement and speculation arose throughout the country when the trial-day approached. The road was ready, as we have stated. Great crowds were assembled from every direction to witness the trial; some, more sanguine, came to witness its success, but far the greater portion came to see the bubble burst. The proceedings began at Brusselton incline, where the stationary engine drew a train up the incline on one side and lowered it down on the other.   These wagons were loaded.

At the foot of this plane a locomotive, driven by Mr. Stephenson himself, was attached to the train.   It consisted of six wagons loaded with coal and flour, next a passenger-coach (the first ever run upon a railroad) filled with the directors and their friends, then twenty-one wagons fitted up with temporary seats for passengers, and lastly came six wagons loaded with coal, making in all twenty-eight vehicles.   The word being given that all was ready, the engine began to move, gradually at first, but afterward, in parts of the road, attained a speed of twelve miles an hour.   At that time the number of passengers amounted to 450, which would, with the remainder of the load, amount to upward of ninety tons.   The train arrived at Darlington, eight and three-quarter miles, in sixty-five minutes.   Here it was stopped, and a fresh supply of water was obtained, and the six coal-cars for Darlington detached, and the word given to go ahead.   The engine started, and arrived at Stockton, twelve miles, in three hours seven minutes, including stoppages.

By the time the train reached Stockton, the number of passengers amounted to over 600.

We will here mention that, when this road was first contemplated, its projectors did not estimate the amount of coal that would be transported over it above 10,000 tons per annum; but before a very few years had elapsed, from the facilities offered by the railroad system, with locomotives instead of horse-power, the amount of coal transported annually amounted to 500,000 tons, and has since exceeded that amount.   At this trial experiment, September 27, 1825, the first passenger-car, or wagon as it was called at that day, was put upon the road.   It had been ordered and made at Mr. Stephenson's works, and had only arrived the day before the trial. It was the vehicle in which the directors and their friends rode upon the occasion. Although built by Mr. Stephenson, it was a very modest and uncouth-looking affair, made more for strength than for beauty. A row of seats ran along each side of the interior, and a long table was fixed in the centre, the access being by a doorway behind, like an omnibus of the present day. This vehicle was named the Experiment, and was the only carriage for passengers upon the road for some time. It was, however, the forerunner of a mighty traffic, and soon after new and more improved passenger-carriages were introduced upon the road, all at first drawn by horses.

Fig. 3.

THE FIRST RAILWAY COACH.

The Experiment was first regularly put upon the road for passenger use on the 10th of October, 1825. It was drawn by one horse, and performed a journey each way daily between the two towns, twelve miles, in two hours. This novel way of travelling soon became popu-

lar among the people, and eventually proved so lucrative and extensive, that the carriage could not contain
the number of applicants for a ride.    Inside and outside
it was crowded, and every available spot was occupied.
The Experiment, however, was not worked by the
railroad company as passenger-cars are now, but was
let to other parties, they paying a certain toll for the
use of the road.    It soon became a lucrative business,
and hotel-keepers and others embarked in the enterprise, and a strong opposition was raised up between
the rival owners or companies.    The old carriage, the
Experiment, was found too heavy for one horse; a new
one was placed in its stead, and the old pioneer was
afterward used as a railroad cabin near Shildon.    To
the driver of the old Experiment the first introduction
of lights being used in passenger-cars, for the comfort of
passengers, is due.    This honest and considerate driver,
whose name was Dixon, nightly purchased a penny
candle, and when he was belated and it became dark in
the carriage, he would light his candle and stick it upon
the table running along the centre of the carriage, between the two rows of seats, which added much to the
comfort of his patrons.

At that time the transportation of freight, like that
of passengers, was not confined to the company alone.
According to their charters, railroads were public highways.    Any individual or company had the right of
using the road with their own private wagons on paying a certain stipulated toll affixed by law.    Like the
passenger-carriages, private individuals owned freight-
wagons for the transportation of produce or their own
manufactures to market, and used the road for the purpose.    This traffic, like the passenger transportation,
soon led to confusion and delays.    Being a single-track

road, with only occasional sidings or turnouts here and there upon its route, the carriages often met upon the way, going in opposite directions. Then would begin a violent contest between the rival drivers, not only in words, but sometimes resulting in blows, to determine who should back to the siding and turn off to allow the other to pass. In these contests not unfrequently the passengers would take sides with their respective drivers, and scenes of riot and pugilistic displays were often the result of these contests, until one party or the other would be compelled to succumb. After a while this difficulty was somewhat diminished by the opposition parties coming to a kind of understanding that, in meeting upon the track, the carriage containing the lightest load should back off to the nearest siding; and finally it became a fixed rule that, whichever carriage arrived last at the half-way post, planted between the two sidings, should back off to allow the other to pass. This plan, though it tended in a great measure to render less frequent these difficulties and contests, subjected the working of the road to much trouble and delay, so that these private enterprises were superseded by the company commencing the regular passenger transportation system, which by that time became a source of much importance in the traffic upon the road, and must be considered as the first introduction of this source of profit upon all railroads of our time, exceeding, in many cases, the income from the freight department.

## CHAPTER X.

### FIRST DELIBERATIONS ON RAILROADS.

WHEN the construction of that great work, the Liverpool and Manchester Railroad, was commenced, and even after it had been in progress for several years, its directors had not determined the motive power to be employed upon it. Horse-power had the strongest advocates. Another method, and one having a number of advocates, was that of stationary engines to draw the trains along. By this method the line of road over which the transport is conducted is divided into a number of short sections, at the extremity of each of which an engine is placed. The wagons or carriages, when drawn by any one of these engines to its own station, are detached and connected with the extremity of the chain worked by the next stationary engine, and thus the journey is performed from station to station by separate engines. It was proposed to divide the Liverpool and Manchester road into nineteen stations, or sections of about a mile and a half each, with twenty-one engines fixed at the different points to work the chains forward. Not a single professional man of any eminence could be found who preferred the locomotive over the fixed-engine power as above, George Stephenson only excepted. He stuck to the locomotive-power; and finally committees were appointed at his suggestion to witness the performance of his locomotives employed in hauling coal upon the Stockton and Darlington Railroad. The report from the chairman of one of these committees states that, "although it would be practicable to go at any speed that the size of the wheel and the number of strokes in the engine might allow, yet it would not be safe to go at a greater rate than nine or ten miles an hour." This was considered a very high rate of speed in those days. The completion of the road was fast drawing nigh. The great tunnel at Liverpool was finished; a firm road over Cheat-Moss was completed; and yet the directors had not settled in their minds what power was to be used upon the road. Prejudice still existed against the use of locomotives. The road had been constructed throughout its entire length in a most substantial manner, and cost upward of £20,000 per mile, amounting to £820,000. The rails used were made of forged iron, in lengths of fifteen feet each, and weighed 175 lbs. each. At the distance of every three feet the rail rests on blocks of stone, let into the ground and containing about four cubic feet each. Into each block, two holes, six inches deep and one inch in diameter, are drilled; into these are driven oak plugs, and the cast-iron chairs into which the rails are fitted are spiked down to the plugs, forming a structure of great solidity, and in every respect calculated for any power that might be determined upon by the Board.

Finally, in the spring of 1829, the directors appointed Messrs. Stephenson and Lock, and Messrs. Walker and Rastrick, experienced engineers, to visit the different railways where practical information respecting the comparative effects of stationary and locomotive engines could be obtained; and from these gentlemen they received reports on the relative merits of the two methods, according to their judgment. The result of the comparison of the two systems was, that the capital necessary to be advanced to establish a line of stationary engines was considered greater than that which was necessary to construct an equal power in

5

locomotives; that the annual expense for maintaining the stationary engines was likewise greater than for the locomotives, and consequently the expense of transportation by a stationary system was greater in like proportion. The system of locomotive-power, therefore, was entitled to the preference. Yet another consideration influenced the directors in its favor, which was this: Should an accident occur on any part of the railroad worked by stationary engines, a suspension of work along the entire road would be involved in the consequences; accidents arising from the fracture of any of the chairs, or from any derangement in the working of any of the fixed engines, would effectually stop the intercourse along the entire line; while in the use of locomotive-power an accident could only affect the particular train of carriages drawn by the engine to which the mishap might occur. "The one system," says Mr. Walker, in his report, "is like a chain extending from Liverpool to Manchester, the failure of a single link of which would destroy the whole; while the other (the locomotive system) is like a number of short and unconnected chains, the destruction of any one of which does not interfere with the effect of the others, and the loss of which may be supplied by others with facility." However, to determine the matter, a prize was offered by the directors of £500 for a locomotive which should be produced by a certain day, and perform a certain duty, as follows:

1. The engine must effectually consume its own smoke.
2. The engine, if of six tons' weight, must be able to draw after it, day by day, twenty tons' weight, including the tender and water-tank, at ten miles an hour, with a pressure of steam upon the boiler not exceeding fifty pounds to the square inch.
3. The boiler must have two safty-valves, neither of which

must be fastened down and one of them completely out of the control of the engineer.

4. The engine and boiler must be supported upon springs and rest on six wheels, the height of the whole not exceeding fifteen feet to the top of the chimney.

5. The engine with water must not weigh more than six tons, but an engine of less weight would be preferred, although drawing a proportionally less load behind it; if of only four and one-half tons, it might be put on four wheels.

6. A mercurial gauge must be affixed to the machine, showing the steam-pressure about forty-five pounds to the square inch.

7 The engine must be delivered, complete and ready for trial, at the Liverpool end of the railway, not later than October 1, 1829.

8. The price of the engine not to exceed £550.

The project and the conditions were thought to be preposterous. An eminent gentleman of Liverpool, afterward inspector of steam-packets, said that "only a parcel of charlatans would have issued such a set of conditions;" that it had been "proved to be impossible to make a locomotive-engine to go ten miles an hour; but, if it was ever done, he would undertake to eat a stewed engine-wheel for his breakfast!"

The Stephenson locomotive factory was still in operation at Newcastle, but for a long time it did not pay expenses. Mr. Stephenson now set about the construction of his far-famed engine the Rocket, to contend for the prize just offered by the Liverpool and Manchester railroad directors. As the name of Mr. Stephenson's Rocket is familiar in the mind of every railroad engineer and machinist of the present day, we will describe it, for the information of all who feel interested in the subject: The boiler of this new engine was cylindrical in form, with flat ends; it was six feet in length and three feet in diameter, the upper half of the boiler used as a reservoir for the steam, the lower half being filled with water; through this lower part twenty-five copper tubes three inches in diameter extended with both ends open, one presented to the furnace or fire-box, and the other end opening into the chimney. The fire-box, two feet wide and three feet high, attached immediately behind the boiler, was also surrounded with water. The cylinders, two in number, were placed on each side of the boiler in an oblique position, the one end being nearly even with the top of the boiler, and the other end pointing toward the centre of the foremost driving pair of wheels, with which the connection was made from the piston-rod by a pin to the outside of the wheel.

Fig. 4.

THE ROCKET LOCOMOTIVE.

The Rocket with its load of water weighed only four and one-quarter tons, and was supported upon four wheels (not coupled). The tender was four-wheeled, and similar in shape to a wagon ; the foremost part contained the fuel, and the hinder part a water-cask.

The engine, when completed, was shipped to Liverpool and ready for the trial, with the most sanguine expectations of Mr. Stephenson of its success.

## CHAPTER XI.

### COMPETITION FOR PRIZES.

A GREAT interest was manifested at Liverpool and throughout the country at the approaching competition. Engineers and scientific men arrived from all quarters of the world, to witness the trial of mechanical skill about to be displayed.

On the day appointed the following engines were upon the spot, and entered for the prize:

THE NOVELTY, made by Messrs. Braithwait and Ericsson.
THE SANS-PAREIL, made by Mr. Timothy Hockworth.
THE ROCKET, made by Messrs. Stephenson and Co., Newcastle.
THE PERSEVERANCE, made by Mr. Burtstall.

The day of trial was changed from the 1st to the 6th of October, in order to give the new engines time to get in good working-order. Many thousand spectators were present. The Rocket, although not the first entered, was, nevertheless, the first ready for the trial. The piece of road to be used for the occasion was two miles in length, upon which the locomotives were to travel to and fro. The distance run by the Rocket was about twelve miles in fifty-three minutes. The

Novelty was next tried. It was a very complicated machine, carrying the water and fuel upon the same wheels as the engine, and the whole weighed three tons one hundred lbs. On account of some difficulty in determining the load she was to draw, she was not tested like the Rocket, but was run over the road, making sometimes twenty-four miles per hour.

FIG. 5.

THE NOVELTY LOCOMOTIVE.

The Sans-pareil was next tried, but no particular experiment was made on that day.

The contest was postponed until the following day, but, before the judges arrived upon the ground, the bellows for creating the draught or blast in the Novelty gave way, and it was incapable of going through its performance. A defect was also discovered in the boiler of the Sans-pareil, and time was allowed to get it repaired. Meantime, Mr. Stephenson, to lessen the disappointment to the vast crowd assembled to witness these experiments by the delay, brought out the Rocket and attached it to a coach containing thirty persons, and ran it along the road at the rate of from twenty-six to thirty miles an hour, much to the delight and gratification of the spectators. The judges then ordered the Rocket to be in readiness the following morning to go through its trial according to the prescribed conditions.

FIG. 6.

THE SANS-PAREIL LOCOMOTIVE.

On the morning of October 8, 1829, the Rocket was again upon the road for the contest. The fire-box was filled with coke, the fire lighted, and the steam raised until it lifted the safety-valve loaded to the pressure of fifty pounds to the square inch. These preparations occupied fifty-seven minutes. The engine being started on its journey, dragged after it thirteen tons' weight in carriages or wagons, and made the first ten trips backward and forward upon the two miles of the road, running the thirty-five miles, including stoppages, in one hour and forty-eight minutes.

The second ten trips were in like manner accomplished in two hours and three minutes. The maximum velocity of the Rocket during the trial-trip was about twenty-nine miles an hour, or three times the speed that one of the judges had declared to be the limit of possibility.

Neither the Novelty nor the Sans-pareil was ready for trial until the 10th. The weight of carriages attached to the Novelty was only seven tons. In starting, the engine went off in fine style for the two miles, but, on returning, the pipe for the forcing-pump burst and put an end to the trial. The pipe having been repaired, the engine made a trial-trip, without a load, and is said to have run from twenty-four to twenty-eight miles an hour.

The Sans-pareil was not ready until the 13th, and, when the boiler and tender were filled with water, it weighed 400 lbs. beyond the prescribed conditions of four-wheel engines; but nevertheless the judges allowed it to run upon the same footing as the others, and it travelled at the average speed of fourteen miles an hour, with its load; but at the eighth trip the cold-water pipe got out of order, and it could proceed no farther. It was then determined by the judges to award the prize to the successful engine on the following day, October 14th.

When the trial commenced, the Novelty again broke down. The builder of the Sans-pareil requested another trial, but the judges decided that she was beyond the prescribed weight, and besides consumed and wasted too much coke to make her a successful competitor, using 692 lbs. of coke per hour when running.

The Perseverance was then tried for the first time, and found unable to move more than five or six miles an hour.

The Rocket was the only engine that had performed all the stipulated conditions, and the prize of £500 was accordingly awarded to its makers. The Rocket had eclipsed all other engines that had as yet been constructed, and determined the question of the use of locomotive power upon the Liverpool and Manchester Railroad.

Our narrative now brings us down to the period when locomotives were first introduced into the United States, A. D. 1829. Two important railroads had been commenced, and were in successful working-order, as far as they had been built. But horse-power upon levels, and stationary engines upon steep inclines, were the only powers resorted to. Locomotives had not yet been introduced. The experiments in England had been heard of in this country, and were frequently discussed by those interested in the success of railroads. The experiments of Mr. Stephenson had been carefully watched. His name and fame, as an eminent engineer, were familiar to the minds of the people of this country. His success with his "Rocket" excited the liveliest interest here, and equally as much so as in England. His bearing off the £500 prize was hailed with rapture by thousands in America, who admired him for his genius and indomitable perseverance.

We will now leave Mr. Stephenson and his improvements in England, and turn to the period of 1829, in the United States, when, although, as before said, two important railroads and two coal-roads were in successful progress, or in operation in different sections of the country, yet, as in England in its earliest day, for mining purposes, only horse-power was used, and no attempt had been made to construct a locomotive, nor had one been imported from abroad.

---

## CHAPTER XII.

### RAILROADS IN AMERICA.

THE first railroad built in the United States was three miles in length, extending from the granite-quarries of Quincy, Massachusetts, to the Neponset River. This road was commenced in 1826, and completed in 1827. It was built with granite sleepers, seven and a half feet long, laid eight feet apart. The rails, five feet apart, were of pine, a foot deep, covered with an oak plate, and these with flat bars of iron.

The second railroad was commenced in January, 1827, and completed in May of the same year, extending from the coal-mines in Mauch Chunk, Pennsylvania, to the Lehigh River, a distance of nine miles. From the summit of the road, and within half a mile of the mines, the descent by a plane was nine hundred and eighty-two feet, inclined two hundred and twenty-five feet to the river, and thence twenty-five feet in a shute to the spot where the cars were discharged into the boats. The cars descended by gravity with the loaded wagons, and were drawn up again by mules. The rails of the road were of timber, laid on wooden sleepers, and strapped with flat iron bars.

In 1828 the Delaware and Hudson Canal Company constructed a railroad from their coal-mines to Honesdale, the termination of their canal. The Baltimore and Ohio Railroad and the South Carolina Railroad were also commenced in the same year.

It is said that at the time (1812) when De Witt Clinton was urging the passage, through the Legislature of New York, of the act for the construction of the Erie Canal, Colonel Stevens, of Hoboken, astonished that body by announcing that he could build a railroad at a much less cost than the proposed canal, and on which the transportation, by means of cars drawn by steam locomotives, could be carried on at a considerably cheaper rate, and at a much higher degree of speed than was possible on any canal. He laid before them the results of his numerous and long-continued researches, but his enemies openly laughed at him, and called him a maniac, and even some of his best friends regarded him as a man who had lost himself in experimental science. Had he lived in the days of poor Solomon de Cause or of Friar Bacon, he would probably, like those eminent men, have been consigned to a dungeon. The nineteenth century contented itself with sneering at him as a visionary, and refused to entertain his propositions. His distinguished, wise, and sensible friend, Chancellor Livingston, in a letter addressed to Stevens, dated at Albany, March 2d, 1811, only a year before, expresses his opinion of the railroad locomotive schemes of which his friend was so strenuous an advocate. The chancellor thus writes:

"I had before read of your very ingenious proposition as to railway communication. I fear, however, on mature reflection, that they will be liable to serious objections, and ultimately prove more expensive than a canal. They must be double, so as to prevent the danger of two such heavy bodies meeting. The wall on which they are placed must be at least four feet below the surface, to avoid frost, and three feet above, to avoid snow, and must be clasped with iron, and even then would hardly sustain so heavy a weight as you propose moving at the rate of four miles an hour on wheels. As to wood, it would not last a week. They must be covered with iron, and that, too, very thick and strong. The means of stopping these heavy carriages without a great shock, and of preventing them from running on each other—for there would be many running on the road at once—would be very difficult. In case of accidental stops or necessary stays to take wood or water, etc., many accidents would happen. The carriage of condensing water would be very troublesome. Upon the whole, I fear the expense would be much greater than that of canals, without being so convenient."

And yet, only fourteen years afterward, such was the rapid development of the steam locomotive, the Legislature of the same State granted a charter incorporating the Mohawk and Hudson Railroad, a line, seventeen miles long, running between Albany and Schenectady; and there are now no less than three thousand one hundred and ninety-five miles of railway in the State of New York alone.

Next to Colonel Stevens, and as early as 1819, we have in the United States another advocate for railroads, with steam locomotion. We learn, by an extract from the current news of that day, copied from a literary paper called *The Villager*, that the following memorial was presented to Congress at the previous session, which was referred to the Committee on Commerce and Manufactures. The following is a copy of the document:

" The memorial of Benjamin Dearborn, of Boston, respectfully represents that he has devised in theory a mode of propelling wheel-carriages in a manner probably unknown in any country; and has perfectly satisfied his own mind of the practicability of conveying mails and passengers with such celerity as has never before been accomplished, and with complete security from robberies on the highway.

" For obtaining these results, he relies on carriages propelled by steam, on level railroads, and contemplates that they be furnished with accommodations for passengers to take their meals and their rest during the passage, as in packets ; that they be sufficiently high for persons to walk in without stooping, and so capacious as to accommodate twenty, thirty, or more passengers, with their baggage.

" The inequalities of the earth's surface will require levels of various elevations in the railroads ; and your memorialist has devised means which he believes will be completely effectual for lifting the carriage, by the inherent power of its machinery, from one level to another, as also for the passage of carriages by each other, on the same road ; and he feels confident that whenever such an establishment shall be advanced to its most improved state, the carriages will move with a rapidity at least equal to a mile in three minutes.

" Protection from the attacks of assailants will be insured ; not only by the celerity of the movement, but by weapons of defence belonging to the carriage, and always kept ready in it to be wielded by the number of passengers constantly travelling in this spacious vehicle, where they would have liberty to stand erect, and to exercise their arms in their own defence.

" The practicability of running steam-carriages on the common road was long since advocated in a publication, by that ingenious and useful citizen, Oliver Evans : your memorialist, therefore, does not assume the merit of originating the idea of steam-carriages, but only of modifying the system in such a manner as to produce the results here stated, which could not be effected on a common road.

" Relying upon the candor of the national council, this memorial is laid before them with the desire that ingenious and scientific artists, in the different sections of our country may be consulted, by direction of Congress, on the probability of accomplishing the purposes here anticipated ; and that an experiment be made, if sanctioned by their favorable opinions ; for if the design can be put into successful operation by the Government, a great revenue would eventually be derived from the establishment, besides the advantages before enumerated."

We never have heard that any report was made by the committee respecting it; yet all these results have been signally realized within a little more than a third of a century.

———— ◆•◆ ————

# CHAPTER XIII.

### FIRST ENGLISH LOCOMOTIVE BROUGHT TO AMERICA.

THE competition in England for the £500 prize attracted many distinguished engineers, scientific men, and enterprising gentlemen, from all parts of the world, to witness the contest. Among the engineers from America was Horatio Allen, Esq., late assistant engineer upon the Delaware and Hudson Canal and Railroad, who was on a trip to England to examine into the improvements in the new mode of intercommunication. Another enterprising gentleman from America, who went out expressly to witness these experiments, was Mr. E. L. Miller, of Charleston, South Carolina. Of this gentleman we shall hereafter have occasion to speak more fully. While in Europe, Mr. Horatio Allen was appointed by John B. Jervis, Esq., the chief engineer of the Delaware and Hudson Canal and Railroad Company, to contract for the iron for the road just graded, and also for three locomotives. Mr. Allen was an excellent person for this important duty, as Mr. Jervis well knew, having been associated with him in the construction of the road; he was an engineer of distinction and experience. We shall have to speak of him hereafter, in connection with the running of the first locomotive imported and put upon a railroad in America.

In this work the author has promised to substantiate every position he may assume, by giving to the readers all the evidence upon which his statements are based, and thereby enable them to judge for themselves as to the correctness of his history.

On this visit of Mr. Allen to England, he purchased for the Delaware and Hudson Canal and Railroad Company three locomotives. The "Stourbridge Lion" was one of these, and the first, which soon after arrived in New York. Its performances in the yard of the works where it was landed (the West Point Foundery Works, foot of Beach Street) were witnessed by thousands, attracted by the novelty of the machine. In a letter addressed to the author by David Matthew, Esq., late of Philadelphia, who resided in New York in 1829, and had charge of the men while fitting up the machinery in the shops of the West Point Foundery Association, to whom the author had addressed a letter making some inquiries, he writes:

" PHILADELPHIA, *December* 6, 1859.

"MR. WM. H. BROWN—

"DEAR SIR: Yours of the 20th November is received, inquiring about the first locomotive imported into this country; the first built here, and on what date and railroad it was run. In compliance with your request, I herewith with pleasure send you the following history, partly from memory and partly from records and memoranda upon the subject in some documents I have preserved among a file of old papers and documents.

"Some time about the middle of May, 1829, the locomotive called the Stourbridge Lion arrived from England, on the ship John Jay. It was landed at the wharf of the West Point Foundery Works, foot of Beach Street, New-York City. This engine was in charge of Horatio Allen, Esq., assistant engineer of the Delaware and Hudson Canal and Railroad Company. The locomotive was blocked up in our yard, and steam put to it from our works, and it became the object of curiosity to thousands who visited the works from day to day, to see the curious "*critter*" go through the motions only, as there was no road for it about the premises.   After a short stay in New York, about the 1st of July, it was shipped up the North River to Rondout, for the Delaware and Hudson Canal Company, and thence by canal to Carbondale, where it was tried upon their railroad at Honesdale, run a few miles out upon the road, then taken off the track, the road not being sufficiently strong to carry it.   It was housed and held for sale for many years."

So much, at present, for Mr. Matthew's letter upon the first English locomotive in America.   To this letter, however, we will hereafter again refer.   Meantime, for the information of such of our readers as may not be acquainted with the character and reputation of Mr. Matthew, we will refer to the following certificates from prominent and well-known citizens:

"NEW YORK, *March*, 1831.

"Mr. David Matthew has served an apprenticeship of four years and eleven months in the steam-engine factory of the West Point Association, as a tinner and fitter-up, in course of which time he has conducted himself to the entire satisfaction of his employers, and I recommend him as a trusty and good workman.                                "WM. KEMBLE,
"*Agent for the West Point Association.*"

"ALBANY, *December* 1, 1831.

"The bearer, Mr. David Matthew, has been employed to run the locomotive De Witt Clinton on the Mohawk and Hudson Railroad, since the opening of the work.   I have often been on the engine with him, and seen much of his management and conduct in reference to his business, and believe him to be a sober, industrious man, and well qualified for such work.   I think him very prudent in managing an engine.
"JOHN B. JERVIS,
" *Chief Engineer Hudson and Mohawk Railroad.*"

"SCHENECTADY, *September* 24, 1835.

"By a resolution of the Board of Directors of the Utica and Schenectady Railroad Company, passed September 23, 1835, David Matthew is employed as chief locomotive engineer, at a salary of one thousand one hundred dollars per year.

"WM. C. YOUNG,
" *Chief Engineer.*"

"OFFICE OF THE UTICA AND SCHENECTADY RAILROAD COMPANY.
"ALBANY, *August* 29, 1842.

" *To whom it may concern:*

"The bearer, Mr. David Matthew, has been employed by the company during the past six and a half years, as chief locomotive engineer and machinist, and in all respects has shown himself honest, industrious, and intelligent, and is worthy of patronage and confidence.

"ERASTUS CORNING."

These and many other evidences of Mr. Matthew's character and reliability could be produced, but the foregoing will no doubt be sufficient.

From a mass of useful information received by the author in several letters from John B. Jervis, Esq., who was in 1829 chief engineer of the Delaware and Hudson Canal Company, we make the following extracts in reference to the arrival of the first locomotive in America:

"ROME, NEW YORK, *July* 17, 1870.

"DEAR SIR: Yours of the 1st inst. was duly received; absence from home and special duties have delayed my answer. As it required the overhauling of papers forty years old, it could not be done promptly. The name of the first locomotive ordered from England, and the first in America, was the Stourbridge Lion, and to your questions when and where it was landed, I will refer you to the following letters addressed to me at the time, by Horatio Allen, Esq., who was in New-York City waiting its arrival, and had contracted for it when in England. On referring to my papers, I find that the engine arrived at Rondout on the way to Honesdale from New York, on the 4th of July, 1829. My recol-

6

lections are that it was put in motion on the Carbondale Railroad, at Honesdale, in August, same year, most probably the early part of August. This locomotive and two or three others were obtained from England for the said road, but only the Lion was set up. It worked very well, and no doubt would have done good service, had the trestle-work (of which there was a large portion on the road) been sufficient to sustain the weight of the engine in working. It was the intention of having engines of one and a quarter ton on a wheel as the heaviest; but the builders of the engine at that time had little experience, and when the machine was constructed it was found to have nearly two tons on a wheel, and this the road was not designed for. Subsequently the road has been made a gravity railroad, all the power in both directions being stationary; which is no doubt the best economy for the circumstances and nature of the traffic.

"Mr. Allen's letters, which follow, will give you all necessary facts relative to the arrival of the first locomotive in America. In regard to the present officers of the Delaware and Hudson Canal Company, I have little acquaintance with them; all the old ones are gone, excepting, perhaps, Isaac N. Seymour, who was for many years treasurer (now retired), and living in New York. He could give you much information, by referring to the file of letters for 1829, in the office of the company in New York, including those of August; they would give the time of the running of the engine at Honesdale, in letters from Mr. Horatio Allen to myself. In your last letter to me, you make some inquiries concerning my invention of the principle of using the truck under the front part of the engine, to support and to govern the machine in running curves. I believe I sent you, some time since, a copy of my work upon railway property, etc. In that work, commencing at page 153, you will find all the information upon that subject you may desire. I shall only say here that I was the inventor, and put in successful operation, the locomotive-truck.

"I notice that they are giving more attention to it in England, where they heretofore had strong prejudices against it, and now they attribute it, as a new thing, to Farlie, who introduced it in some new and small machinery in England. All that Farlie has done is simply to adopt my truck. Wishing you great success in your undertaking, I am very truly yours,

"JOHN B. JERVIS."

We will hereafter notice the improvement alluded to by Mr. Jervis, in the last paragraph of his highly-interresting letter, viz., the introduction of the truck under the front part of the engine.   Of this improvement he is, no doubt, the inventor, having put it in successful operation in this country, nearly forty years ago, as we are prepared to show, England's claim to the contrary notwithstanding.

"NEW YORK, *May* 12, 1829.

"JOHN B. JERVIS, ESQ.:

.   .   .   .   "We at length have something definite on the subject of our locomotive.   The Canada, that sailed from Liverpool April 15th, arrived this afternoon, and brings us news of the shipment of our locomotive, on April 8th, on the John Jay, which has not yet got in, though it sailed one week before the Canada.

"Yours,

"HORATIO ALLEN."

"NEW YORK, *May* 17, 1829.

"JOHN B. JERVIS, ESQ.:

.   .   .   .   "The John Jay has arrived, as I informed you.   On Monday the engine is to be landed, and sent to Kemble's establishment.   I hope to have it all together and in operation by Saturday next.                          Yours, .

"HORATIO ALLEN."

## CHAPTER XIV.

### DATE OF ITS RUNNING.

THE exact date of the arrival and landing of the first English locomotive that was ever run upon a railroad in America being now settled by Mr. Horatio Allen's letters to John B. Jervis, Esq., the next object of the author was to learn upon what day that engine was first run upon a railroad.   For this purpose, by advice of Mr. Jervis, he addressed a letter to C. F. Young, Esq., the present general superintendent of the Delaware and Hudson Railroad and Canal Company. Previously to receiving Mr. Young's answer, the author addressed a letter to Thomas Dickson, Esq., the president of the company, to which he received the following reply.

> " DELAWARE AND HUDSON CANAL COMPANY,
> "SCRANTON, *February* 26, 1870.
>
> "WM. H. BROWN, ESQ.,—
>
> "DEAR SIR: I have yours of the 19th inst.  C. F. Young, of Honesdale, Pennsylvania, our general superintendent, has been looking up, for you, the matters you refer to, and has doubtless written you ere this.  In a conversation I had with Mr. Young, a few days ago, he told me that the time of the trial-trip he had found *positively* to have been between the 3d and 8th of August, 1829.  That it was in 1829, and on one of *the days mentioned*, there is not the shadow of a doubt, and that it was the first locomotive run upon this continent is beyond question.
>
> " We take pleasure in affording you every opportunity in making your investigation; and, that there may be no mistake, I will enclose your letter to Mr. Young, that his attention may be called to it again.
>
> " Very truly yours,
> "THOMAS DICKSON, *President.*"

Almost the same mail brought the long-looked-for letter from Mr. Young; and, as he gives the date of the first day's trial near to the consummation of the author's desire upon that subject, we will, as we promised our readers, present Mr. Young's letter, just as it was written, as every portion of it is of interest:

> " OFFICE OF GENERAL SUPERINTENDENT,
> " DELAWARE AND HUDSON CANAL COMPANY,
> "HONESDALE, PA., *February* 23, 1870.
>
> "WM. H. BROWN, ESQ.,—
>
> "DEAR SIR: I owe you an apology for the long delay in furnishing you what information I might be able to obtain respecting

the date of the experimental trip of the first locomotive-engine imported by our company. I waited to hear from a gentleman who was to have examined a file of newspapers, published at Montrose, Susquehanna County, in 1829; but I have not yet heard from him. I have not been able, from any thing I can find in the books or papers of the company, to fix the exact day on which the trial-trip took place. I find from our collector's books, at Eddyville, that two locomotive-engines were cleared at that office, and started up the canal, July 16, 1829. I do not find any record of their arrival at Honesdale, which was probably five or six days thereafter.

"The old inhabitants of this place, who were present at the time, agree that the experimental trip was made in August, 1829. Hon. John Torry informs me that he finds in the books of his father, Jason Torry, a charge against the Delaware and Hudson Canal Company, dated August 3, 1829, for labor of men and horses, drawing stones, 'this day,' to load a railroad-car. This car, loaded with stone, is understood and believed to be the one which was to be attached to the locomotive on its trial-trip. I find many, who were present at the time, remember the car-load of stone designed to be attached to the locomotive on its trial-trip. At the celebration, on the day the experiment was made, a young man, by the name of Alva Adams, had his arm badly shattered by the premature discharge of the cannon which was used. Dr. E. T. Losey, who is now living here, assisted in amputating the arm and afterward attended the patient. Dr. Losey finds the charge on his books, for amputating, dated August 8, 1829. The trial-trip, no doubt, took place some time from the 3d to the 8th of August, 1829. Dr. Losey thinks the arm was amputated the same day on which the injury was received; but says he might have omitted to make the charge for three or four days, but is not certain of this.

"I have had the file of letters for 1829 examined, at our office in New York, without finding any letters from John B. Jervis or Horatio Allen which fix the date of the experiment. I am of opinion that there were such letters, and that they have been lent to some previous explorer, who has failed to return them.

"John B. Jervis's annual report for 1829 I have examined (it is now in our New-York office); but, while he speaks of the causes of failure as to the success of the locomotive, he does not give the day on which the experiment was made.

"I am sorry that I am unable to fix the exact day on which the trial-trip of the first locomotive was made, but there is no doubt it occurred some time from the 3d to the 8th of August, 1829.                  "Yours very truly,
                "C. F. YOUNG,
                        "*General Superintendent.*"

Determined to leave no stone unturned and no effort untried to establish the exact day the first locomotive was run upon a railroad in America, the author (taking the hint from Mr. Young's letter) addressed the postmaster of Montrose, relative to the old file of newspapers said to be in existence, stating the object of his inquiry.   In a few days he received a reply from a lady, Miss Emily C. Blackman, offering her aid and services in examining the said file, and through her energy and perseverance he received much valuable information, by following which, he was rewarded with complete success.   In one of Miss Blackman's letters, she corroborates Mr. Young's information, by the following extract from the Montrose paper:

"*Melancholy Accident.*—We are informed that a young man, by the name of Adams, was severely injured on Saturday last, at Honesdale, by the sudden and unexpected discharge of a cannon. Adams and others were engaged in firing signals on starting the locomotive-engine."—*From the Dundaff Republican, but no date.*

Through the kindness of Miss Blackman, the author learned that a file of the *Dundaff Republican* of 1829 could be obtained from Dilton Yarrington, Esq., of Carbondale; who, on application, kindly forwarded the same to the author.   From this file, under date of Thursday, August 13, 1829, we extract the following:

"*Melancholy Accident.*—We are informed that a young man, by the name of Adams, was severely injured on Saturday last, at Honesdale," etc., etc.

"Saturday last," before Thursday, 13th, was the 8th day of August, 1829, and, without a shadow of doubt, the day the first locomotive turned a driving-wheel upon a road on the American Continent.

———————

# CHAPTER XV.

## LANDING IN AMERICA.

THE author was next at a loss how to account for the long interval, some six weeks or more, which elapsed after the Stourbridge Lion arrived in New York, by Mr. Allen's letter, before its first appearance upon the railroad at Honesdale; when the prompt and indefatigable lady correspondent, Miss Blackman, again came to his relief with a statement abstracted from her own private journal, which was as follows:

*From Morning Courier and New York Enquirer, June 12, 1829.*

"*Locomotive-Engines.*—We yesterday attended the first exhibition of a locomotive-engine, called *The Lion*, imported by the Delaware and Hudson Canal Company, to be used upon their railway. On Wednesday, the engine, just imported, was tried, and gave such general satisfaction, that the present exhibition was unanimously attended by gentlemen of science and particular intelligence. The engine was put up in Mr. Kemble's manufactory, by Horatio Allen, Esq., who went to England to purchase it for the company, and it gives us great satisfaction to say that the most important improvements which have lately been made in the construction of these engines originated with him. It is of nine-horse power, having a boiler sixteen and a half feet long, with two cylinders, each of three-feet stroke. It is calculated to propel from sixty to eighty tons, at five miles per hour. The power is applied to each wheel at about twelve inches from the centre, and the adhesive power of the wheel, arising from the weight of the engine, will give locomotion to the whole structure.

"The steam was raised by the *Lackawaxen* coal, and sustained (although there was no friction) at between forty and fifty pounds to the inch.

"We were delighted with the performance of the engine, and have no doubt but the enterprising company to whom it belongs will reap a rich reward for their enterprise and perseverance.

"Pleased as we were, however, with the engine, we were much more pleased with the practical demonstration offered, of the importance and usefulness of the coal which the company propose to bring to market. It is now reduced to a certainty that the Lackawaxen coal will generate steam in sufficient quantity to answer all the purposes to which it is applied, and this fact is not only of great importance to the company, but is worth millions to our State."

To the kindness of Mr. Yarrington, of Carbondale, Pennsylvania, we are indebted for the opportunity to examine an old file of the *Dundaff Republican*, published in Susquehanna County, Pennsylvania, for the year 1829. Under date of July 23, 1829, we find the following, announcing the arrival at Honesdale of the Stourbridge Lion from New-York, *via* Delaware and Hudson Canal:

"The boats begin to arrive with the travelling-engines and railroad machinery ; all is bustle and business. The engine intended for this end of the road is a plain, stout work of immense height, weighing about seven tons, and will travel four miles per hour, with a train of thirty to thirty-six carriages, loaded with two tons of coal each ; the engine is called the Stourbridge Lion, its boiler being built something in shape of that animal, and painted accordingly. Now imagine to yourself the appearance of that animal, the body at least twelve feet in length and five in diameter, travelling at the rate of four or five miles per hour, together with a host of young ones in train, and you will have some idea of the scene before us ; but the enchantment is broken, and in a few days the whole will be set in motion, and we will now give you information that, when the whole is in operation, we shall give a general notice that we intend to hold a day of rejoicing on the completion of the same, and shall give a general invitation to our fellow-citizens to attend.

"We have procured a large cannon, and intend to station it on the top of the high peak, to sound on the occasion.

"A STRICT OBSERVER."

The following description of the locomotive Stourbridge Lion and its first experimental trip, from the pen of the Hon. John Torry, a resident of Honesdale, and a spectator of the events on that occasion, we will present in his own language :

"HONESDALE, *March* 28, 1870.

"WM. H. BROWN, ESQ.,—

"DEAR SIR: Yours of the 16th inst., asking for information and particulars respecting the trial-trip of the first locomotive in Honesdale, came duly to hand. I have conversed with numerous persons who I thought would be likely to remember incidents concerning it, and have seen my brother, who kept my father's accounts in 1829 (but who was in Minnesota when C. F. Young, Esq., was seeking information).

"From his memorandum made at the time, the precise *date* of the trial is determined (viz., August 8, 1829). I have prepared a statement embodying so many of the incidents as it seems to me you would think of any interest, and probably including some which might better be omitted, as well as some which you will have obtained from other sources, and have appended as foot-notes such copies of the entries I have found as relate to the subject.

"The statements I have made are partly from *my own* knowledge, partly such as I have obtained from interviews with persons who were present, and whose statements I consider reliable, and partly from written memoranda, from which I have made extracts. You can use so much of it as you think advisable, and in such form as you please.

"Dr. Losey, to whom you wrote, died on the 9th inst.

"The first locomotive run by the Delaware and Hudson Canal Company, on their railroad at Honesdale, was constructed in Stourbridge, England (a manufacturing town on the river Stour, some fifteen miles westward from Birmingham).

" Its plan of construction was much less simple than that of
those now in use.   From the great number of its rods and joints,
some who were observers of its experimental trial on the road,
describe it as looking like a mammoth *grasshopper*, having three
or four times the usual number of legs.   Its driving-wheels were
of oak-wood, banded with a heavy wrought-iron tire, and the front
was ornamented with a large, fierce-looking face of a *lion*, in bold
relief, and it bore the name of ' *Stourbridge Lion.*'

" This locomotive and two others, purchased by or made for
the company in England, arrived in New York in May, 1829, and
it was expected the company's railroad would be completed in
time to have the celebration of the opening of the railroad, and of
the running of the first locomotive upon it, on the 4th of July of
that year.   But the month August came before the railroad was
so far completed that the formal opening could be attempted.

" The locomotive having been transported by canal to Honesdale, the ' Stourbridge Lion ' was elevated, by the use of a temporary inclined plane, to the level of the railroad, and put in running order, and placed upon the rails; and every thing thus got
in readiness for the trial.   On Saturday, August 8, 1829, the fire
was kindled and steam raised, and, under the management of Mr.
Horatio Allen, the ' wonderful machine' was found capable of
moving, to the great joy of the crowd of excited spectators.
After running it back and forth on the portion of the road
between the canal basin and the high railroad-bridge across the
west branch of the Lackawaxen, Mr. Allen started it, with no person accompanying him, and without any car being attached, and
ran it with good speed around the curve and across the bridge, and
up the railroad about one and a half mile, to where the railroad
was crossed by a common road-bridge, placed too low to admit of
the passage of the locomotive under it.   Here he reversed the
engine and ran it back to the place of starting, greeted by the
shouting cheers of the people and the booming of cannon.   Mr.
Alva Adams, a mechanic, while assisting to fire the cannon, had
his arm so badly shattered that amputation became necessary.

" After repeating the trial a few times, the ' Stourbridge Lion '
was removed from the track and left standing by the side of the
railroad, with no covering but a temporary roof, until the approach
of winter.

" These experiments demonstrated that the manner of construction of the railroad was not sufficiently firm and substantial

for a locomotive-road, the rails being of hemlock-timber, six inches thick by twelve inches deep, keyed (or wedged) into gains cut in cross-ties of hemlock-timber, placed ten feet apart, with a flat bar of iron fastened by screws upon the top of the rail—the gauge (or width) of track being *four feet three inches*. They also demonstrated that the plan of construction of the locomotive was not such as to afford a probability of its being successfully used for the purpose designed, with any such changes in the road as were then deemed reasonable.

"The failure of success was a great disappointment, not only to the directors and stockholders of the company, but also to the community, who were interested in the prosperity of the county.

"While thus standing by the side of the railroad, it was an object of great dread to timid children who were obliged to pass by it; and many, now residing in Honesdale, remember the care they were accustomed to take, when children, to avoid passing near the fierce-looking 'lion.' In November, 1829, it was housed in with rough boards, as it thus stood beside the railroad, though some of the boards on the sides were soon displaced, to give opportunity *for the curious* to examine it more readily. It remained where thus housed some fourteen or fifteen years, until so many of its parts were detached or broken, that it was entirely disabled and considered worthless as a locomotive; when the boiler was removed to Carbondale, and used with a stationary engine in one of the company's shops, and the wheels, axles, and loose parts, were sold for old iron. Some of the loose parts are still kept as mementos of *the first locomotive run upon a railroad in America*. The boiler is now in use in Carbondale.

"In the original 'Labor Account' kept by Mr. Stephen Torry, for his father's Honesdale business, in 1829, is the following entry:

" 'SATURDAY, *August* 8, 1829.

" ' The locomotive-engine "Stourbridge Lion" was started by steam this morning.—Alva Adams had his arm blown off while firing the cannon.

" ' No work was done until after the middle of forenoon.'

"In the accounts kept by Stephen Torry for his father, in 1829, is a charge to the Delaware and Hudson Canal Company, under date of 'November 7, 1829,' for 'boards to cover the steam-engine.'

"The foregoing extracts are true copies from the original papers relating to Jason Torry's business.

"Respectfully,

"JOHN TORRY."

Annexed we give a sketch of the "Stourbridge Lion" from an original drawing of the machine, together with a description of the engine by Mr. David Matthew, who had charge of the men who were employed to fit up the engine when it arrived in New York, and had been landed at the works of the West Point Foundery, New York.

Mr. Matthew writes, under date of December 6, 1859:

"The 'Stourbridge Lion' was a four-wheeled engine, all drivers, with all four wheels connected by pins in the wheels. The boiler was a round, cylindrical one; no drop part for the furnace, and the smoke-box had a well-painted lion's head on it. The cylinders were vertical, placed at the back and each side of the furnace, with grasshopper-beams and connecting-rods from them to the crank-pins in the wheels. The back wheels and the side-rods between them and the front wheels; the front end of the beams were supported by a pair of radius rods which formed the parallel motion. This engine was built by Foster, Rastrick & Company, at Stourbridge, England."

## CHAPTER XVI

### MORE FACTS OF THE STOURBRIDGE LION.

IN September, 1829, a locomotive built by George Stephenson, at his works in Newcastle-upon-Tyne, arrived in New York and was to be seen, for some time, in the yard of E. Dunscomb, Water Street; its wheels

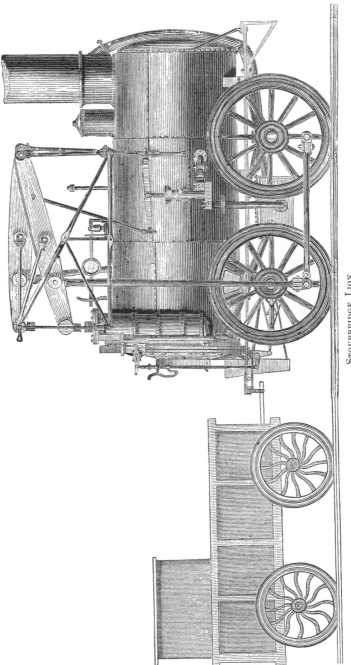

STOURBRIDGE LION.

were raised above the ground and kept running for the amusement of the crowds attracted by its novelty. Of this engine Mr. Horatio Allen speaks in a letter to the author as follows:

"This locomotive, or motive (but not progressive motion), was not the engine which made the first run on the railroad at Honesdale, Pennsylvania. This engine (built by Stephenson at Newcastle-upon-Tyne) was set up at an iron-yard on the East-River side of New York, and being blocked up, so that the wheels could not touch the ground, the engine could go through the motions without running."

As we are determined that our history of the first locomotives in America shall lack no evidence to sustain the facts we record, we cannot close our testimony in the case of the "Stourbridge Lion" without removing an impression which many persons entertain, and have often declared to the author, that this same old engine, which came from England and made the first trip on a railroad in America, is still in existence somewhere in New England. Such is not the fact. Notwithstanding the testimony upon this point to be found in the latter part of the Hon. John Torry's letter to the author, where he distinctly records the ultimate fate of the Lion, we have another letter from an old citizen of that region, the same gentleman who favored us with the file of the *Dundaff Republican*, Mr. Dilton Yarrington, from which we will extract such parts as relate to the final disposition of this locomotive, thus:

"As far as the locomotive was concerned, it was considered a failure from the very first time it was used. It stood around for some years, and by degrees was taken to pieces and wasted away like an old cripple. I worked up some of the fragments of it in the shop in 1849.

. . . . "The boiler is now in use here in Carbondale, in a foundery, where it has been in use for twenty years past, and is

still considered reliable.  The iron plates composing it are full
half an inch thick.

"Respectfully yours,

"D. YARRINGTON."

Mr. Yarrington was in the company's employ, an
old citizen of that region, and lived in Dundaff from
1825 to 1847.

We will now close our description of the events incident to the first locomotive in America, by giving our
readers Mr. Allen's account of his ride alone upon the
"Stourbridge Lion," in a speech made by him in 1851,
at Dunkirk, on the occasion of the celebration in honor
of the completion of the New York and Erie Railroad,
and transmitted by him to the author.  After alluding
in terms of commendation to those who, by their talents
and perseverance, had carried through to a successful
completion the great work just finished, Mr. Allen
continued:

" Having occupied your time with these statements of perhaps
no great interest, but the omission of which would have been an
act of injustice, I have thought that, on this great railroad occasion,
a reference to some of the incidents in the early railroad history
of this country might be appropriate.  To bring before you as
strikingly as in my power, it has occurred to me to lead your imagination to the conception of the scene which would present
itself if, on some fine morning, you were placed at an elevation,
and gifted for the moment with a power of vision which would
command the railroad movements of the whole United States.
There would be presented an exciting picture of activity, in a
thousand iron horses starting forth from the various railroad
centres, or traversing the surface of the continent in all directions.
When the imagination has attained to some conception of the
scene, let it seek to go back to the time when only one of these
iron monsters was in existence on this continent, and was moving
forth, the first of his mighty race.  When was it? where was
it? and who awakened its energies and directed its movements?
It was in the year 1829, on the banks of the Lackawaxen, at the

commencement of the railroad connecting the canal of the Delaware and Hudson Company with their coal-mines, and he who addresses you was the only person on that locomotive.

"The circumstances which led to my being left alone on the engine were these : The road had been built in the summer, the structure was of hemlock-timber, and the rails, of large dimensions, notched on to caps placed far apart. The timber had cracked and warped, from exposure to the sun. After about five hundred feet of straight line, the road crossed the Lackawaxen Creek on a trestle-work about thirty feet high, and with a curve of three hundred and fifty or four hundred feet radius. The impression was very general that the iron monster would either break down the road or that it would leave the track at the curve and plunge into the creek. My reply to such apprehension was, that it was too late to consider the probability of such occurrences; that there was no other course but to have the trial made of the strange animal which had been brought here at such great expense, but that it was not necessary that more than one should be involved in its fate; that I would take the first ride alone, and that the time would come when I should look back to this incident with great interest. As I placed my hand on the throttle-valve handle I was undecided whether I would move slowly or with a fair degree of speed; but believing that the road would prove safe, and preferring, if we did go down, to go down handsomely and without any evidence of timidity, I started with considerable velocity, passed the curve over the creek safely, and was soon out of hearing of the cheers of the large assemblage present. At the end of two or of three miles, I reversed the valves and returned without accident to the place of starting, having thus made the first railroad trip by locomotive on the Western Hemisphere."

Our readers are doubtless now satisfied that to the Delaware and Hudson Canal Company is justly due the credit of having introduced and run upon their railroad the first locomotive that made a revolution with its driving-wheel upon the American Continent. And although this engine proved to be impracticable under the circumstances, it was caused by no defect in its construction, or the principle involved, nor from a lack of power and ability to perform all the duties that might have been required; but from this cause alone, that the road had not been built to sustain such a weight as it was called upon to bear when this new instrument of power was placed upon it. The road had been constructed for horse-power alone, as all other roads were in this country at that early period, and for a long time after, even in England. No idea of a locomotive had then been conceived in this country. Nevertheless, this machine was the forerunner of a mighty race of iron monsters, which only twoscore years after were to be seen traversing every section of the country, even stretching their course from the Atlantic to the Pacific.

We are informed by a letter just received from our faithful correspondent, Miss Blackman, that the boiler of the Stourbridge Lion may now be seen alongside of the road near Carbondale, Pa., and offered for sale. It has been removed from its position in the furnace, to give place to a larger boiler required for the work. The present owners demand $1,000 for it, as a relic of the first locomotive in America.

## CHAPTER XVII.

### FIRST MEETING OF THE BALTIMORE AND OHIO RAILROAD COMPANY.

The first meeting for the purpose of forming a railroad company in the United States, to connect the waters of the East with the waters of the West, was held in the city of Baltimore, on the 12th day of February, 1827. The practicability of the project was left to a committee who soon after reported at the second meeting, on the 19th, and a resolution was passed to obtain a charter from the Legislature. The charter was obtained, and on April 24, 1827, the company was organized, and the first board of directors elected.

The construction of the road was commenced by laying a corner-stone, July 4, 1828, attended by one of the most magnificent processions of the military and civil associations, trades, and professions, ever witnessed on any occasion in the United States. The author was in Baltimore at that time, and participated as one in the vast crowd assembled to take part in the imposing ceremonies of that eventful day. Never in his life (and he has been present on many demonstrations on other occasions) has he witnessed a more magnificent display than was made on that day.

The venerable Charles Carroll, of Carrollton, then over ninety years of age, the only survivor of the signers of the Declaration of Independence, was present on the occasion and laid the corner-stone of this stupendous fabric, with appropriate ceremonies. It is related that, on this occasion, after the imposing ceremonies were over, the venerable patriot made use of the expression to one of his friends present: " I consider this among the most important acts of my life, second only to my signing the Declaration of Independence, if even it be second to that;" and to the end of his life he continued a firm friend of the work.

The construction of the Baltimore and Ohio Railroad was commenced in 1828, and completed in 1852. On January 12, 1853, in honor of the completion of the road, a magnificent banquet took place in Wheeling, its western terminus. At that time it was the longest railroad in the world.

7

At this banquet Mr. Swann, the president of the company, in his address, made this beautiful allusion to the venerable and patriotic Carroll: "There are those present who witnessed the enthusiasm which attended the laying of the first stone, by the illustrious Charles Carroll, of Carrollton. *Clarum et venerabile nomen.*" He then produced the trowel which had been used by Mr. Carroll, and was still preserved by the company, with this memorandum on it: "This trowel was used by Charles Carroll, of Carrollton, to lay the first stone of the Baltimore and Ohio Railroad, July 4, 1828." This interesting relic was received by the assembled company with rapturous applause. Mr. John B. Morris, who delivered the address for the president and directors, took occasion to remark of Mr. Carroll, in connection with the interesting event: "In the full possession of all his mental powers, with his feelings and affections still buoyant and warm, he now declares that the proudest act of his life, and the most important in its consequences to his country, was the signature of the Declaration of Independence; the next, the laying of the corner-stone of the work which is to perpetuate the union of the American States, and to make the East and the West as one household in the facilities of intercourse and the feelings of mutual affection." Benjamin H. Latrobe, Esq., then followed in a few brief remarks, in reply to the beautiful and flattering allusion made to his services by the president of the road. Mr. Latrobe was the chief engineer of the long work just completed, and to his great energy and ability, as well as to his indomitable perseverance in overcoming all obstacles, the success of this stupendous undertaking is largely to be attributed. To the kindness of Mr. Latrobe, also, is the author indebted for much of the valuable information contained in these pages, and also for the pen-and-ink drawing of the Peter Cooper engine, of which we will speak in its proper place, and the sketch and experiments of Mr. Thomas's sailing-car and several other machines that succeeded it.

As soon as the corner-stone of the road was laid, preparations were made to push the work through with as much energy and expedition as could be exercised in the manner of construction for a railroad deemed absolutely necessary at that early day.  The amount of expense involved in the prosecution of this work, when compared with the construction of railroads at the present day, only fills our minds with the more wonder and admiration at the boldness displayed by the projectors of such a stupendous undertaking as the Baltimore and Ohio Railroad.  We will briefly describe the mode of construction of this early road, as it will no doubt prove interesting to our readers who are only conversant with the present method of building railroads.  The method of construction was reported to the author by a gentleman now living in Baltimore, who was engaged in one of the branches of the enterprise at the time, thus :

"After the ground was brought to a level for the track, two square holes were dug, four feet apart, twenty inches wide, two feet long, and two feet deep.  In these holes broken stones were put, sufficient to fill to the surface.  They were then securely rammed down.  Each particle of stone was tested and passed through an iron ring, to insure its proper dimensions.  On this point great care was taken that every stone should be of the uniform size required.  After the foundation is made, a trench six inches deep, and filled with stone, broken and tested with the ring as at first, is extended across the track from one of the filled-up holes to another opposite, upon which a sleeper made of cedar, seven feet long, is laid.  By this process the foundation of the

rails is protected from the effects of dampness or frosts, and firm-
ness and stability are imparted to it. These cedar cross-pieces
were laid with great accuracy and care; a spirit-level was used to
adjust them properly. In each end of these cedar cross-pieces,
immediately above the stone foundation, notches were cut and carefully levelled; into these notches were laid wooden rails or string-
pieces, and securely kept in their places by wedges. These string-
pieces were of yellow pine, from twelve to twenty-four feet long
and six inches square, and slightly bevelled on the top of the
upper side, for the flange of the wheels, which at that time was on
the outside. On these string-pieces iron rails were placed and
securely nailed down with wrought-iron nails, four inches long.
The earth between these cedar sleepers was carefully removed, so
as not to come in contact with the bottom of the string-pieces, and
thus the decay, which otherwise might take place, was prevented.
Yet, with all these difficulties to contend with, our pioneers of the
Baltimore and Ohio Railroad persevered until they brought their
work to a successful termination. After several miles of this
description of road had been made, long granite slabs were substituted for the cedar cross-pieces and the yellow-pine stringers.
Beyond Vinegar Hill, these huge blocks of this solid material
could be seen deposited along the track, and gangs of workmen
engaged in the various operations of dressing, drilling, laying, and
affixing the iron.

"When the track was finished to Vinegar Hill, a distance of
about seven miles, cars were put upon it for the accommodation
of the officers, and to gratify the curious by a ride."

---

# CHAPTER XVIII.

## FIRST BRIGADE OF CARS.

SOME of the newspaper notices of the events of that
day, and the schedules advertised by the company, will
no doubt be interesting to our readers and to railroad
men of the present time. We will give them as we

copied them from old files of the Baltimore newspapers. The *Baltimore American*, May 20, 1830, said:

"We understand that a critical examination of the entire line of the first division of the Baltimore and Ohio Railroad, between this city and Ellicott's Mills, was made on Thursday last, by the president and engineer of the company, for the purpose of testing the solidity of the work. A car was loaded with double the weight intended hereafter to be transported on a single wagon, and was passed over the whole of the first and those parts of the second track which are finished, and it is highly gratifying to learn that, notwithstanding the recent heavy rains, which have placed the work in the most unfavorable condition, it sustained the pressure to the entire satisfaction of those interested in the work. About seven and a quarter miles of the single track are laid on wooden sleepers, and the remaining six and three-quarter miles on stone slabs. Such is the stability of this mode of construction that, in about 16,000 blocks, only forty were observed to be the least affected by the pressure. The horse-path and 'turn-outs' are finished, and the necessary arrangements for horses and drivers having been already made, we understand that it is the intention of the company to open the road for public travel on Monday next, the 24th inst."

The *Baltimore American*, May 24, 1830, said:

"A brigade of cars will run three times a day each way from Baltimore to Ellicott's Mills—passage 25 cents.

"This morning at nine o'clock, in pursuance with previous arrangements of the mayor and the members of the two branches of the City Council, the president, directors, engineer, and officers, of the Baltimore and Ohio Railroad, the editors of the different papers of the city, and a number of strangers, left the depot at the intersection of the railroad with Pratt Street, on an excursion to Ellicott's Mills. The procession was headed by the splendid car Pioneer, in which, together with a number of others, rode the venerable Charles Carroll, of Carrollton. Although the brigade was of large dimensions and filled with passengers, it was drawn with great ease by one horse at a rapid rate. The appearance which they presented was novel and interesting in the extreme. A great number of persons, attracted by the novelty of the sight, attended at the depot and along the course of the road, and all, as far as we could learn, were unanimous in the expression of the opinion that the experiment was calculated to dissipate the doubts of those (if there be any such) who are yet skeptical as to the manifold advantages of this over all other modes of fostering our internal commerce.

"P. S.—Since the above was written, we learn that the party of excursionists had returned, accomplishing the distance (thirteen miles) in one hour and four minutes."

Another extract reads as follows:

"The weather yesterday being remarkably mild and pleasant, vast numbers availed themselves of the opportunity to examine the road and viaduct, and enjoy the gratification of a ride in one of Winans's carriages. The Hon. the Postmaster-General, having reached the city, and being desirous of visiting the road, accompanied the gentlemen attached to the road. A carriage being brought out, the party, consisting of twenty-four ladies and gentlemen, including the Postmaster-General, were drawn to the viaduct by one horse, in actually a little less than six minutes. After alighting to view the magnificent granite structure, the party again seated themselves, and were conveyed back to Pratt Street at the extraordinary rate of fifteen miles per hour. In order to show the perfect ease and rapidity with which heavy loads can be transported over well-constructed railroads, three carriages were attached to each other, and, being filled with more than eighty persons, were rapidly drawn by one horse, at the rate of eight miles per hour. Average each person at 150 lbs., and estimate the carriages at two and a half tons, a single horse actually drew a load of eight and a half tons, at a speed of eight miles per hour, and this extraordinary result was accomplished without any apparent distress to the animal, or indeed uncommon exertion on his part."

In another number of the *American*, we read that an experiment was made for the transportation of two hundred barrels of flour, with a single horse, with the most triumphant success. The flour was deposited in a train of eight cars, and made, together with the cars and the passengers, an entire load of thirty tons. The train was drawn, from Ellicott's Mills to the Relay House, six and a half miles in forty-six minutes. The horse was then changed, and the train, having again started, reached the depot on Pratt Street in sixty-nine minutes, thus accomplishing the thirteen miles in one hour and fifty-four minutes, or at the rate of six and three-fourths of a mile an hour.

We will close these extracts with the following copy of an advertisement, made forty years ago, for the Baltimore and Ohio Railroad:

"RAILROAD NOTICE.—A sufficient number of cars being now provided for the accommodation of passengers, notice is hereby given that the following arrangements for the arrival and departure of carriages have been adopted, and will take effect on and after Monday morning, the 5th inst., viz.: A brigade of cars will leave the depot in Pratt Street at 6 and 10 o'clock A. M. and at 3 to 4 o'clock P. M., and will leave the depot at Ellicott's Mills at 6 and at 8½ o'clock A. M., and at 12½ and 6 o'clock P. M.

"Way-passengers will provide themselves with tickets at the office of the company in Baltimore, or at the depot at Pratt Street or Ellicott's Mills, or at the Relay House, near Elk Ridge Landing.

"The evening way-car for Ellicott's Mills will continue to leave the depot, Pratt Street, at 6 o'clock P. M. as usual.

"N. B.—Positive orders have been issued to the drivers to receive no passengers into any of the cars without tickets. P. S. —Parties desirous to engage a car for the day, can be accommodated after July 5th."

When we compare our present mode of travelling from one city to another, over hundreds and thousands of miles by railroads, being comfortably seated in the most magnificent cars by day, and snugly resting by night in commodious sleeping-cars, we cannot refrain from wonder in attempting to conceive how our forefathers, forty years ago, could content themselves to make a journey even in the most urgent cases, and at all seasons of the year, in the old-fashioned stage-coaches over a rough turnpike, or in canal-packets. But at that time nothing better was known; and the fast line of stages, and the packet-line on the canal, were the best the country could boast of, if we except the beautiful steamers that navigated some of our rivers. The early methods of travelling when railroads were first brought to notice were only one remove, in convenience and improvement, from those we have just described.

In connection with the early operations of the Baltimore and Ohio Railroad, as compared with the present, the following "travelling memoranda," published in the *New-York Gazette*, in May, 1831, furnish some reminiscences worthy of preservation.

"TRAVELLING MEMORANDA.

"*Messrs. Lang, Turner & Company:*

"Having, last week, business in Philadelphia, Baltimore, and the city of Washington, I started at six A. M. on Monday. In order to show the facilities afforded at the present day to do much business in a short time, I send you a sketch of my excursion.

"Left New York at six A. M. on Monday. Arrived in Philadelphia at five P. M. Called on four persons. Settled my business with them by nine. Went to bed; and started on Tuesday morning at six for Baltimore, where I arrived at five P. M. Got through with my business there at half-past nine. Went to bed. Started at four A. M. on Wednesday for Washington, and arrived a little after nine A. M. Dressed, called on the President, and finished my business with him. Dined at Gadsby's. Took a hack in the afternoon, rode several miles, and completed my business with four persons. Took tea with a friend. Slept at Gadsby's. Started at four A. M. on Thursday, on my return. Arrived at Baltimore at ten, visited the cathedral, Washington Monument and the waterworks, before dinner. Dined at Barnum's splendid hotel. Partook of a bottle of wine with three Albanians; at three mounted a car, with twenty-two passengers, on railroad. Visited Ellicott's Mills, thirteen miles from Baltimore. Returned to Baltimore before

dark. Took tea, and afterward, in a hack, visited the venerable
Mr. Carroll, of Carrollton. Returned to Barnum's. Went to bed;
and started for Philadelphia, where I arrived at half-past six P. M.
Made several friendly visits. Went to bed. Started on Saturday
and reached New York at half-past five the same day. Was thus
absent nearly six days—travelling about six hundred miles, and
completing all my business at the expense of forty dollars and
seventy cents.

"The observations that I made were, that Baltimore and Philadelphia are looking up. In both places the bustle of business
reminded me of home, that is to say, New York. The canal which
connects the Delaware with the Chesapeake, through which I
passed in two hours, is a great and useful work. The railroad,
which already passes several miles beyond Ellicott's Mills, is a
most delightful and useful mode of conveyance. The car in which
I took my passage to Ellicott's Mills (four others in company)
contained twenty-two passengers, drawn by one horse, and the
time going the thirteen miles was one hour and a quarter. By the
1st of July the locomotives will be in operation upon the railroad,
when the same distance will be travelled in thirty minutes.

"Yours, etc., J. L."

Those who have seen and travelled only in the
comfortable and convenient passenger-cars of the present
day cannot comprehend the tedious progress with which
such improvements have been made.

The first passenger-car was like a market-car on rail-
road-wheels. Then came cars resembling the old-fashioned stage-coach, with the same springs and leather
braces, and carrying nine passengers each, with a driver's
seat perched upon either end, as there was no such contrivance as a turn-table at that early day. For a long
time the cars were gaudily painted, with a small increase
in the size. One of those, built by Mr. Richard Imlay,
is thus described in the *Baltimore American*, August 4,
1830:

"A number of persons visited Monument Square, yesterday,
for the purpose of examining a very elegant railroad passenger-

carriage, just finished by Mr. Imlay, and intended to be immediately placed on the road.

"The arrangement for the accommodation of passengers is, in some respects, different from any other which has yet been adopted. The body of the carriage will contain twelve persons, and the outside seats at either end will receive six, including the driver. On the top of the carriage is placed a double sofa, running lengthwise, which will accommodate twelve more. A wire netting rises from two sides of the top of the carriage, to a height which renders the top seats perfectly secure. The whole is surmounted by an iron framework, with an awning to protect from the sun or rain. The carriage, which is named the 'Ohio,' is very handsomely finished, and will, we have no doubt, be a great favorite with the visitors to the railroad, the number of whom, we are gratified to learn, continues to be as great as it was at the opening of the road."

———— ✦•✦ ————

# CHAPTER XIX.

## ROSS WINANS'S IMPROVEMENTS.

THE road to Ellicott's Mills was opened on May 24, 1830. Trains of cars like the above were called brigades, and were continued until Ross Winans, Esq., placed upon the track the first eight-wheel car ever built for passengers, and called it by the appropriate name of "Columbus." This car was a large box, such as any carpenter could make; it had a truck of four wheels at either end, the same as the eight-wheel cars of the present time; it also had seats on the top, like the other cars hitherto used, which were reached by a ladder at one of the corners. This was followed by several odd-shaped contrivances; one was nicknamed the "Sea-serpent," another was known by the *sobriquet* of the "Dromedary;" next came the Winchester pattern; and this was followed by the "Washington," each an improvement on its predecessor. The latter resembled three coach bodies combined in one, and divided in the interior into three separate apartments, and entered by doors on each side of each apartment. The author remembers well, as if but yesterday, riding in cars of this construction, in October, 1833, upon the railroad between South Amboy and Bordentown, which connected by steamboats both with New York and Philadelphia. As the passengers landed and approached the cars to take their seats, each car appeared surmounted with the letter A, B, C, etc., in order, and each apartment was numbered 1, 2, or 3. Thus the passenger, on examining the ticket furnished to him on the steamboat, entered the car and apartment designated thereon. These carriages continued on all the roads then operating between the principal cities—as Boston and Providence, Philadelphia and New York, Philadelphia and Baltimore, and Baltimore and Washington—until the eight-wheel passenger car was brought into use, with the passage-way the entire length between the seats, which were placed on the sides, as at present.

When the design for this style of car came before the board of directors of the Baltimore and Ohio Railroad Company, there was quite a discussion whether there should be an aisle in them, with entrances at each end, and seats as at present, or whether the cars should be in compartments, with entrances at the sides, with a ledge outside for the conductor; and one of the arguments against the aisle, verified by the result, as we know, was the apprehension that it would often be one long spittoon! The possibility of this was admitted;

but other considerations prevailed in favor of the aisle, which has continued to the present day.

Horatio Allen, Esq., in one of his letters to the author, once said, in alluding to the improvements in every department of railroad machinery, locomotives, cars, etc.:

"It is generally believed that the railroad system was imported into this country from England, full grown, but such is not the case. This will be exemplified in no better instance than the fact that in September, 1832, steel springs were first placed upon the locomotive 'York' and tender, as an experiment only, and they demonstrated their utility and necessity in regulating the motion and greatly diminishing the jar and consequent injury to the road. This also suggested the propriety of making a further experiment, by placing some of the burden-cars on springs, by which it was found that they admitted of one-third more loading, without any increase of damage to the road or car."

Two years earlier than this, however, other and important improvements had been made. One of the great desideratums in the beginning of railroad enterprise in this country, and to which no example could be applied, was a plan to reduce the large amount of friction.

In the early period of the Baltimore and Ohio Railroad, when no one dreamed of steam, horses were expected to do the work, and to reduce the friction of the axles in the boxes was the object to be achieved. In this extremity, Ross Winans, Esq., now living, a venerable citizen of Baltimore, came to the rescue with his inventive genius. Dr. William Howard, an accomplished and scientific gentleman, had already patented the application of the ordinary friction-wheel to a car, where the main journal revolved on the exterior periphery; but Mr. Winans suspended his wheel by a projecting flange, on the interior periphery of which the

main axle revolved. This was the *ne plus ultra* of the
friction-wheel, and Mr. Winans became immortalized.
B. H. Latrobe, Esq., describes a scene in one of the upper
rooms of the Baltimore Exchange, where the venerable Charles Carroll, of Carrollton, who was the great
man, on all important occasions, was seated in a little
railroad car, drawn by a small weight attached to a
string passing over a pulley and dropping into the hall
below. Around him were all the prominent men of
Baltimore; all were as much pleased as children with a
new toy. In fact, there was a verdant freshness about
all railroad objects in those days which it is wonderful
to conceive in this period of advance and improvement.

Not only was friction sought to be avoided, but all
sorts of experiments were tried, to improve the road.*
To ride in a railroad-car, in those days, was literally
to go "thundering" along. The roll of the wheel was
hammering the iron rails out of existence. When this
became known, after tens of thousands of dollars had
been thrown away, one of the directors, a man, too, of
general information, proposed to lay a thin slab of lead
between the iron and the stone, to relieve the concus-
sion. Luckily, this costly experiment, which would
have furnished the sportsmen of the interior with slugs
and bullets without cost, was not carried into effect.
We only mention this now, to show how crude were
the notions of the wisest men, touching railroads in their
infancy, in this country, and to indicate the obstacles
our forefathers had to contend with in the early days
of their construction. With no example before them
to follow, with no experience before them to govern,
every thing had to be tested by actual experiment.

---

* Iron strips were laid, for miles and miles, on stone curbs, on the Baltimore and
Ohio Railroad.

# CHAPTER XX.

## FIRST EXPERIMENTAL LOCOMOTIVE.

The first locomotive ever built in the United States was constructed to determine a principle, at that early period, susceptible of a great diversity of opinions, even among the engineers and scientific men of that day, viz., the ability of a locomotive to keep upon the track in running a curve.    When steam made its appearance on the Liverpool and Manchester Railroad, in England, it attracted much attention in this country, and the question of its early adoption became the subject of a great deal of speculation and argument.    There was this difficulty in the way of introducing an English engine upon an American road : In England the roads were virtually straight, or with very long curves; but in America they were full of curves, sometimes of as small a radius as two hundred feet.    There was not capital enough in the United States, applicable to railroad purposes, to justify engineers in setting Nature at defiance in their construction.    If a tunnel through a spur could be saved, in an American railroad, by a track round it, the tunnel would be avoided, and a circuitous route adopted, although the distance was increased for miles in consequence ; so, if embankments could be saved by heading valleys in place of crossing them, it was done.    This led to sharp curves upon the American roads, where there would be straight lines in England.

No better illustration of this is to be seen than near the Relay House, or Washington Junction, of the Baltimore and Ohio Railroad, where the curve, as the road turned into the gorge of the Patapsco, was originally located, with less than three hundred feet radius, to avoid the necessity of the cut that has since been made through the rocky northern jaw of the gorge. A tunnel, too, is now cut at the Point of Rocks, through the hard intractable material which is there met with, in a spur of the Catoctin Mountain. In the first instance, the road was located to avoid it.

THE first locomotive, then built to demonstrate its adaptability to a curved road, was constructed by Mr. Peter Cooper, of New York, long and most favorably known as the founder of the far-famed Cooper Institute in that city. Mr. Cooper's locomotive was built at the St. Clair Works, near Baltimore, and was first run upon the Baltimore and Ohio Railroad in the summer of 1829, nearly two years before that first really successful locomotive (as it was described in the *Ledger*, and built by Messrs. Tyler and Baldwin) was tried upon the Germantown and Norristown Railroad, in 1832. What success Mr. Cooper's locomotive displayed on its first trial-trip we will describe:

The Baltimore and Ohio Railroad, as we have before stated, was the first of any extent begun in America; and the first built for the purposes of trade and commerce, as nearly all are at the present day. Previous to the year 1826, no railroad, even in England, had been constructed for the general conveyance of passengers or merchandise between two distant points. A few railroads had been constructed for local purposes, such as the conveyance of coal or ores from the mines to the points of shipment on navigable streams; but, for general purposes of travel or transportation, they were still regarded as an untried experiment, and the question had not been settled whether stationary engines or horse-power would be the most available. The Stockton and Darlington Railway, the Killingsworth, and several others in England, all coal-roads, had experimented with locomotives, but no one of them was satisfied that the locomotive would ever advantageously super-sede horse-power. The Liverpool and Manchester Rail-road had just been completed, but the question had not been settled what power should be used upon it. The same might be said of railroads in America—one or two short roads, for mining purposes, having been construc-ted, using horse-power.

We have devoted the foregoing remarks to the early history of the Baltimore and Ohio Railroad, not only from the fact that it was the first railroad in the United States, commenced for the actual traffic and commerce of the community between two distant sec-tions of the country, the far-off West with the East, but because it was the railroad upon which the first locomotive built in the United States was successfully introduced. We allude to the machine constructed by Mr. Peter Cooper, in 1829;* and, although this was but a liliputian affair, it nevertheless became the forerun-ner of a race of iron giants who sprang into existence as soon as the principle was established, for the demonstra-tion of which Mr. Cooper had brought forth his "Tom Thumb" locomotive. The cause which led him, at this time, to deviate from the path of his legitimate business, to become the builder of the first American locomotive, will be better explained by the perusal of his letter to the author, in answer to some inquiries upon that sub-ject, dated

* First experiment made in that year, then altered and successfully experi-mented with in 1830.

NEW YORK, *May* 18, 1869

MR. WILLIAM H. BROWN—

"MY DEAR SIR: In reply to your kind favor of the 10th inst., I write to say that I am not sure that I have a drawing or sketch of the little locomotive placed by me on the Baltimore and Ohio Railroad, in the summer of 1829, to the best of my recollection.

"The engine was a very small and insignificant affair. It was made at a time when I had become the owner of all the land now belonging to the Canton Company, the value of which, I believe, depended almost entirely upon the success of the Baltimore and Ohio Railroad.

"At that time an opinion had become prevalent that the road was ruined for steam locomotives, by reason of the short curves found necessary to get around the various points of rocks found in their course. Under these discouraging circumstances many of the principal stockholders were about abandoning the work, and were only prevented from forfeiting their stock by my persuading them that a locomotive could be so made as to pass successfully around the short curves then found in the road, which only extended thirteen miles, to Ellicott's Mills.

"When I had completed the engine, I invited the directors to witness an experiment. Some thirty-six persons entered one of the passenger-cars, and four rode on the locomotive, which carried its own fuel and water; and made the first passage, of thirteen miles, over an average ascending grade of eighteen feet to the mile, in one hour and twelve minutes. We made the return-trip in fifty-seven minutes.

"I regret my inability to make such a sketch of the engine as I would be willing to send you at this moment, without further time to do so.

"Yours with great respect,
"PETER COOPER."

The following letter from Benjamin H. Latrobe, Esq., the chief engineer of the Baltimore and Ohio Railroad during its construction, addressed to the author, and containing a description and sketch of the sailing-car invented by Mr. Evan Thomas, and experimented with upon the road, and also his promise of a future sketch

8

of the Peter Cooper locomotive, will no doubt be interesting to our readers:

EAST HAMPTON, LONG ISLAND, *August* 4, 1869.
WM. H. BROWN, ESQ.—

"DEAR SIR: Your letter to me, of the 26th July, has been
forwarded to me at this place, where I am on a visit with my
family. It will give me pleasure to give you what information I
can upon the subject upon which you inquire, but I cannot do this
so well here, as I could after my return to Baltimore, and communicating with my brother, who, as counsel of the Baltimore and Ohio
Railroad Company, entered its service a couple of years before I
did, as a subordinate in the engineer corps, on the 1st of July, 1830.

"I well recollect the little experimental locomotive of Mr.
Peter Cooper, and also the sailing-car of Mr. Evan Thomas; but
I could not give you a reliable sketch of the former at present,
but, as to the latter, it was 'a basket body,' like that of a sleigh,
and had a mast, and, if I recollect, 'a square sail, and was mounted
upon four wheels of equal size.' It ran equally well in either direction, but of course only in that in which the wind happened to be
blowing at the time, although it would go with the wind abaft the
beam, but at a speed proportioned to the angle with a line of the
sails. It was but a clever toy, but had its use at the time in showing how little power of propulsion was necessary upon a railway,
compared with the best of the roads that had preceded it. Mr.
Cooper's engine had, I remember, a vertical tubular boiler, and
he was, at the time of its being placed on the Baltimore and Ohio
Railroad in the summer of 1829, regarded as the first suggester of
that form of boiler,* although Mr. Booth, the treasurer of the
Liverpool and Manchester Railway, had proposed it for the Rocket
engine about the same time; upon this point, however, I am not
posted. Were I at home I would refer to some books and memoranda there, which, together with an interchange of recollections
with my brother, would enable me to speak more specifically. The
mode of applying the power to the wheels I do not remember. I
had just entered the company's service, and my thoughts were
directed more to learning the use of the levelling instrument and
transit, and how to run curves with the latter, than to the rolling
machinery of the railroad.

* Mr. Cooper has since informed the author that, for want of regular tubes (not
then ever used), he substituted gun-barrels for tubes.

"I recollect very distinctly, however, a trip which this little locomotive of 'Alderman Cooper's,' as he was then called, made to Ellicott's Mills, where I was stationed. It must have been in July or August, 1830. It brought out several of the directors, and my brother was one of the party, and I remember following it a little distance down the road, after it had started with much puffing and leaking of steam from some of its joints.

" It was in size (and power too, I might say) about the scale of Evan Thomas's sailing-car; yet it was, as the first step in the use of steam on that road, a highly important one.

" Its fuel, I think, was anthracite coal, the use of which, in the engines which succeeded it, was a favorite idea with the company, and influenced the form of the locomotives employed upon the road for several subsequent years.

" The Baltimore and Ohio Railroad, stimulated by the example of the Liverpool and Manchester Railway, next year (1830) offered a premium of $500 to the constructor of the locomotive which would draw fifteen tons, gross weight, fifteen miles an hour. This advertisement brought upon the road an odd collection of four or five original American ideas, of which it is much to be regretted that photographs and indeed detailed drawings have not been preserved. Among these was a rotary engine, by a Mr. Childs, which, I believe, never made a revolution of its wheels, certainly not in the form of *the locomotive*. The engine which took the premium was built by Mr. Phineas Davis, which was the model for those built after it for three or four years.

"I cannot add more just now, and, as I shall not be in Baltimore (except to post this) for three or four weeks, I must delay writing until then.

" Respectfully and truly yours,

" BENJAMIN H. LATROBE."

# CHAPTER XXI.

## PETER COOPER LOCOMOTIVE.

MR. LATROBE's next letter informed the author that he had then a rough sketch of the Peter Cooper machine, taken by his brother, John H. B. Latrobe, Esq., counsellor for the company; but he desired to submit the sketch to Mr. Ross Winans, for his examination and opinion, before he transmitted it.

BALTIMORE, *November* 20, 1869.

WM. H. BROWN, ESQ.—

"DEAR SIR: I have now seen Mr. Winans, and shown him the rough sketch of the Peter Cooper locomotive, referred to in my former letter. I send, upon the next page, a copy of the sketch, which presents as near an approach to a picture of the machine as at this distant day is possible to exhibit. Mr. Ross Winans tells me that Mr. Cooper brought the boiler from New York, in the spring or early in the summer of 1829; and it was on a frame, and rested on four wheels belonging to the company; the road was then used thirteen miles to Ellicott's Mills, and with horse-power. The boiler was tubular, and upright in position. Mr. Winans does not recollect the dimensions of it, although he says it lay in his shops for several years. He thinks it was not more than twenty inches in diameter, and, perhaps, from five to six feet high. There was a single cylinder of three and one-quarter inches in diameter, fourteen and one-quarter inches stroke, that projected its piston-rod and connecting-rod, so as to take hold of the crank by direct action.

"On the crank-shaft, which rested on the frame of the car, was a spur-wheel which geared with a pinion on the forward road-wheels so as to increase speed; the road-wheels being only two and one-half feet in diameter.

"The fuel was anthracite coal, and an artificial draught, in the fire-box at the bottom of the boiler, was created by a fan, driven by a belt passing around a wooden drum attached to one of the road-wheels, and a pulley on the fan-shaft as shown in the sketch.

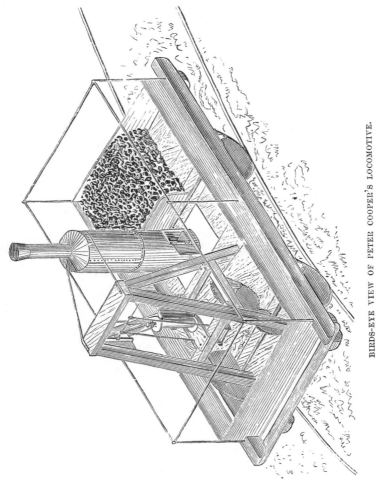

BIRDS-EYE VIEW OF PETER COOPER'S LOCOMOTIVE.

"Mr. Winans says that Mr. Cooper at first proposed to communicate the reciprocating motion of the piston-rod to the road-wheels by an arrangement which I cannot accurately describe, but the experiment did not satisfy Mr. Cooper on trial, and the common crank action was substituted, and the favorable results obtained, which are described in Mr. Winans's letter of August 28, 1830, published in the *Railroad Record* of Cincinnati, on the 8th of July last. Mr. Cooper, if applied to, could perhaps furnish some interesting additional particulars about this engine, which was undoubtedly the *very first* American locomotive.

"Mr. Winans, after examining the sketch, pronounces it substantially correct as to the general features of the engine ; the details, many of course ideal, must be very defective. The number, size, and length of the tubes are not known, only their position in the boiler.

"The road-wheels were two and a half feet in diameter; the axles had outside bearings upon Winans's friction wheels. The axle on which the pinion was fixed was kept from lateral or longitudinal movement, so as to preserve its position with respect to the spur-wheel.

"Your friend's sketch of the horse-car, you sent for my inspection, gives the general idea of it, and it is made with a spirit that shows him to be a good draughtsman and knowing to the 'points of a horse,' better than myself—the thing was as much like one of those horse-powers, of which we see so many, along railways at the stations, for cutting-up wood for the locomotives. The hinged or slatted platform, on which the horse walked, turned round a drum ; on this was a spur-wheel working in a pinion on the road-wheel axle; so that this gearing gave considerable speed to the car, with a moderate one to the horse. I remember well the adventure with the cow, mentioned by my brother in his lecture, to which you refer. I agree with him and Mr. Winans that the successful experiment with the Cooper engine was in 1830, as it was the year I entered the Baltimore and Ohio Railroad Company's service, and some of the particulars are permanently fixed upon my memory.

"I cannot add more just now, and, as I shall not be in Baltimore for three or four weeks, I must delay writing.

"Respectfully and truly yours,

"BENJ. H. LATROBE."

In 1829 Mr. Cooper made some experiments with his little locomotive, built upon the principle he first adopted; but, as it did not perform as well as he expected and desired, he changed his plan, and, after some delays, made, as one may say, the first actual experimental trip on Saturday, August 28, 1830. A full and particular account of this experiment has been given the author by Mr. Winans himself, who was present on the occasion, and took a lively interest in the result. Mr. Winans writes:

" On Saturday, the 28th of August last, 1830, the first railroad-car propelled by steam proceeded the whole distance from Baltimore to Ellicott's Mills, and tested a most important principle—that curvatures of 400 feet radius offer no material impediment to the use of steam-power on railroads, when the wheels are constructed with a cone, on the principle ascertained by Mr. Knight, chief engineer of the Baltimore and Ohio Railroad Company, to be applicable to such curvatures. The engineers in England have been so decidedly of opinion that locomotive steam-engines could not be used on curved rails, that it was much doubted whether the many curvatures on the Baltimore and Ohio Railroad would not exclude the use of steam-power. We congratulate our fellow-citizens on the conclusive proof, which removes forever all doubt on this subject, and establishes the fact that steam-power may be used on our road with as much facility and effect as that of horses, at a very reduced expense.

" The engine " (Cooper's locomotive-engine) " started from Pratt Street depot, taking the lead of a train of carriages. The power of the engine is a little, if any, over that of one horse, and it can therefore only be regarded as a working model. Immediately on front of, and connected with it, was a passenger-carriage containing (including the engine attendants) twenty-four persons. The aggregate weight of carriages, persons, fuel, and water, as nearly as could be ascertained, was estimated to be from four to four and a half tons. Notwithstanding the great disproportion of the moving power to the load, the following highly-gratifying results were obtained; the time was accurately noted by disinterested gentlemen, of the first respectability:

*First mile*—performed in six minutes and ifty seconds, the steam in the onset not being fully raised.

*Second mile*—performed in five minutes ; one minute was lost in altering the switch, to pass from one track to the other.

*Third mile*—travelled in six minutes ; two minutes lost in changing from one track to the other, the switch not being in the right place.

*Fourth mile*—was travelled in four minutes and thirty seconds.

*Fifth mile*—occupied five minutes and twenty-five seconds.

*Sixth mile*—travelled in six minutes ; one minute was lost in changing to the other track.

*Seventh mile*—travelled in five minutes and thirty seconds ; the engine stoped at the middle depot for fifteen minutes to receive a supply of water.

*Eighth mile*—performed in six minutes.

*Ninth mile*—performed in five minutes and forty-five seconds, the engine traversing an ascent of thirteen feet per mile, and encountering the numerous curves which abound in this part of the road.

*Tenth mile*—performed in seven minutes ; the engine still ascending at the rate of thirteen feet per mile, and the road much curved.

*Eleventh mile*—in seven minutes and thirty seconds ; the same disadvantages of an ascending and curved line of road being still encountered.

*Twelfth mile*—in seven minutes and thirty seconds ; the ascent here being increased to eighteen feet per mile and the line curved.

*Thirteenth mile*—in six minutes and thirty seconds, the same disadvantages of an ascending and curved line being encountered as on the preceding mile.

" Making the aggregate passage of thirteen miles, under the circumstances detailed, in the space of one hour and fifteen minutes.

" On the return of the locomotive-engine at six o'clock in the evening, the following results were realized, there being four additional passengers, or thirty in all, seated in the attached carriage :

*First mile*—travelled in five minutes.

*Second mile*—travelled in four minutes.

*Third mile*—travelled in four minutes six seconds.

*Fourth mile*—travelled in four minutes.

*Fifth mile*—travelled in four minutes four seconds.

*Sixth mile*—travelled in four minutes five seconds.

(Four minutes occupied in taking in a supply of water.)

*Seventh mile*—travelled in five minutes.

*Eighth mile*—travelled in three minutes fifty seconds.

*Ninth mile*—travelled in four minutes twenty-five seconds.

*Tenth mile*—travelled in four minutes ten seconds.

*Eleventh mile*—travelled in four minutes forty seconds.

*Twelfth mile*—travelled in four minutes fifty seconds.

*Thirteenth mile*—travelled in four minutes fifty seconds.

Making the entire passage of thirteen miles in sixty-one minutes, including the four minutes lost in taking in water at the middle depot. If this be deducted, it will give precisely fifty-seven minutes in travelling the distance.

"It should also be borne in mind that these are experiments merely, and that several material improvements have already suggested themselves to the inventor. The result, under all the circumstances, is highly satisfactory, and constitutes another triumph of the efforts of American genius."

# CHAPTER XXII.

### THE "TOM THUMB'S" RACE WITH THE HORSE-CAR.

As much as we have written and quoted respecting this first experimental locomotive of Mr. Peter Cooper, we still cannot leave the subject without giving our readers a description of that first trip, from the pen of H. B. Latrobe, Esq., the counsellor of the company, who was one of the passengers on that occasion. Mr. Latrobe thus describes the adventure:

"For a brief season it was believed that this feature of the early American roads would prevent the use of locomotive-engines. The contrary was demonstrated by a gentleman still living in an active and ripe old age, honored and beloved, distinguished for his private worth and for his public benefactions; one of those to whom wealth seems to have been granted by Providence that men might know how wealth might be used to benefit one's fellow-creatures. The speaker refers to Mr. Peter Cooper, of New York. Mr. Cooper was satisfied that steam might be adapted to the curved roads which he saw would be built in the United States; and he came to Baltimore, which then possessed the only one on which he could experiment to vindicate his belief, and he built an engine to demonstrate his belief. The machine was not larger than the hand-cars used by workmen to transfer themselves from place to place; and, as the writer now recalls its appearance, the only wonder is, that so apparently insignificant a contrivance could ever have been regarded as competent to the smallest results. But Mr. Cooper was wiser than many of the wisest around him. His engine could not have weighed a ton, but he saw in it a principle which the forty-ton engines of to-day have but served to develop and demonstrate.

" The boiler of Mr. Cooper's engine was not as large as the kitchen boiler attached to many a range in modern mansions; it was of about the same diameter, but not much more than half as high. It stood upright in the car, and was filled above the furnace, which occupied the lower section, with vertical tubes. The cylinder was but three and a half inches in diameter, and speed was gotten up by gearing. No natural draught could have been sufficient to keep up steam in so small a boiler; and Mr. Cooper used, therefore, a blowing-apparatus, driven by a drum attached to one of the car-wheels, over which passed a cord that in its turn worked a pulley on the shaft of the blower. Among the first buildings erected at Mount Clare was a large car-house, in which railroad-tracks were laid at right angles with the road-track, communicating with the latter by a turn-table, a liliputian affair indeed compared with the revolving platforms, its successors, now in use.

" In this car-shop, Mr. Cooper had his engine, and here steam was first raised; and it seems as though it were within the last week that the speaker saw Mr. George Brown, the treasurer of the company, one of our most estimable citizens, his father Mr. Alexander Brown, Mr. Philip E. Thomas, and one or two more, watch Mr. Cooper, as with his own hands he opened the throttle, admitted the steam into the cylinder, and saw the crank-substitute operate successfully with a clacking noise, while the machine moved slowly forward with some of the by-standers, who had

stepped upon it. And this was the first locomotive for railroad
purposes ever built in America; and this was the first transportation of persons by steam that had ever taken place on this side
of the Atlantic, on an American-built locomotive.

"Mr. Cooper's success was such as to induce him to try a trip
to Ellicott's Mills, on which occasion an open car, the first used
upon the road already mentioned, having been attached to the
engine, and filled with the directors and some friends, the speaker

Fig. 9.

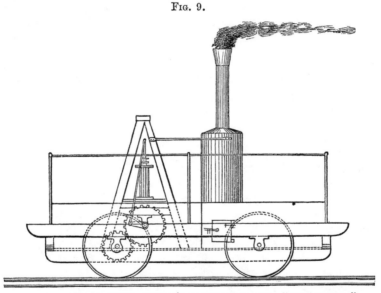

A SIDE VIEW OF PETER COOPER'S LOCOMOTIVE, THE "TOM THUMB."

[From an original drawing expressly for this work.]

among the rest, the first journey by steam in America on an
American locomotive was commenced. The trip was most interesting. The curves were passed without difficulty, at a speed of
fifteen miles an hour; the grades were ascended with comparative
ease; the day was fine, the company in the highest spirits, and
some excited gentlemen of the party pulled out memorandum-books,
and when at the highest speed, which was eighteen miles an hour,
wrote their names and some connected sentences, to prove that
even at that great velocity it was possible to do so. The return trip

*Exciting Trial of Speed between Mr. Peter Cooper's Locom*

The trial took place on the Baltimore and Ohio Railroad, on the 28th August, 1830.   The sketch

(See Mr. Latrob

*Tom Thumb,"* *and one of Stockton & Stokes's Horse-Cars.*

the moment the Engine overtook and passed the Horse-Car, the passengers filled with excitement.

tior, page 116.)

from the Mills, a distance of thirteen miles, was made in fifty-seven minutes. This was in the summer of 1830, but the triumph of this Tom Thumb engine was not altogether without a drawback. The great stage proprietors of the day were Stockton and Stokes; and on that occasion a gallant gray, of great beauty and power, was driven by them from town, attached to another car on the second track—for the company had begun by making two tracks to the Mills—and met the engine at the Relay House, on its way back. From this point it was determined to have a race home; and, the start being even, away went horse and engine, the snort of the one and the puff of the other keeping time and time.

"At first the gray had the best of it, for his *steam* would be applied to the greatest advantage on the instant, while the engine had to wait until the rotation of the wheels set the blower to work. The horse was perhaps a quarter of a mile ahead, when the safety-valve of the engine lifted, and the thin blue vapor issuing from it showed an excess of steam. The blower whistled, the steam blew off in vapory clouds, the pace increased, the passengers shouted, the engine gained on the horse, soon it lapped him— the silk was plied—the race was neck and neck, nose and nose— then the engine passed the horse, and a great hurrah hailed the victory. But it was not repeated, for just at this time, when the gray master was about giving up, the band which drove the pulley, which moved the blower, slipped from the drum, the safety-valve ceased to scream, and the engine, for want of breath, began to wheeze and pant. In vain Mr. Cooper, who was his own engineer and fireman, lacerated his hands in attempting to replace the band upon the wheel; in vain he tried to urge the fire with light wood: the horse gained on the machine and passed it, and, although the band was presently replaced, and steam again did its best, the horse was too far ahead to be overtaken, and came in the winner of the race. But the real victory was with Mr. Cooper, notwithstanding. He had held fast to the faith that was in him, and had demonstrated its truth beyond peradventure. All honor to his name! In a patent-case, tried many years afterward, the boiler of Mr. Cooper's engine became, in some connection which has been forgotten, important as a piece of evidence. It was hunted for and found among some old rubbish at Mount Clair. It was difficult to imagine that it had ever generated steam enough to drive a coffee-mill, much less that it had performed the feats here narrrated. In the *Musée d'Artillerie* at Paris there are preserved old cannon, contemporary, almost, with Crecy and Poictiers.

In some great museum of internal improvement, and some such will at a future day be gotten up, Mr. Peter Cooper's boiler should hold an equally prominent and far more honored place ; for, while the old weapons of destruction were ministers of man's wrath, the contrivance we have described was one of the most potential instruments in making available, in America, that vast system which unites remote people, and promotes that peace on earth and good-will to men which angels have proclaimed."

WE will also take pleasure here in laying before our readers the following highly-interesting letter from Ross Winans, Esq., the inventor of the friction-wheels now in general use on the Baltimore and Ohio Railroad. It gives a comparative view of the performance of the locomotive-engine of the Messrs. Stephenson, of England, contrasted with that of Mr. Cooper:

BALTIMORE, August 28, 1830.

PHILIP E. THOMAS, ESQ., *President Baltimore and Ohio Railroad Company—*

" SIR : The performance of the working model of experimental locomotive-engine of Mr. Cooper has been such to-day as to induce me to attempt a hasty comparison of its dimensions and performances with some of the late celebrated English locomotives, having witnessed the grand locomotive exhibition at Liverpool in October last, for the £500 purse, and many other interesting experiments by the Novelty and Rocket since that time. As Mr. Cooper's engine has been got up in a temporary manner, and for experiment only, and has been on the road but a few days, it will be no more than justice to make the comparison with some of the early experiments of the English engines. I have, therefore, selected the experiment of the Rocket in October, on the result of which the premium of £500 was awarded to Mr. Stephenson, its builder, for having produced the most efficient locomotive-engine, etc.

" The Rocket is professedly an eight horse-power when working at a moderate speed, but, when working at high velocities, she is said to be more than eight horse-power. Its furnace is two feet wide by three feet high ; the boiler is six feet long and three feet in diameter.

" The furnace is outside of the main boiler, and has an external casing, between which and the fireplace there is a space of three inches filled with water and communicating with the boiler. The heated air from the furnace is circulated through the boiler by means of twenty-five pipes of two inches internal diameter. It has two working cylinders of eight inches internal diameter and fifteen inches in length each, or thereabouts. The road-wheels to which the motion is communicated are four feet eight and a half inches in diameter. Mr. Cooper's engine has but one working cylinder of three and one-fourth inches diameter, and fourteen and a half inch stroke of piston, with a boiler proportionably small, or nearly so. The wheels of the engine to which the motion is communicated are two and a half feet in diameter, making it necessary to gear with wheel and pinion to get speed, by which means a considerable consumption of power is experienced. You will perceive by the foregoing that the capacity, or number of cubic inches, contained in the cylinder of Mr. Cooper's engine is only about one-fourteenth part of that contained in the two cylinders of the Rocket; consequently, it can only use one-fourteenth the quantity of steam under the same pressure when each engine is making the same number of strokes per minute, which is nearly the case when the two engines are going at equal speed on the road. The total weight moved in the experiment above alluded to by the Rocket, including her own weight, was seventeen tons on the level road at an average speed of twelve and a half miles the hour, thereby exhibiting (agreeably to Vignoles's late table of the power of loco-motive-engines) a little less than a six-horse engine.

" Mr. Cooper's engine has to-day moved a gross weight of four and a half tons from the depot to Ellicott's Mills and back in the space of two hours and ten minutes, which, as you are aware, the distance being twenty-six miles, gives an average speed of twelve miles to the hour. As the engine returned with its load to the same point whence it started, the acclivities and declivities of the road were, of course, balanced; and at least as much time and power (if not more) were required to traverse the whole distance as would have been on a level road; therefore (agreeably to the aforesaid tables of M. Vignoles) Mr. Cooper's engine exhibited an average force during the time it was running of 1.43 horse power, or nearly one and a half, which is more than three times as much power as the Rocket exhibited during the experiment above described, in proportion to the cylindrical capacity of the respective engines. This, no doubt, originated in a considerable degree from the steam being used in Mr. Cooper's engine at a higher pressure than in the Rocket. We are, however, not able to come to any very correct conclusion as to what extent this cause prevailed (Mr. Cooper's steam-gauge not being accurately weighed), which prevents a more minute comparison being made. It may be said that subsequent practice and experience with the Rocket have enabled her constructor to produce more favorable results, which is no doubt the case; but we have every reason to expect a similar effect with regard to Mr. Cooper's engine, judging from what we have witnessed, each exhibition of its power being, as yet, an improvement upon the one that preceded it. It is, however, too small and too temporary in its construction to expect a great deal, from the friction of the parts; the heat lost in a small engine being much greater in proportion to the power than in a large one. But to-day's experiments must, I think, establish, beyond a doubt, the practicability of using locomotive steam-power on the Baltimore and Ohio Railroad for the conveyance of passengers and goods at such speed and with such safety (when compared with other modes) as will be perfectly satisfactory to all parties concerned, and with such economy as must be highly flattering to the interests of the company. It has been doubted by many whether the unavoidable numerous short curves on the line of your road and inclined planes would not render the use of locomotive-power impracticable; but the velocity with which we have been propelled to-day by steam-power round some of the shortest curves (to wit, from fifteen to eighteen miles per hour) without the slightest appearance of danger, and with very little, if any, increased resistance, as there was no appreciable falling off in the rate of speed, and the slight diminution in speed in passing up the inclined planes, some of which were nearly twenty feet to the mile, must, I think, put an end to such doubts, and at once show the capability of the Baltimore and Ohio Railroad to do much more than was at first anticipated or promised by its projectors and supporters.

" Very respectfully,

"Ross Winans."

# CHAPTER XXIII.

## HORSE AND SAILING CARS.

As we stated in a previous page, a competitor that steam had to contend with on the Baltimore and Ohio Railroad was " horse-power." A horse was placed in a car and made to walk on an endless apron or belt,

Fig. 10.

HORSE-POWER LOCOMOTIVE.

and to communicate motion to the wheels, as in the horse-power machines of the present day. The machine worked indifferently well; but, on one occasion, when drawing a car filled with editors and other representatives of the press, it ran into a cow, and the passengers, having been tilted out and rolled down an embankment, were naturally enough unanimous in condemning the contrivance. And so the horse-power car, after countless bad jokes had been perpetrated on the cowed editors, passed out of existence, and probably out of mind.

Following the horse-power car came the Meteor. This was a sailing-vehicle, the invention of Mr. Evan Thomas, who was, perhaps, the first person, as already mentioned, who advocated railroads in Baltimore. The Meteor required a good gale to drive it, and would only run when the wind was what sailors call abaft, or on the quarter. Head-winds were fatal to it, and Mr. Thomas was afraid to trust a strong side-wind lest the vehicle might be upset; so it rarely made its appearance except a northwester was blowing, when it would be dragged out to the farther end of the Mount Clair embankment, and come back, literally with flying colors. The Baltimore and Ohio Railroad being the first in operation in this country, and almost the first in the world for the transportation of passengers and merchandise, of course was visited by crowds from almost every section of the United States, as well as from parts of Europe. Among them was Baron Krudener, envoy from Russia, who, by invitation of Mr. Thomas, made an excursion in the sailing-car, managing the sail himself. On his return from the trip, he declared he had never before travelled so agreeably. Mr. Thomas caused a model sailing-car to be constructed, which he presented to the baron, with the respects of the company, to be forwarded to the emperor. This courtesy on the part of Mr. Thomas was handsomely acknowledged by the baron.

Like the horse-car, the sailing-car had its day. It was an amusing toy—nothing more—and is referred to now as an illustration of the crudity of the ideas prevailing forty years ago in reference to railroads.

FIG. 11.

SAILING-CAR.

It was after the demonstration by Peter Cooper that the Baltimore and Susquehanna Railroad Company, now the Northern Central, imported the Herald from England. It ran off the track continually, and was useless. Its unfitness, with its large wheels, for use on our curved roads was at once apparent, and it had to be altered to obviate the difficulty. It was, however,

9

antedated by the engine of Mr. Cooper and other locomotives, as we shall show; yet it excited great admiration
for its beauty, and even its driver, an Englishman named
John, became a person of consequence.   When he came
down from the engine to oil it, the crowd surrounded
him, as the boys at a race surround the dismounted
jockeys on the course.   The whole American world
were railroad children in the days we speak of.

The contest for the right of way along the Potomac
between the Baltimore and Ohio Railroad and the
Chesapeake and Ohio Canal Companies—the prelimi-
nary proceedings, in which counsel on both sides, with
surveyors at their heels like moss-troopers, scouted the
banks of the river from the Point of Rocks to Williams-
port, ferreted out the proprietors of almost inaccessible
cliffs, besieged them in their dwellings to obtain grants
of the right of way, described what railroads were,
oftentimes to men whose knowledge of highways was
confined to mountain-paths, made diagrams and drawings of cars and tracks unlike any thing that ever existed before or which ever came afterward, and were
believed by an ignorance that was only greater than
their own—these proceedings alone would furnish more
than a dozen chapters, but our limits will not allow us
to record them.   The route to the mountains lay up the
valley of the Potomac, and the struggle for priority of
claim was a prolonged and exciting one.

COOPER UNION.    C.B. COGSWELL, Sot.

PETER COOPER.

# CHAPTER XXIV.

## PETER COOPER.

Mr. Peter Cooper, of New York, like his great contemporary, George Stephenson, of England, may be justly looked upon as the pioneer of the locomotive system in America. Undoubtedly he built the first locomotive ever constructed here; and although (as we have stated before) his little machine was not intended for practical purposes or employment upon a railroad, yet it was designed to demonstrate a fact then very much doubted, namely, the ability of a locomotive to travel on the short-curved roads in this country, which Mr. Cooper's successful performance set at rest forever. Like George Stephenson, Mr. Cooper commenced his career in life from the very foot of the ladder, and, like him also, by his indomitable perseverance and industry, clambered step by step from one round to another, ascending until he reached the proud pinnacle of the topmost round, as a pioneer in the great achievements of the locomotive, now an indispensable necessity for the successful prosecution of trade and commerce throughout the world.

*From New York Evening Mail, July 1, 1869.*

"The history of a poor boy, without education or influential friends, who, by honesty, industry, and persistence, raised himself to a position of wealth and reputation, cannot but be interesting. Such, if properly told, would be the life of Peter Cooper—a man who, perhaps, as much as any other citizen of New York, has left his mark on his associates, and has placed his name in imperishable remembrance.

"He was born in the city of New York, February 12, 1791. His maternal grandfather, John Campbell, was Mayor of New York, and deputy quartermaster-general during the Revolutionary War, in which his father also served as a lieutenant. Mr. Cooper's father was a respectable hatter, and, as soon as young Cooper was old enough to pick fur from the rabbit-skins used in making hats, he was set to work. He had no opportunities for education, and only attended school one or two months in his life. 'I have never had any time to get an education,' he once almost pathetically remarked, 'and all that I know I have had to pick up as I went along.'

"He remained in the hat business with his father until he had mastered it in all its branches, and during much of the time, after he had finished his labors for the day, he would work until late at night with some carver's tools which his grandmother gave him, in order to eke out his small wages.

"We, who go to our places of business at nine, or less, and leave at five, can little realize the toil which falls to the lot of mechanics. The Cooper Institute is the result of the recollections of those early days, and was intended to help poor boys in the same situation as he had been. Young Cooper afterward went into the brewing business, at which he remained about two years. He then served the usual apprenticeship to coach-making, and finally went into the cloth-shearing business with his brother. For some time he succeeded very well, but after the War of 1812 his business was so injured by the introduction of foreign cloths that he left it and began cabinet-making. He gave this up after a while, and opened a grocery-store on the present site of the Cooper Union, where he carried on a small retail trade for some time. He finally bought a woollen factory with his savings, and since that time has steadily prospered. He has since tried his hand at other kinds of business, but the largest part of his fortune was gained by the manufacture of glue and by his iron-works. He has shown a Yankee talent for undertaking different speculations, as well as great shrewdness and prudence in conducting them.

"In 1830 he erected extensive iron-works at Canton, near Baltimore, where he built from his own designs the first locomotive ever turned out on this continent. He carried on large wire and rolling mills at Trenton, New Jersey, and was the first person to roll wrought-iron beams for fire-proof buildings. He has been much interested in the progress of telegraphy, and has been an officer in several leading telegraph associations.

"It was while serving as an alderman, forty years ago, that Mr. Cooper conceived the idea of the 'Cooper Union.' A fellow-officer who had visited the *Écoles d'Industrie*, in Paris, and been much impressed with their utility and attractions, described them to him and suggested that they would be well suited for introduction into this country. The thought thus planted in Mr. Cooper's mind, remained for long years, germinated, took root, and grew into the accomplishment of his design.

"Let those who think it an easy thing to do good, ponder the lesson taught by Mr. Cooper's experience in building the Institute. The mere saving and donating the money for the purpose was but a fraction of the work performed. Great difficulties had to be overcome in designing so unique a building. Mr. Cooper was determined that it should be fire-proof, consequently a separate foundery had to be erected to forge the iron used in the construction; when this was done, the estimated outlay fell short twenty-five thousand dollars of the actual cost. Countless other obstacles had to be overcome, and finally the Institute was completed, at an immense cost over its estimated expense. In fact, it took all Mr. Cooper's money to finish it, and he was comparatively a poor man when all the bills were paid; but, as if to reward his sacrifices, his business has since improved, until he is now richer than ever.

"What greater triumph could be desired, than to have accomplished such a work as the Institute as it now stands, with its classes for young men and women, its scientific, literary, art, and music schools, reading-room, and other features, and what greater honor could be desired than to go down to posterity as its founder? Let the voices of those who have received its benefits be a pæan to the memory of its originator, and let his name share the glory of their deeds!

"But nothing is complete in life without its disagreeable side, and noble as have been Mr. Cooper's motives, and open as were his plans in erecting this institution, not a few persons have avowed their belief that it was all done with self-interested views.

"After this, who can expect gratitude from the world?

"Mr. Cooper's personal appearance is familiar to every New-Yorker. He is of middle stature, with silver locks and beard, and a venerable and benevolent face. He is best known by his old white hat, which, like Horace Greeley's, is characteristic of the man. He commonly drives about in an old-fashioned one-horse chaise, drawn by a steady mare, the whole turn-out looking as if it belonged to some well-to-do farmer or retired tradesman, rather than a millionnaire.

"The key to Mr. Cooper's life and deeds is to be found in those few words which we have heard from his own lips : ' I resolved that I would repay every benefit which I had received by conferring an equal benefit on some of my fellow-men.'

" His success in business has been greatly due to a faculty for taking up enterprises which had been abandoned by other people, and by dint of perseverance and hard work making them succeed. In the main, however, he has gained his ends by attending to his affairs in person, and has always strictly followed Dr. Franklin's principle—'The eye of the master is worth all of his servants.' Even at his present advanced age he does not neglect this rule, but keeps a strict eye upon the affairs of the Cooper Union."

We cannot leave Mr. Cooper, even now, without devoting a few pages of our work to record his last act of generosity, benevolence, and philanthropy, toward the meritorious poor and industrious classes of our community, in his munificent bequest of one hundred and fifty thousand dollars to be used in the establishment and endowment of a library, where the hard-working and deserving classes, who desire repose and relaxation after the toils of the day, can seek recreation and information from the great store of useful books he has placed within their reach, where all may participate who feel a desire of so doing, and know that they are welcome.

On the day of this munificent bequest, Mr. Cooper reached his eightieth birthday, February 12, 1871. On that occasion a most interesting interview took place between the graduating class of the Institute and their venerable benefactor and friend. Being assembled in the large hall of the Institute, the class, in an interesting address, expressed their heart-felt gratitude to the venerable donor for the valuable gift he had that day bestowed upon them—a gift which they hoped and trusted would, from the results for many years to come, bring to their minds the eightieth anniversary of his birth, a period of life prolonged, by the providence of Almighty God, beyond the term usually allotted to a ripe old age, yet retaining all that vigor of body, strength of mind, and warmth of heart, which promise many years of usefulness and honor.

To their address Mr. Cooper replied in a most feeling and interesting manner, and we only regret now that our limited space will not allow us to embody in our present work his appropriate remarks upon this deeply interesting occasion, as we feel assured that they would prove most useful and instructive to many of our readers, who, no doubt, may be found among the mechanics and working-classes of the community.

## CHAPTER XXV.

### PRIZE FOR BEST LOCOMOTIVE.

WE will now resume our history of the early locomotives in America, believing that our readers will pardon our digression.

As it may be interesting to railroad engineers and machinists, we insert here the conditions required and the premium offered by the Baltimore and Ohio Railroad Company for the best locomotive of American manufacture, which were referred to in Mr. Latrobe's letter to the author:

"OFFICE OF THE BALTIMORE AND OHIO RAILROAD COMPANY,
"*January* 4, 1831.

"The Baltimore and Ohio Railroad Company, being desirous of obtaining a supply of locomotive-engines of American manufacture, adapted to their road, the president and directors hereby give public notice that they will pay the sum of four thousand dollars for the most approved engine which shall be delivered for trial upon the road, on or before the 1st of June, 1831 ; and they will also pay three thousand five hundred dollars for the engine which shall be adjudged the next best, and be delivered as aforesaid, subject to the following conditions, to wit :

" *First.* The engine must burn coke or coal, and must consume its own smoke.

" *Second.* The engine, when in operation, must not exceed three and one-half tons' weight, and must, on a level road, be capable of drawing, day by day, fifteen tons, inclusive of the weight of the wagons, fifteen miles per hour. The company to furnish wagons of Winans's construction, the friction of which will not exceed five pounds to the ton.

" *Third.* In deciding on the relative advantages of the several engines, the company will take into consideration their respective weights, power, and durability, and, all other things being equal, will adjudge a preference to the engine weighing the least.

" *Fourth.* The flanges are to run on the inside of the rails. The form of the cone and flanges, and the tread of the wheels, must be such as are now in use on the road. If the working-parts are so connected as to work with the adhesion of all the four wheels, then all the wheels shall be of equal diameter, not to exceed three feet ; but if the connection be such as to work with the adhesion of two wheels only, then those two wheels may have a diameter not exceeding four feet, and the other two wheels shall be two and a half feet in diameter, and shall work with Winans's friction-wheels, which last will be furnished upon application to the company. The flanges to be four feet seven and a half inches apart, from outside to outside. The wheels to be coupled four feet from centre to centre, in order to suit curves of short radius.

" *Fifth.* The pressure of steam not to exceed one hundred pounds to the square inch, and, as a less pressure will be preferred, the company, in deciding on the advantages of the several engines, will take into consideration their relative degrees of pressure. The company will be at liberty to put the boiler, fire-tube, cylinder, etc., to the test of a pressure of water not exceeding three times the pressure of the steam intended to be worked, without being answerable for any damage the machine may receive in consequence of such test.

" *Sixth*. There must be two safety-valves, one of which must be completely out of the reach of the engine-man, and neither of which must be fastened down while the engine is working.

" *Seventh*. The engine and boiler must be supported on springs and rest on four wheels, and the height from the ground to the top of the chimney must not exceed twelve feet.

" *Eighth*. There must be a mercurial gauge affixed to the machine, with an index-rod, showing the steam-pressure above fifty pounds per square inch, and constructed to blow out at one hundred and twenty pounds.

" *Ninth*. The engines which may appear to offer the greatest advantages will be subjected to the performance of thirty days' regular work on the road; at the end of which time, if they shall have proved durable, and continue to be capable of performing agreeably to their first exhibition, as aforesaid, they will be received and paid for as here stipulated.

"P. E. Thomas, President.

" N. B.—The railroad company will provide and will furnish a tender and a supply of water and fuel for trial. Persons desirous of examining the road, or of obtaining more minute information, are invited to address themselves to the president of the company. The least radius of curvature of the road is four hundred feet. Competitors who arrive with their engines before the 1st of June, will be allowed to make experiments on the road previous to that day.

" The editors of the *National Gazette*, Philadelphia, *Commercial Advertiser*, New York, and *Pittsburg Statesman*, will copy the above once a week, for four weeks, and forward their bills to the Baltimore and Ohio Railroad Company."

As Mr. Latrobe says in his letter before quoted, Phineas Davis's engine, built at York, Pennsylvania, was the only one which came up to the requirements of the company. After a trial, and several modifications and changes, each as it suggested itself, late in the summer of 1831, the Davis (or rather "Davis and Gartners") engine was found capable of pulling on the part of the road between Baltimore and Ellicott's Mills, thirteen miles, four loaded cars of the gross weight of fourteen tons, in about one hour.

This engine was mounted on wheels like those of the ordinary cars, thirty inches in diameter, and its velocity was effected by means of gearing with a spur-wheel and pinion on one of the axles of the road-wheels.

In the construction of the road from Baltimore to the Point of Rocks, every mode hitherto suggested by science or experience had been tested, and thus the work must be regarded as having the honor of solving most of the problems which presented themselves in this early period of railroads in this country. The granite, and the iron rail; the wood and iron, on stone blocks; the wood and iron on wooden sleepers, supported by broken stone; the same supported by longitudinal ground-sills in place of broken stones; the log-rail, formed of trunks of trees, worked to a surface on one side to receive the iron, and supported by wooden sleepers; and the wrought-iron rails of the English mode—had all been laid down, and as early as 1832 formed different portions of the work. Great credit is therefore due to the engineers and workmen of this road, for the patience displayed in carrying out their work, at that time the longest in the world; nothing in England could approach it in the magnitude and extent of its plan. These men labored long, at great cost, and with a diligence which is worthy of all praise. Their road and workshops have been a lecture-room to thousands who are now practising and improving upon their hard-earned experience.

# CHAPTER XXVI.

## FIRST AMERICAN LOCOMOTIVE.

WHILE these events were transpiring in Maryland, through the progress of the Baltimore and Ohio Railroad, a similar enterprise, nearly equal in its magnitude, and fully so in importance, had been started in another section of the country. The practicability of establishing a railroad communication between the city of Charleston, South Carolina, and Hamburg, on the western border of the State, a distance of one hundred and thirty-six miles, must have been talked of, and even some primary steps taken for its consummation, as early as 1827. We have seen, in an old file of the *Charleston Courier*, dated December, 1827, the following copy of a letter from Columbia, the capital of the State, where the Legislature was in session at the time. It says:

"The committee to whom the Charleston memorial was referred is divided in opinion on the propriety of an appropriation for the survey of the country between Charleston and Hamburg. Some of the committee think that if the railroad is to be the work of a company, who is to receive all the profits, the whole expense should be borne by the company. And again, that if a survey be effected by the State, it would not be done so satisfactorily to the community as it probably would be if managed by individuals immediately interested."

However, a bill, granting a charter for the South Carolina Railroad, was passed December 19, 1827. Fifteen days after, on January 4, 1828, a meeting of the citizens was called, and a committee appointed to report on that charter at the next meeting. The second meeting was called in the *Charleston Courier*, January 7, 1828, as follows:

"A meeting of the citizens is requested at the City Hall, this day, at 1 o'clock, to take into consideration the report of the committee on the subject of the railroad from this city to Hamburg. At a previous meeting on January 4th, the sub-committee had reported unfavorably. This committee pointed out many parts of the General Act of the Legislature for incorporating companies for constructing turnpike-roads, bridges, and ferries, that were inapplicable to a railroad company, as the bill now before the Legislature."

On the reassembling of the Legislature, January 21, 1828, after the usual Christmas recess, Mr. Black presented a memorial praying amendments to the act of the last session, and a new bill was reported on the 22d.

January 29, 1828, the present charter of the South Carolina Railroad was granted. A motion had been made to strike out the provision exempting the property of the road from taxation. The yeas and nays were taken—yeas 13, nays 22—and the bill passed.

The stockholders organized as a company on the 12th of May, 1828, being the second railroad company formed in the United States for commercial purposes and the transportation of passengers and freight.

At one of the earliest meetings of the projectors, Horatio Allen, Esq. (before mentioned), well known as an experienced engineer, had been invited by them to fill the position of chief engineer of the contemplated work. In compliance with their request, Mr. Allen made a report at the first meeting, five days after their organization, recommending the kind of road to be constructed and the kind of power best calculated to be used upon the road. Having visited England to examine the progress so far made in railroads and locomotive power, and having been requested, while in England, by John B. Jervis, Esq., chief engineer of the Delaware and Hudson Railroad, to contract for the iron for that road, and procure for it three first-class locomotives, the Charleston Railroad directors had confidence in his skill and judgment. In his report at this first meeting, Mr. Allen used all the arguments at his command to recommend the construction of the road for locomotive-power, and with such success that at the meeting on January 14, 1830, when the report was acted upon, the Hon. Thomas Bennett offered a resolution to the effect that the locomotive alone should be used upon the road, and in selecting that power for its application to railroads, the maturity of which will be reached within the time of constructing the road, would render the application of ·animal power a great abuse of the gifts of genius and science. The resolution was unanimously carried.

At the celebration in Dunkirk, New York, in 1852, in commemoration of the completion of the New York and Erie Railway, Mr. Allen, alluding to this subject in his address, makes use of the following language:

"At the same period, that is, prior to the great locomotive trial in England, and when the Baltimore and Ohio Railroad Company were so strongly impressed in favor of horse-power, it became necessary for me, as engineer of the South Carolina Railroad Company, to decide for what power that road should be built. The road was one hundred and thirty-six miles long. From the character of the country, the plan of the road would be naturally influenced by the kind of power adopted. Stationary power was out of the question, but the opinion was held, by many of great intelligence, that horse-power should at least be commenced with. In the report I made on this important question, I submitted such comparative estimate of the results of horse-power and locomotive-power as the information then to be had appeared to me to sustain. That estimate was in favor of locomotive-power, but I rested the decision of the question on the position that, what the performance of a horse was and would be, every one knew; but the man was not living who would undertake to say what the locomotive was yet to do; and I may add that, after more than thirty years have elapsed, during every one of which the soundness of this position has gained new grounds to sustain it, he would be a bold man who would say that we had attained the limit in the performance, and especially in the economy of performance, of this great mechanical blessing to mankind. In the recommendation of this report in favor of locomotive-power the Board of the South Carolina Railroad Company unanimously concurred, and, as this decision was the first on any railway built for general freight and passenger business in this country or in England, it has been referred to as one of the interesting facts in the early history of railroads."

The preparations for the work were at once commenced, and the road was begun in 1829. Six miles were completed in that year.

Like the Baltimore and Ohio Railroad, a number of experiments were tried with different powers.

The company offered a premium of $500 for the best locomotive by *horse-power*. This premium was awarded to Mr. C. E. Detmold, who invented one worked on an endless-chain platform. When this horse-power locomotive was completed and tested upon the road, it carried twelve passengers at the rate of twelve miles an hour.

A sailing-car, or a car propelled by the wind, was also tested upon the road in 1829–'30. A description of one of the trips upon this machine we copy from the *Charleston Courier*, March 20, 1830:

"SAILING ON LAND.—A sail was set on a car on our railroad yesterday afternoon, in the presence of a large concourse of spectators. Fifteen gentlemen got on board and flew off at the rate of twelve to fourteen miles an hour. Thirteen persons and three tons of iron were carried about ten miles an hour. The preparations

Horse-power locomotive invented by C. E. Detmold, the successful competitor for the prize of $500 offered by the South Carolina Railroad, as it appeared on this road in 1829–'30.

for sailing were very hastily got up, and of course were not of the best kind; but owing to this circumstance the experiment afforded high sport. The wind blew very fresh from about northeast, which, as a sailor would say, was 'abeam,' and would drive the car either way with equal speed. When going at the rate of about twelve miles an hour and loaded with fifteen passengers, the mast went by the board, with the sail and rigging attached, carrying with them several of the crew. The wreck was descried by several friendly shipmasters, who kindly rendered assistance in rigging a jury-mast, and the car was again soon put under way. During the afternoon the wind changed so as to bring it nearly ahead when going in one direction; but this did not stop the sport, as it was ascertained that the car would sail within four points of the wind. We understand it is intended by some of our seamen to rig a car properly, and shortly to exhibit their skill in managing a vessel on land."

The president of the road, Mr. Tupper, in one of his reports to the board, informs them that on March 1, 1830, the committee to whom the matter was referred had reported that they had accepted the offer of Mr. E. L. Miller, of Charleston, to construct a locomotive at the West Point Foundery, in New York, and that it should perform at the rate of ten miles per hour, instead of eight, as first proposed, and carry three times her weight, which was required the year before, on the Liverpool and Manchester Railroad, at the trial for the premium of £500.

Mr. Miller immediately set about the construction of his locomotive. His plans and specifications were drawn out by the same Mr. Detmold, who had invented the horse-power locomotive on the Charleston road, and who was then living in New York.

Meantime the work on the road was pushed forward, and another mile completed, making seven miles ready for use, and many more under contract and fast approaching completion.

# CHAPTER XXVII.

## FURTHER TRIALS.

Mr. David Matthew, who was foreman of the hands fitting up machinery in the West Point Foundery, and had charge of those fitting up the Stourbridge Lion, when she came from England, also had charge of the men fitting up the " Best Friend," the first loco- motive ever built in America, for actual service on a railroad. In the same letter, which he addressed to the author in 1859, after describing the Stourbridge Lion, he thus continues :

" The first American-built locomotive for actual service upon a railroad was called the 'Best Friend of Charleston.' I had charge of the hands fitting up this engine ; this was in 1830, shortly after the Stourbridge Lion had been tried in our yard, and some modi- fications made to it. The locomotive ' Best Friend of Charleston ' was contracted for by Mr. E. L. Miller, of Charleston. The Best Friend was a four-wheel engine, all four wheels drivers. Two in- clined cylinders at an angle, working down on a double crank, inside of the frame, with the wheels outside of the frame, each wheel connecting together outside, with outside rods. The wheels were iron hub, wooden spokes and felloes, with iron tire, and iron web and pins in the wheels to connect the outside rods to.

" The boiler was a vertical one, in form of an old-fashioned porter-bottle, the furnace at the bottom surrounded with water, and all filled inside full of what we called teats, running out from the sides and top, with alternate stays to support the crown of the furnace ; the smoke and gas passing out through the sides at several points, into an outside jacket ; which had the chimney on it. The boiler sat on a frame upon four wheels, with the connect- ing-rods running by it to come into the crank-shaft. The cylin- ders were about six inches in the bore, and sixteen inches' stroke. Wheels about four and a half feet in diameter. The whole machine weighed about four and a half tons. It was shipped to Charleston, South Carolina, for the Charleston and Hamburg Railroad, in the fall of 1830, and was put upon that road during the winter.

" It was the first locomotive built in America, was exhibited at our shop under steam for some time, and visited by many. She was shipped to Charleston on board of the ship Niagara, in October, 1830."

Prof. Samuel Henry Dickson, of the Jefferson Medical College of Philadelphia, in a recent letter to the author, describes his visit to the West Point Foundery-works in New York, in 1830. At this time the " Best Friend of Charleston," the first locomotive ever built in America, for actual service upon a railroad, was just completed, and about to be shipped to Charleston. Prof. Dickson writes as follows:

"PHILADELPHIA, *May* 30, 1871.
" WM. H. BROWN, ESQ.—

" DEAR SIR : In reply to your courteous letter of inquiry, just received, I regret that I can give you nothing better than general though very definite reminiscences. Dates, circumstantial details, and printed statements, such as would best suit your purpose, have faded from my mind, and all written memoranda of that distant time have perished amid the general ruin at the South.

" But I recollect that, being on a tour among my Northern friends in the summer of 1830, I was written to on the part of the board of directors of the Charleston and Hamburg Railroad (the South Carolina Railroad), and requested, as one of that body, to visit the foundery of Mr. Gouverneur Kemble, to look at a locomotive-engine which he was building for our road, and report as to its general appearance, and the prospect of its completion by the appointed time.

" Our contract had been made with Mr. E. L. Miller, who engaged with Mr. Kemble to build the machine. Mr. Miller accompanied me to the workshop, where I saw with intense interest and great satisfaction, not unmixed with some pride too, the first locomotive constructed in this country. Never having seen a locomotive, and being neither engineer nor mechanic, I could not of course presume to pronounce upon its merits, and was as curious

10

and anxious about the result of our experiment as any one interested. But I had read and heard a good deal on the subject, and did not hesitate to recommend the prompt acceptance of the engine from the contractor, and to congratulate my fellow-directors upon its promise of decided utility and advantage to our great enterprise.

"Mr. Miller named it, I think, 'The Best Friend,' and it was forwarded to Charleston late that fall or early in the winter, when it was at once put upon the road. It did not disappoint our hopes, but proved in capacity and serviceable qualities all that we had expected. It was run long and successfully, under the charge of Mr. Darrell, one of our young native machinists. I am under the impression that it was one day blown up through the carelessness of a negro fireman, that it was soon repaired and replaced upon the road. Of its ultimate fate I am not certain, but believe that, after having attained a ripe old age, in process of time it finally wore out, and was thrown aside, the common destiny of man and all his works.

"I am glad to hear of the gratifying progress of your book, and know that its publication will not long be delayed. Wishing you the large and profitable success, as an author, which your energy and perseverance so richly deserve, and all other forms of happiness and prosperity,

"I remain, very truly,

"Your friend and obedient servant,

"SAMUEL HENRY DICKSON."

The author examined the order-book recently at the West Point Company's Foundery, at Cold Spring, Putnam County, on the Hudson River, for some reminiscences of the old "Best Friend," but all he could find (the old books having been lost or mislaid) was the following order from the New-York office, dated April 6, 1830, as follows: "Two cylinders, see pattern locomotive-engine, nozzles for exhaust cast right and left."

The above shows that the engine was commenced, as Mr. Matthew states, in the spring of 1830.

The following paragraph appeared in the *Charleston Courier*, October 23, 1830:

"LOCOMOTIVE STEAM-ENGINE.—"We understand that the steam-engine intended for our road is on board the ship Niagara, which arrived in the offing last night."

As no machinist came out with the locomotive, the superintendent of the railroad applied to Mr. Thomas Dotterer, of the firm of Dotterer & Eason, machinists and engineers, to put the machine together and prepare her for the road. These gentlemen appointed Mr. Julius D. Petsch, who was foreman in their workshops, to discharge this duty. Mr. Petsch, at their request, undertook the task, and selected as an assistant Mr. Nicholas W. Darrell, a young man just out of his time in their workshops. These gentlemen (Mr. Petsch and his assistant Mr. Darrell) immediately set about fitting up the "Best Friend" for the road, and so energetically did they work that in a few days all was ready. Before the 1st of Nov., 1830, several experimental trials, at short distances, were made to see that all was right; and on the 2d of November, with Mr. Darrell in charge, Mr. Miller, accompanied by several gentlemen in a car, made a trial-trip.

The result of this trial-trip we learn from the following letter from the chief engineer, Horatio Allen, in the *Charleston Courier*, November 3, 1830:

"The public will regret to learn that an accident has happened to a pair of the wheels of the locomotive-engine lately put upon the railroad. To prevent any misunderstanding or exaggeration, it is proper to communicate the facts. The change of direction which takes place when a carriage enters a curved part of a road is effected by the action of the flange which is attached to the rim against the iron rail. A lateral strain is then brought to act on the spokes of the wheel, and in this present instance they have proved too weak to resist it, and from this circumstance the accident has originated. The spokes were discovered to spring, and fears were entertained by Mr. Miller, shortly after he commenced running his engine. Yesterday he experimented with it for this especial purpose, and after having proceeded to the extremity of the road, and almost completed his return, during which time the operation of the engine was in the highest degree satisfactory, the forward wheel was sprung inward, so much so as to leave the rail entirely; and the engine, after proceeding about twenty feet, was stopped with both the front wheels off the rail, and some of the spokes much injured.

"It is as singular as satisfactory that no other part of the frame, machinery, or boiler, exhibited the least derangement, affording the most decisive proof of the correctness of the proportions and the excellence of the work. It is but justice to state that the wheels were made after the English wheels, the most approved until the construction of the wrought-iron ones. A short time will be required to replace the wheels, when the engine will again be put in motion.

"No personal injury happened to any of the individuals, either on the passenger-car or engine.

"HORATIO ALLEN."

We next hear of the "Best Friend" through the report of President Tupper to the board of directors. After speaking of Mr. Miller's contract to furnish a locomotive, etc., he continues:

"On the 14th and 15th of December, 1830, the engine was tried, and proved her force and efficiency to be double that contracted for; running at the rate of sixteen to twenty-one miles an hour, with forty to fifty passengers in some four or five cars, and, without the cars, thirty to thirty-five miles per hour."

"Jockey of York," an amusing sporting writer, gives an account of a trip on Christmas-day, in his peculiar style, in the *Charleston Courier*, December 29, 1830:

"SPORTING INTELLIGENCE.—Our distant friends no doubt are desirous to know the result of our Christmas sports. The celebration season was altogether novel and interesting. The iron horse 'Best Friend' was entered for the purse, about a fortnight since, to 'run against time.' The 'heat' was, that he should run ten miles an hour, carrying three times his own weight. He was trained every day preparatory to the great trial of speed. Doubts were at first entertained as to 'his wind,' when everybody acknowledged he had sufficient 'bottom.' The 'Best Friend' is out of a horse bred by Messrs. Watt & Bolton, and of the same breed as the Novelty and Rocket, which contended for the purse of £500, at the late Liverpool and Manchester races. By crossing the breed with a Columbian sire, he has 'eclipsed' his progenitors upon the European, and stands unrivalled upon the American turf. The knowing ones have already hinted that his dam was 'half salamander, half alligator' as he eats fire, breathes steam, and feeds upon light-wood. All doubts, however, of his being 'short-winded' have been dissipated, and it is now confidently believed that he can run one hundred miles without 'flagging,' for, like Pat, after the foot-race at Donnybrook Fair, when being questioned if he was 'out of breath,' he replied, 'No, faith, I'm only likely to be troubled with too much of it.' But, Mr. Editor, allegory apart, I am the 'odd fellow' of the one hundred and forty-one persons who were drawn or rather whisked through the air by the iron horse or locomotive-engine, on Christmas-day—

> 'Which sped through the air like a meteor swift,
> While the crowds from around it did fearfully drift
> To the right and the left, as it passed.'

"We flew on the wings of the wind at the varied speed of fifteen to twenty-five miles an hour, annihilating 'time and space,' and, like the renowned John Gilpin, 'leaving all the world behind.' A venerable friend of mine, seventy-five years of age, gravely remarked he thought it was passing through life rather too quick, as the journey at least was a very short one. 'Very true, my good sir,' said I. 'We cannot, however, just now take time for those sage reflections on matters and things in general so necessary to our mental and moral improvement.' It was nineteen minutes five and one-fourth seconds since we started, and we discovered ourselves beyond the forks of the State and Dorchester roads. Somebody exclaimed the engine was 'waltzing.' I looked around, and 'tis a fact, Mr. Editor; notwithstanding the apparent absence of every moving principle of grace or agility, it turned round as nimbly as a miss of sixteen: but I swear by the spectacles I shall one day or other wear, that either the road or the engine turned round like a top—in proof of which I appeal to my own pumps—if it did not afterward *chassé* to the left and remain there until the three cars led off a country-dance before it. Never did reviewing general present a more warlike front to troops passing on line of march than did this same knight-errant, 'clad in his iron-bound armor.' As each car came in front, it gave us three whiffs of steam in acknowledgment that the compliment to our company was felt and appreciated. Never were the three ruffles of the drum more gratifying to my feelings when military ardor 'fired my breast.' On our return, it again headed the column. We came to Sans-Souci in quick and double-quick time. Here we stopped to take up a recruiting-party—darted forth like a live rocket, scattering sparks and flames on either side—passed over three salt-water creeks, hop, step, and jump, and landed us all safe at the Lines before any of us had time to determine whether or not it was prudent to be scared. It beats the Dumb Chess-Player all hollow.          Your obedient servant,

"JOCKEY OF YORK."

It will be borne in mind, from the foregoing extract of "Jockey of York," that the "Best Friend" made an excursion trip on Christmas-day, December 25, 1830.

These extracts, from one of the most respectable journals of the time, will tend to prove that as early as the months of November and December, 1830, and January, 1831, the "Best Friend" was in existence, and running upon the South Carolina Railroad:

*From the Charleston Courier, January 17, 1831.*

"On Saturday last, the first anniversary of the commencement of the railroad was celebrated. Notice having been previously given, inviting the stockholders, about one hundred and fifty assembled in the course of the morning at the company's building in Line Street, together with a number of invited guests. The weather the day and night previous had been stormy, and the morning was cold and cloudy. Anticipating a postponement of the ceremonies, the locomotive-engine 'Best Friend, of Charleston,' had been taken to pieces for cleaning, but upon the assembling of the company she was put in order, the cylinders new packed, and at the word, the apparatus ready for movement. The first trip

# The " Best Friend," the First Locomotive built i

The " BEST FRIEND " was built at the West Point Foundery Shops, in New York City, for the South Carolina Ra
1830, made the first excursion trip, as above, on Saturday, 15th January, 1831, being t

e United States for actual service on a Railroad.

ved in Charleston by ship Niagara October 23d, and after several experimental trials, in November and December,
ary of the commencement of the road. (See extract from *Charleston Courier*, page 152.)

was performed with two pleasure-cars attached, and a small carriage, fitted for the occasion, upon which was a detachment of United States troops and a field-piece which had been politely granted by Major Belton for the occasion.

"Upon the return of the engine, it was found necessary to tighten the packing, which occasioned some little delay. At about one o'clock she again started with three cars attached, upon which were upward of one hundred passengers. At two o'clock a Federal salute was fired by the detachment of troops stationed upon the remains of the fortification erected during the Revolution near the Quarter House. At four o'clock the company commenced returning, and were all safely landed at Line Street before six. The number of passengers brought down, which was performed in two trips, was estimated at upward of two hundred. A band of music enlivened the scene, and great hilarity and good-humor prevailed throughout the day."

The "Best Friend" continued to do the necessary work of the road, hauling materials, workmen, ballast, lumber, etc., used in the construction, during all of which time she was in charge of Mr. Nicholas W. Darrell, who had assisted Mr. Petsch in putting her together and on the road when she first came out to Charleston.

## CHAPTER XXVIII.

### EXPLOSION OF "BEST FRIEND."

On Friday the 17th of June, 1831, the boiler of the "Best Friend" exploded. As this is the first boiler-explosion upon a locomotive on record in America, we will give the account of the accident and its consequences, from an article in the *Charleston Courier*, June 18, 1831:

"Saturday Morning, *June* 18, 1831.

"The locomotive 'Best Friend' started yesterday morning to meet the lumber-cars at the Forks of the Road, and, while turning on the revolving platform, the steam was suffered to accumulate by the negligence of the fireman, a negro, who, pressing on the safety-valve, prevented the surplus steam from escaping, by which means the boiler burst at the bottom, was forced inward, and injured Mr. Darrell, the engineer, and two negroes. The one had his thigh broken, and the other received a severe cut in the face and a slight one in the flesh part of the breast. Mr. Darrell was scalded from the shoulder-blade down his back. The boiler was thrown to the distance of twenty-five feet. None of the persons are dangerously injured except the negro, who had his thigh broken. The accident occurred in consequence of the negro holding down the safety-valve while Mr. Darrell, the engineer, was assisting to arrange the lumber-cars, and thereby not permitting the necessary escape of steam above the pressure the engine was allowed to carry."

The wreck of the old "Best Friend" was taken by Mr. Julius D. Petsch for repairs and such alterations as were found upon experiment to be necessary.

Railroad men of the present day will no doubt ask, "Why was the engineer, Mr. Darrell, not at his post upon the engine, and why was he attending to the arrangement of the lumber-cars, leaving his engine in charge of his negro fireman?" To these questions we will reply by stating that, at that early day in railroad affairs, no such officers of a train as conductors, flagmen, or brakemen, had been instituted. The engineers of locomotives, like the drivers of the old-fashioned stage-coaches in by-gone days, and of the horse-cars used upon railroads, had to do their own hitching up, etc. Hence the reason why Mr. Darrell was not on the engine during the arrangement of the train. At that time every thing had to be learned as the necessity demanded it. Previous to the explosion of the "Best Friend," an accident occurred at a switch, which is explained by Mr. Allen, the chief engineer, and which called for a new order from the directors, which we will insert as an illustration of our remarks in the case of the explosion:

"CHARLESTON, *May* 14, 1831.

"To ELIAS HORRY, ESQ., PRESIDENT—

"SIR: I hasten to communicate the causes which produced the accident of yesterday afternoon. It originated in the wild derangement of the tongue, which guides the wheel through the turnout, by some ill-disposed person, and was rendered injurious to the car by the imprudent speed allowed by those who had the management of the engine—the tongue having been nailed to its proper position, but was made loose by removing the fastening, and was probably shaken from its place by the speed with which the engine and one car had preceded the one injured. Directions have been given to pass the turnout at moderate speed, and the attention of the person in charge to be constantly kept on the road in advance of the engine.

"Respectfully, your obedient servant,

"HORATIO ALLEN."

Extract from the minutes, July 3, 1831, in reference to the order above alluded to by Mr. Allen:

"*Resolved*, That in future not over twenty-five passengers be allowed to go on each car. That the locomotive shall not travel at a greater speed when there is attached:

"One car and passengers at fifteen miles an hour.

"Two cars and passengers at twelve miles an hour.

"Three cars and passengers at ten miles an hour.

"And that directions be given to that effect."

The foregoing will no doubt draw a smile upon the faces of engineers and railroad-men of the present day. It only serves to show the crudeness of railroad experience, at that early day, of locomotives.

The following letter from Mr. Nicholas W. Darrell,

the first locomotive-engineer in America, will, we trust, be read with interest, especially by his fellow-engineers and railroad-men. It was received in answer to some inquiries made of him by the author, in reference to the "Best Friend."

"CHARLESTON, *September* 2, 1869.

"MR. WM. H. BROWN—

"DEAR SIR: Your letter came to hand a few days ago, and I now hasten to reply to it, with all the information I can give you upon the subject at this distant day, drawn from memory alone, as I have no notes to which to refer.

"In the spring of 1830, Mr. E. L. Miller, of our city, entered into a contract to furnish the South Carolina Railroad with a locomotive that should travel ten miles an hour, and draw three times its own weight.

"Under this contract Mr. Miller brought out his engine, which was built at the West Point Foundery in New-York City.

"The engine arrived by the ship Niagara in Charleston, in the latter part of October, 1830. The engine was called the 'Best Friend, of Charleston.' Mr. Julius D. Petsch and myself had served our apprenticeship with Mr. Thomas Dotterer, of the firm of Dotterer & Eason, as machinists and engineers, and were engaged to put this engine together, and made the first run or trial-trip, when she proved equal to double the stipulations of the contract, running at the rate of sixteen to twenty-one miles an hour, with forty or fifty passengers in four or five cars, and making thirty to thirty-five miles per hour without cars. From this date I was regularly engaged as the engineer of the 'Best Friend,' the first locomotive ever built and run in this country, in the actual service of a company.

"In June, 1831, the boiler of the 'Best Friend' exploded, while in charge of myself. She was rebuilt by Mr. Julius D. Petsch, who substituted straight axles and cast wheels and wrought tires, for crank-axles and wood wheels with iron tires. Her name was also changed, and called the 'Phœnix.'

"In February, 1831, after the arrival of the 'Best Friend,' a second engine, called the 'West Point,' arrived in Charleston, and was put upon the road. Of this engine I was also engineer. When the 'Friend' was repaired, she was run by Henry Raworth as engineer, and name changed to Phœnix.

"I continued to run the 'West Point' until the first eight-wheel engine was brought out, called the 'South Carolina,' built in New York, after plans of Mr. Horatio Allen, then chief engineer of the South Carolina Railroad.

"Julius D. Petsch, Nicholas W. Darrell (myself), John Eason, and Henry Raworth, were the first to run locomotives. We were all apprentices of Mr. Thomas Dotterer, and natives of Charleston. I have been constantly in the employ of the South Carolina Railroad from December 8, 1830, to the present time; was born on the 12th day of November, 1807.

"Attached is a rough sketch of the 'Best Friend,' made from recollection alone, yet I was so long upon the machine, and had her so many years before my eyes, that her general form and appearance can never be forgotten. I have shown the sketch to many of the old hands now living, and they all exclaim at once, 'There is the old "Best Friend!"'

"When I run the 'Best Friend,' I had a negro fireman to fire, clean, and grease the machine. This negro, annoyed at the noise occasioned by the blowing off the steam, fastened the valve-lever down and sat upon it, which caused the explosion, badly injuring him, from the effects of which he died afterward, and scalding me.

"I hope this information will be of service to you. If you require any other facts in reference to the first engines, let me hear from you.

"Yours with great respect,
"NICHOLAS W. DARRELL,
"*First Superintendent of Machinery,*
"*South Carolina Railroad.*"

The following letter from James M. Eason, Esq., of Charleston, South Carolina, who is a manufacturer of steam-engines, boilers, and machinery, will serve to establish the fact that, not only was the South Carolina Railroad the very first in the world built expressly for locomotives, but it was also the pioneer in having the first locomotive for actual service in America built for their use; also the first to order a locomotive to be built in their midst and by one of their own native mechanics and citizens:

"Office of J. M. Eason & Brother, Manufacturers of
"Steam-Engines, Boilers, and Machinery.
"Charleston, S. C., *September* 24, 1869.

"William H. Brown, Esq.—

"Dear Sir: I enclose you a note from old Mr. Darrell, and also a photograph of him which I prevailed upon him to have taken for you.

"If of any interest to you, I could send you a photograph of Thomas Dotterer, who, in early railroad days, built the 'Native,' the first locomotive ever built with outside connections and straight axles.    After the explosion of the 'Best Friend,' Mr. Petsch took the wreck to Mr. Dotterer's shop to rebuild, as the railroad company had at that time no shop.    In repairing the 'Best Friend,' Mr. Petsch changed the double-crank axle to a straight axle, made cast-iron wheels, changed the position of the cylinders, and made the first outside connection, so universal at the present day, and was then appointed master-machinist of the road.

"I remember the first trip of the 'Native.'    She had been started out to run up the road, and I well remember the great prejudice which Mr. Dotterer had to encounter against his plan of outside connections, which was then urged to this effect : that the power, being applied to the end of the axle, would rack the road to pieces and the engine too ; that the *thing* (not calling it an engine) would not do, etc.    But, nothing daunted, he made the engine and sent it out.    Evening came, and the locomotive, probably the second ever run on the road, certainly the first after the 'West Point,' did not arrive with the train.    Great uneasiness was manifested by the officers of the company, for in those days everybody interested attended at the arrival of a locomotive.    Finally night came on ; neither the regular train nor the *little* 'Native' (for she only weighed about four tons) was in sight, and the murmurings could be heard in knots of persons and officials, that the damned *thing* had broken the road, or blown up, or some other casualty had happened to her, and prevented the arrival of the other locomotive and train.

"Now, my dear sir, imagine Mr. Dotterer's feelings ; but behold him, the man of genius, standing amid the bickerings of men, almost fearing that his little engine was the cause of the delay, when a voice cried out, 'She's coming!' and the sparks from the smoke-pipe were observed (for in those days spark-arresters were not perfected).    Then a general rush to hear the news, to see what caused the detention, and learn the fate of the poor home-made 'Native,' when lo ! a cry from a faithful friend of Mr. Dotterer, ' Why, 'tis the Native pulling locomotive and train!' Then look at Thomas Dotterer, with a heart full, with tear-drops in his eyes, as the smile of successful championship and confidence in his work played upon his countenance. I stood beside him at that moment, and shared with him in his pride. If I had the time and the ability, I could gather many interesting facts of early railroad times here in our old city, for I can remember many things. But I only intended to enclose to you Mr. Darrell's letter and his photograph, and trust you will excuse me for thus intruding on your valuable time.           Very respectfully, yours, etc.,

" JAMES M. EASON."

## CHAPTER XXIX.

### SECOND AMERICAN LOCOMOTIVE.

THE second locomotive for the South Carolina Railroad, and also the second built in this country, arrived at Charleston by the ship Lafayette on Monday, February 28, 1831. This engine was ordered from the West Point Foundery, and constructed from plans sent by Horatio Allen, Esq., the chief engineer of the road. Of this locomotive, Mr. David Matthew, after describing in his letter to the author, in 1859, the " Stourbridge Lion " and the " Best Friend " locomotives, thus continues :

" American locomotive number two was called the ' West Point.' This engine was contracted for by Horatio Allen, and was commenced by me, *David Matthew*, in the fall of 1830, and completed and shipped to the Charleston and Hamburg Railroad about the middle of February, 1831. This locomotive had the same size of engine, frame, wheels, and cranks, as the ' Best Friend,' but had a horizontal tubular boiler.   The tubes were two and a half inches in diameter and about six feet long."

After this engine was run upon the road for some time, a trial of her speed was made, which is thus described in the *Charleston Courier*, March 12, 1831:

"On Saturday afternoon, March 5, 1831, the locomotive 'West Point' underwent a trial of speed, with the barrier car and four cars for passengers, on our railroad.   There were one hundred and seventeen passengers, of which number fifty were ladies in the four cars and nine persons on the engine, with six bales of cotton on the barrier car, and the trip to the Five-mile House, two and three-fourths miles, was completed in eleven minutes, where the cars were stopped to oil the axles about two minutes.   The two and one-fourth miles to the forks of Dorchester road were completed in eight minutes.   The safety has been insured by the introduction of the barrier-car * and the improvements in the formation of the flange of the wheels, which we learn was made by a young mechanic of this city, Mr. Julius D. Petsch, in the company's service. The new locomotive worked admirably, and the safety-valve being out of the reach of any person but the engineer, will contribute to the prevention of accidents in future, such as befell the 'Best Friend.'"

As we before stated, Mr. Nicholas W. Darrell was the engineer who ran this machine from the time it was put on the road.   He thus describes it in a letter to the author:

"CHARLESTON, S. C., *September* 23, 1869.
"MR. WILLIAM H. BROWN—

"RESPECTED SIR: I have received your favor of the 22d of August, and would have answered it before this time, but, being quite indisposed in health, I have been prevented.

"It gives me pleasure to know that the information and sketch of the 'Best Friend' I sent in my last letter is of any service to you.   I will now give you such information of the second locomo-

---

* A car with bales of cotton fixed up as a rampart between the locomotive and passenger cars.

tive for our road as my memory serves. The engine was named the 'West Point.' The boiler was horizontal, with tubes or flues running lengthwise with the boiler, about five or six feet long and, I think, about three inches in diameter. I think their number was six or eight. These tubes, or flues, or whatever you may call them, were riveted to the fire-box and to the other end of the boiler. They were made of iron, and the water in the boiler surrounded them, and the flame and smoke passed through the tubes into the smoke-box.

"The engine was similar in every respect to the 'Best Friend,' except in the boiler. I herewith send you a rough sketch of the machine as near as I can recollect.

"Several persons now living, and who saw the engine at that time, think that the sketch looks very much like the old 'West Point.' Hoping that this brief information may lead to some more important results from some more valuable source, I remain, dear sir, Very respectfully, etc.,

"NICHOLAS W. DARRELL,

"*Formerly Superintendent of Machinery, South Carolina Railroad.*"

Tristram Tupper, Esq., the president of the South Carolina Railroad, in one of his reports under the head of "The History of the Road," gives an extract from the report of the Hon. Thomas Bennett, four days after the building of the road had commenced, as follows:

"The locomotive shall alone be used. The perfection of this power in its application to railroads is fast maturing, and will certainly reach, within the period of constructing our road, a degree of excellence which will render the application of animal power a gross abuse to the gifts of genius and science."

"This," continues Mr. Tupper, "was assuming a great deal, when animal power was used, years afterward, on all the other railroads then in progress in this country. But what, then, were our expectations as regards the performance of a locomotive?

"On March 1, 1830, a committee reported that they

had accepted the offer of Mr. E. L. Miller to construct a locomotive-engine in New York, at the West Point Foundery; and that she should perform at the rate of *ten miles an hour*, instead of *eight* as first proposed, and carry three times her weight, which was required the year before on the Liverpool and Manchester Railroad, at a trial of engines for the premium of £500, which Mr. Miller went out to witness. Mr. Miller's engine, under this contract, was brought out by him in the fall of 1830, and on the 14th and 15th of December, 1830, had her trial and proved her power and efficiency to be double those contracted for. She was the first locomotive-engine built in the United States to run on a railroad. She was first called the 'Best Friend,' but having her boiler burst in June, 1831, and renewed in Charleston, she was afterward called the 'Phœnix.' This engine was built according to the plan and under the personal direction of our talented and enterprising fellow-citizen E. L. Miller, Esq."

At the time this engine was engaged, 1830, Mr. Miller led the van among the advocates of steam over horse or any other power for railroads. Public opinion was, at that time, much divided on the subject; the Baltimore and Ohio Railroad Company leaned in favor of horse-power; but, nothing daunted by the weight of their authority, Mr. Miller persevered, and, with an unyielding fixedness of purpose, proposed to construct an engine, on his own responsibility, equal to the best then in use in England. He succeeded, and to him belongs the honor of planning and constructing the "Best Friend," the *first locomotive ever built and worked* on a *railroad* in the United States.

The directors of the South Carolina Railroad, therefore, are not only entitled to the credit of having had

# The "West Point," the Second Locomotive built

The "WEST POINT" was built at the West Point Foundery Works, in New York City, for the South Carolina Railroad, forwarded to Charleston
(See extract from (

e United States for actual service on a Railroad.

fayette, and after several experimental trials, in February, 1831, made the first excursion trip, as    ove, on Saturday afternoon, March 5, 1831.
ourier, page 154.)

built for their railroad, and run upon it, the first locomotive built in the United States, for the practical use of
their road, but they are also entitled to the credit of
being the pioneers in having their railroad the first, not
only in America but the first in the world, constructed
from the very beginning for the use of locomotive-
power.

When the Baltimore and Ohio Railroad was commenced, nearly a year before, from the lack of experience
and under the advice of the best English engineers, the
track was designed and constructed for horse-power,
and not until it had been built as far as Ellicott's Mills,
a distance of thirteen miles, did the subject of locomotives come under deliberation; as Mr. Peter Cooper states
in his letter to the author: "The road, in the opinion
of the largest stockholders, was considered ruined for
locomotives, which at that time began to show some
signs of advancement and improvement in England,
and they refused, in many instances, to advance another
dollar toward its completion;" when Mr. Cooper's little
locomotive, the "Tom Thumb," demonstrated the fact
that, although the road was really built for horse-power,
locomotives could be run upon it successfully. But
with the Charleston Railroad directors there was no
such doubt. At the first meeting of the board, the
chief engineer of the road, Horatio Allen, made his able
report on the kind of power the road should be constructed to sustain, and this report was followed by
that memorable resolution of Mr. Bennett that it should
be built for locomotive-power; and this resolution was
unanimously adopted and acted upon in the contract
with Mr. Miller to furnish a locomotive.

11

## CHAPTER XXX.

### FIRST LOCOMOTIVE-ENGINEERS.

WE have mentioned the name of Mr. Nicholas W. Darrell (whose likeness is herewith presented) as the first engineer of the two first-built locomotives in America; and we are also indebted to him for the descriptions and the sketches of these pioneer machines for railroad usefulness, the "Best Friend, of Charleston," and the "West Point."

A few months only after we received from Mr. Darrell's own hand these letters of description and sketches, the old veteran in railroad service, from his age and infirmities, yielded up his spirit to the God that gave it, and died in Charleston, the place of his nativity, and of his long career of usefulness, on the 4th of December, 1869, beloved and regretted by all who knew him.

In December, 1830, Mr. Darrell stood upon the platform of the "Best Friend" as its engineer. What imagination could then have conceived any thing like our present system of railroads, covering a continent with a net-work of iron stretching out its arms from the Atlantic to the Pacific? Yet, at that very time and place, 1830, at Charleston, existed one of the small beginnings. The man who helped to give the initial impulse to the wheels of locomotion has recently departed this life, beloved and respected by a large circle of friends and acquaintances, but almost unknown to the public; yet, in Charleston, he was known and appreciated. His body was attended to its last resting-place by the entire force of officials and employés of the South Carolina

N. W. DARRELL.

Railroad Company, and numerous friends, and the work-shops were closed in token of respect for the first loco-motive-engineer in America.

Next to Nicholas W. Darrell comes the veteran engineer, Mr. Henry G. Raworth, another employé of the South Carolina Railroad from its very beginning. When the Best Friend was blown up through the ignorance of the negro fireman, the wreck was taken by Mr. Julius D. Petsch to Mr. Dotterer's shop for repairs, as we mentioned in another chapter. Young Raworth, an apprentice of Mr. Dotterer, assisted Mr. Petsch in the work upon the engine, and when again ready for the road, and the name changed to the "Phœnix," Mr. Raworth ran it as engineer, and in that capacity has continued to serve the company up to the present time, and is now running an engine on the road, a period of consecutive service of over forty-two years. During all this time Mr. Raworth was never in the service of any other railroad, and never out of the service of the South Carolina Railroad, excepting only once during the Seminole War, when the Government applied to the South Carolina Railroad for an engineer to run the engine of a small steamboat engaged in transporting troops and supplies in the Everglades of Florida. On this duty Mr. Raworth was engaged ten months, then returned to his old position, resumed his engine, and is running now (August 1, 1873). In the fall of 1871, the author (when he visited South Carolina to examine the records of the old roads for statistics for his "History of the First Locomotives in America") had the pleasure of several interviews, and a ride upon the locomotive over his entire route, with Mr. Raworth, and received much valuable information as to the early

history of the road.   During the ride on the locomotive
with Mr. Raworth, the author saw and conversed with
another veteran in the service of the South Carolina
Railroad, in the person of Mr. Raworth's old negro
fireman.   This faithful assistant has been Mr. Raworth's
fireman on the locomotive successively from one to
another, as occasion required a change, for a period
of over nineteen years, and during all that time never
quitted Mr. Raworth.   Between these two, Mr. Raworth and his fireman, the most friendly understanding
has existed.

In one of Mr. Raworth's letters to the author, June
17, 1872, he states that his old negro fireman, " Adam
Perry," was formerly the property of Major John
Schmidt, of Barnwell District, South Carolina, who
hired him to Mr. George B. Lythgoe, who was employed
on the road as assistant civil engineer at that time;
that Adam had been with him, in October coming,
nineteen years ; and in reference to his character would
say that he was faithful, industrious, strictly temperate,
and a most moral negro ; always respectful to his
superiors when a *slave*, and since a freeman, and has
been working on the road in different positions thirty-
seven years.   Mr. Raworth also wrote that he had
a white fireman for seventeen years, whose name was
Thornton Randall, who died two years ago.   When
running on Aikin Hill, he had both firemen.   The
most perfect friendly relationship existed between
these men.   " You would " (he writes) " never hear an
improper word from them ; they were always kind to
each other."

The president of the road informed the author,
when in Charleston, that, during all the period of Mr.
Raworth's service, as a locomotive-engineer, the engine

ADAM PERRY.

HENRY G. RAWORTH.

was never in the shops an hour for repairs, excepting only when actually worn out from constant hard work, and some of its parts required renewing. Both Mr. Raworth and his firemen, white and black, have been total-abstinence men all their lives, and much, if not all, of this remarkable exemption from accident and disaster of all kinds incident to railroad running, may be attributed to that excellent trait in their characters.

During the author's ride on the locomotive last fall with Mr. Raworth, the veteran was well, hearty, and in the finest spirits, and in his own peculiar way he said that he had been running so long, a period now of nineteen consecutive years, over the same route and between the same two points, that he had become so familiar with every feature on it, that if the division boss removed one of the spikes, or put another in its place, he was sure to notice it. The same was the case with his old fireman. He thought he would be fit for service for ten years yet, and then the company would switch him off on some comfortable siding, put a shed over him, and take care of him the rest of his life, as they had done with old Darrell, another of their faithful servants, as the first and second locomotive-engineers in America.

Since the foregoing was prepared for our present volume, we received, on August 16th, from the railroad veteran, Mr. Raworth, the following letter, enclosing the photographs of himself and his old negro fireman:

" AIKEN, S. C., *August* 11, 1873.

" MR. WM. H. BROWN—

" DEAR SIR: Yours is received. I am very sorry I had to keep you so long for our photographs. My old fireman has been very sick, which is the reason why I could not send them earlier.  Adam Perry has worked on the South Carolina Railroad thirty-seven years, and nineteen years with me as my fireman.  Hoping the photographs will be in time for you,

" I remain, very respectfully,

" H. G. RAWORTH."

# CHAPTER XXXI.

### HORATIO ALLEN'S LETTER.

WE will now close our history of the first and second American-built locomotives, by giving in this place Horatio Allen's communication to the author on several points of interest, to which we have alluded in the preceding pages.  Mr. Allen's letter is as follows:

"NEW YORK, March 1, 1869.

" MR. WILLIAM H. BROWN—

" DEAR SIR : You ask me for some incidents in the early history of railroads and locomotives in this country, of which I have personal knowledge.

" Being one of the first of American engineers who gave attention to the subject, at the time when the indications were that a new era in intercommunication was about to open, and having visited England to obtain the information that existed at that time, and having given special attention to what was to be, and proved to be, the vital element of the new era—the locomotive—I, of necessity, was a party to many events of interest at this day. It has always been my intention to place on record some of the earlier incidents; but the postponement to a more convenient time, which the business engagements of life have led to, will leave this intention unfulfilled.

" At your request, and, as you say, it may be of some value to you personally, I will briefly refer to one or two events of the character of that contained in the quotation sent me. The quotation is from remarks made by me at the opening of the New York and Erie Railroad in 1852.

"It is often and, perhaps, generally thought that the railroad system was imported full grown. Such is not the fact, and it would greatly interest many Americans to have presented the part that was taken in this country in the development of this great instrumentality of modern times. I have not the time to present it, but I will refer to one or two events. One was the running of the first locomotive on a railroad on this continent. Herewith I send the remarks made by me at the opening of the New York and Erie Railroad, to which I will only add, that the locomotive was built under my directions in England, set up and run as described in 1829.

"The first decision in the world to build a railroad expressly for locomotive-power, for general freight and passenger business, was in this country, and at a period of time which gives especial interest to that decision. In the year 1829, it was my duty, as chief engineer of the South Carolina Railroad, to report to the directors as to the plan of construction of that work, in length one hundred and thirty-five miles.

"At that time, the question of motive power was in the following position: In England, the Liverpool and Manchester company had referred the question of motive-power to a commission of two engineers of great eminence, James Walker, of London, and John W. Rastrick, of Stone Bridge. These gentlemen, after a thorough examination of the whole subject, united in an elaborate report, accompanied by maps, etc., showing how the system recommended was to be carried out, and that system was a series of stationary engines, placed one to three miles apart, which, through long ropes, were to draw the trains from one engine to the other.

"On this side the water, the Baltimore and Ohio Railroad Company had sixteen miles in operation by horse-power. By correspondence with the gentlemen who had the beginning of that great enterprise in hand, I was informed that they were advised by English engineers, consulted on the subject, to build their road for horse-power.

"At this time, and with this intimation before me, I made my report to the directors of the South Carolina Railroad Company. In that report I made such comparison between horse-power and locomotive-power as the information at the time enabled me to make. I presented my conclusion that the comparison was in favor of locomotive-power, and I based my recommendation, that the road should be built for locomotive-power, essentially on the ground that there was no reason to believe that the breed of horses would be materially improved, but that the present breed of locomotives was to furnish a power of which no one knew its limit, and which would far exceed its present performances. At the meeting where this report was submitted, the directors, before they left their seats, passed the resolution unanimously that the South Carolina Railroad should be built solely for locomotive-power.

"To one other circumstance in connection with the same road I will refer. I had early come to the conclusion that to make the locomotive the instrument that would be required, it must furnish more power in one instrument and one engineer; that it was plain that the materials, and that, too, of the road which carried the locomotive, limited the weight to rest under each wheel, and that, as more power required more weight, there must, of necessity, be more wheels, and that, if more wheels are required, power must be made in reference to curves and change of grade. In reports made in 1830–'31, I set forth the combinations by which such provision could be made. At that time the locomotives in England were all on four wheels, and it was maintained by a strong English influence that it was not for us, in America, to depart from English usage. The subject was matter of discussion for a winter. I took the position (English usage to the contrary notwithstanding) that no long road for general passenger and freight purposes could maintain itself without the use of eight-wheel locomotives, and that probably ten-wheel locomotives would also be found desirable. Experience has amply sustained my position. My efforts were successful, and in 1831 the first eight-wheel locomotives were built on my plans and under my direction. The combinations by which provision was made for curves and changes of grade are substantially those so generally used on eight-wheel locomotives and eight-wheel passenger-cars.

"It is of some interest that their introduction, without patent, was in a great degree the means of saving the railroad companies and the public from charges for their use.

"It is with difficulty that I have found time to put on paper, in this brief way, this reply to your inquiries.

                    "Yours respectfully,
                              "HORATIO ALLEN.

# CHAPTER XXXII.

## CLAIMS TO FIRST LOCOMOTIVES.

In previous pages the author has stated that he was mainly induced to compile this history in consequence of the numerous statements in the public journals, giving what they supposed to be correct accounts or histories of the first locomotive built and run upon a railroad in the United States, and his desire to settle that much-disputed question of the first locomotive that was in the actual service of a company. The following from the Philadelphia *Public Ledger*, of January 18, 1869, is a sample of those statements which have, from time to time, been spread before the public, as the true history of the first locomotive. Since this statement was published in the *Ledger*, the author has been frequently told that the first American locomotive was built in Philadelphia, and run upon the Germantown and Morristown Railroad, in 1832. The communication in the *Ledger* reads thus:

"The first really effective locomotive in America," says Mr. Haskell, in the *Coachmaker's Journal*, "was built in Philadelphia, from a draught by Rufus Tyler, a brother-in-law of the late Matthias Baldwin, of Philadelphia. Messrs. Tyler & Baldwin had formed a co-partnership and entered into business at the corner of Sixth and Miner Streets, Philadelphia, where the plans and patterns were made and the building of the iron horse commenced. In consequence of a misunderstanding, the partnership was dissolved, and Mr. Baldwin continued the business, removing to a shop in Lodge Alley, where the engine was completed. Mr. Tyler was at that time considered the best mechanic in America. The wheels of the engine were made of wood, with broad rims and thick tires, the flange being bolted on the side. It was called 'Old Ironsides,' and was built in 1832. At eight o'clock in the morning, she was first put in motion on the Germantown and Norristown Railroad at their depot, Ninth and Greene Streets. She ran a mile an hour, and was considered the wonder of the day. On trial, it was ascertained that the wheels were too light to draw the tender, and to obviate this difficulty we had the tender placed in front of the engine, which kept the wheels on the track. Mr. Baldwin, the machinist, and myself, pushed the engine ahead, until we obtained some speed, when we all jumped on the engine, our weight keeping the wheels from slipping on the track. The boiler being too small for the engine, steam was only generated fast enough to keep the engine in motion a short time, so that we were compelled to alternately push and ride until we arrived at Germantown depot, where we rested and took some refreshments at the expense of the hotel-keeper at that place.

"At four o'clock we started on our return to Philadelphia, alternately riding and pushing in the same manner that we had come. Upon arriving at a turn on the road, at the up-grade, the engine suddenly stopped, when, upon examination, it was found that the connecting pipe between the water-tank and the boiler had been frozen, and the steam was all out of the boiler. It was then about eight o'clock, and was growing each moment colder. 'Necessity knows no law,' and so, after a short consultation, we made a summary appropriation of sundry panels of a post-and-rail fence close to the track, and started a fire underneath the pipe to thaw it. In a short time thereafter we had steam up and resumed our journey toward Philadelphia, arriving at the depot about eleven o'clock. Several successive trials were made during the following year; after each, Mr. Baldwin added improvements and made alterations in the machinery. In about a year it was found that the grease had saturated the hubs and loosened the spokes, and they finally went to pieces, and were replaced by new ones. This same engine is still in existence in Vermont."

When the author read this description in the *Ledger*, with the astounding caption that preceded it, viz., "The first really effective engine in America," he could not restrain his wonder. His surprise was only increased when he tried to imagine what the editor could be thinking about when he suffered such a communication to enter the columns of his valuable journal. When the author tried to imagine the appearance of this excursion-party to and from Germantown—first pushing awhile, then jumping on for a ride, then off again for another push, and on again for another ride—he was forcibly reminded of a scene he has often witnessed after the boss and his hands, on a railroad division, had knocked off for dinner, when a parcel of school-boys amused themselves with a ride upon the unoccupied hand-car.

If Philadelphia will claim this specimen of a locomotive as her share in the enterprise of introducing this indispensable machine into the United States, and as late as 1832, she is welcome to enjoy it; and her mechanics may be justly proud of their handiwork; for they had certainly made no improvement upon the English locomotives, several of which were at that time (December, 1832) in this country; besides the fact that there had been built in this country, between the years 1829 and '31, one most successful experimental locomotive by Mr. Peter Cooper, of New York, which we describe in full, and also there had been built in 1830 and '31 several American locomotives for actual railroad service, which were in successful operation, as we have already shown, viz., the "Best Friend" and the "West Point," for the Charleston Railroad. Another article upon the subject of early locomotives, or rather, as it is headed, "The first train of cars by steam in America," we read in the *Boston Advertiser* of January, 1869, as follows:

"THE FIRST STEAM-TRAIN IN AMERICA."—In the superintendent's office at the Providence Railroad Station, in this city, is a picture of the first steam railroad train in America, run from Albany to Sehenectady, over the Mohawk and Hudson Railroad, in

1831.  The train consisted of a locomotive, tender, and two cars. The locomotive, named the 'John Bull,' and imported from England, was of very simple and uncouth construction, and might be mistaken in these days for a pile-driver.  Its cylinders were five and a half inches in diameter, and sixteen inches' stroke, and the connecting-rods worked on double cranks on the front axle.  It weighed four tons.  John Hampson, an Englishman, was the engineer.' The tender was a simple frame, with a platform, upon which were placed a heap of wood used for fuel, and two crates filled with similar combustibles.  This vehicle had also a passenger-box in the rear.  The cars were patterned after the old stage-coaches, resembling somewhat the railroad-coaches still used in England, and were coupled with three links instead of one, as at present.  Twelve passengers occupied the inside seats, and three were seated outside.  Among them were Mr. Thurlow Weed and ex-Governor Yates.  Their portraits, and those of their fellow-passengers, which the picture gives in sombre and sharply-defined *silhouette*, would readily be recognized by any one acquainted with them when they made the excursion.  The picture is photographed by Messrs. J. L. Howard & Co., of Springfield, from the original, in the possession of the Connecticut Historical Society."

The original picture of the engine and train of cars, from which the photograph just described was taken, was executed by the author of this history, and presented by him to the Connecticut Historical Society at Hartford.  This photograph copy has since been lithographed for Thomas Jarmy, at the lithographic establishment of Sage & Son, Buffalo, in 1865.

The original picture, presented by the author to the Connecticut Historical Society, was done on the very day the engine made its first trip with a train of cars.  Attached to this lithograph Mr. Jarmy has given a kind of history of the machine, as follows: " View of the first American railroad train, as it appeared ready for starting, on the Mohawk and Hudson Railway, the first part of the New York Central Railroad from Albany to Schenectady, about the 31st of July, 1832, executed at the time on black paper with a pair of scissors, by a Mr. Brown, of Pennsylvania, and lithographed from a photograph of the original picture in the possession of the Connecticut Historical Society." Mr. Jarmy also goes on to describe and name the passengers in the cars, and gives the cost and charges of the importation of the engine at the custom-house, New York, and the date, November 12, 1831, as the freight of said locomotive, the "John Bull," per schooner Eclipse, from New York to Albany. With regard to this lithograph, which, no doubt, many railroad men look upon as authentic, the author will say that, so far as the representation of the engine and train of cars, together with the passengers, is concerned, the copy really is correct, nor can the author complain at his name being given as the artist who took the original sketch in the Connecticut Historical Society rooms; but the public should be informed of the utter inaccuracy in the historical portion of the lithographic copy. The locomotive drawn by the author on that occasion was not the English engine, "John Bull," as Mr. Jarmy represents, but the American-built locomotive "De Witt Clinton." It was sketched on the 9th day of August, 1831, the day of the first excursion-trip with a train of cars attached. Several experiments during the previous month of July had been made with different kinds of fuel, to discover that which would be best suited for its use.

# CHAPTER XXXIII.

## FIRST LOCOMOTIVE IN NEW YORK.

THIS locomotive, the " De Witt Clinton," stood upon the track already fired up, and with a train of some five or six passenger-coaches attached to it (two only were represented in our sketch, for want of room.) These passenger-coaches were of the old-fashioned stage-coach pattern, with a driver's seat or box upon either end outside. They had hitherto been used upon the road for passengers, and drawn by horse-power. At this early day when the road was just built, passengers took a car at the foot of the inclined plane in Albany, and were drawn up by a stationary engine to the top of the hill where the regular track commenced. Horses were then hitched to the cars and proceeded to the other end of the road, where another inclined plane, not then built, but soon after completed, with a stationary engine, lowered the cars into Schenectady. (Both these planes are now removed.) On arriving at the top of the plane at Albany on this memorable occasion, the engine and train were seen standing upon the track. The peculiar appearance of the machine and train (the first ever seen by the author) arrested his attention, and he at once resolved to make a sketch of the singular-looking affair and its equally singular-looking appendages. Drawing from his pocket a letter just received of a few lines only, written upon a whole sheet of paper (no envelopes were used at that day), and substituting his hat for a desk, he commenced his sketch of the unique machine standing before him. Meantime the excursionists were entering the cars, and the author had taken a hasty, rough drawing of the machine, the tender, the individual standing on the platform of the machine as its engineer, and the shape of the first passenger-coach, when a tin horn was sounded and the word was given, "All aboard," by Mr. John T. Clark, the master of transportation, who acted as conductor on that memorable occasion. No such officer as a conductor had been required upon a railroad before locomotives and long trains of cars were adopted. Before this event, in place of conductors, the drivers of the single-horse cars collected the tickets or fare, as omnibus-drivers do at the present time.

On this occasion, the two first cars, or coaches, as they were then called, and the third also, were just as the two are represented in our sketch. The remainder of the cars on the train were surmounted with seats made of rough plank to accommodate the vast crowd of anxious expectants assembled to witness the experiment and participate in this first ride on a railroad train drawn by a locomotive. The cars were crowded inside and outside; not an available position was unoccupied. Two persons stood ready for every place where one could be accommodated, and the train started on its route, leaving hundreds of the disappointed standing around.

As there were no coverings or awnings to protect the deck-passengers upon the tops of the cars from the sun, the smoke, and the sparks, and as it was in the hot season of the year, the combustible nature of their garments, summer coats, straw hats, and umbrellas, soon became apparent, and a ludicrous scene was enacted among the outside excursionists before the train had run the first two miles.

The author was an inside passenger on that evermemorable occasion. We say memorable, for it was one never to be forgotten. It was on the 9th day of

August, 1831, when what was represented and known to be the first American locomotive ever run upon a railroad in the State of New York. Thus the sketch in our work, representing a locomotive, tender, and two passenger-cars attached, is, as we before stated, a truthful representation of one of the first railroad trains in America, and the very first run in the State of New York, and followed soon after the last successful locomotive experiments by Mr. Peter Cooper on the Baltimore and Ohio Railroad, and the advent of the first American-built locomotives for actual service upon the Charleston and Hamburg Railroad, in South Carolina. It was the third locomotive built in America for actual service. This engine was named the "De Witt Clinton," and is thus described by Mr. David Matthew, in his letter to the author in 1859:

"American engine No. 3 was called the 'De Witt Clinton.' It was contracted for by John B. Jervis, Esq., at the West Point Foundery, and was commenced by me to fit up in April, 1831, soon after the engines 'Best Friend' and 'West Point' were completed and forwarded to Charleston.

"I left New York with the 'De Witt' on the 25th of June, 1831, and had steam on to commence running in one week from that time. The 'De Witt' had two cylinders five and a half inches in diameter and sixteen inches' stroke; four wheels, all drivers, four and a half feet diameter, with all the spokes turned and finished. The spokes were wrought-iron, hubs cast-iron, and the wheels tired with wrought-iron, inside crank and outside connecting-rods to connect all four wheels; a tubular boiler with drop furnace, two fire-doors, one above the other; copper tubes two and a half inches in diameter and about six feet long; cylinders on an incline, and the pumps worked vertically by bell-crank. This engine weighed about three and a half tons without water, and would run thirty miles an hour with three to five cars on a level, with anthracite coal, and was the first engine run in the State of New York on a railroad."

On this first excursion, on the 9th day of August, 1831, as no such officer as a conductor had been required upon the road, where hitherto no connected train of cars had been run, but where each driver officiated as collector of fares, Mr. John T. Clark, as the first passenger railroad conductor in the North, stepping from platform to platform outside the cars, collected the tickets which had been sold at hotels and other places through the city. When he finished his tour, he mounted upon the tender attached to the engine, and, sitting upon the little buggy-seat, as represented in our sketch, he gave the signal with a tin horn, and the train started on its way. But how shall we describe that start, my readers? It was not that quiet, imperceptible motion which characterizes the first impulsive movements of the passenger-engines of the present day. Not so. There came a sudden jerk, that bounded the sitters from their places, to the great detriment of their high-top fashionable beavers, from the close proximity to the roofs of the cars. This first jerk being over, the engine proceeded on its route with considerable velocity for those times, when compared with stage-coaches, until it arrived at a water-station, when it suddenly brought up with jerk No. 2, to the further amusement of some of the excursionists. Mr. Clark retained his elevated seat, thanking his stars for its close proximity to the tall smoke-pipe of the machine, in allowing the smoke and sparks to pass over his head. At the water-station a short stop was made, and a successful experiment tried, to remedy the unpleasant jerks. A plan was soon hit upon and put into execution. The three links in the couplings of the cars were stretched to their utmost tension, a rail, from a fence in the neighborhood, was placed between each pair of cars and made fast by means

12

of the packing-yarn for the cylinders, a bountiful supply being on hand (as the present brass-ring substitute had not then been invented). This arrangement improved the order of things, and it was found to answer the purpose, when the signal was again given, and the engine started.

In a short time the engine (after frightening the horses attached to all sorts of vehicles filled with the people from the surrounding country, or congregated all along at every available position near the road, to get a view of the singular-looking machine and its long train of cars; after causing thus innumerable capsizes and smash-ups of the vehicles and the tumbling of the spectators in every direction to the right and left) arrived at the head of the inclined plane at Schenecta-dy, amid the cheers and welcomes of thousands, assem-bled to witness the arrival of the iron horse and its living freight.

After some time passed in the ancient city of Sche-nectady, and ample refreshments had been afforded, the word was given by conductor Clark to prepare for the return. The excursionists resumed their seats, and in due time, without any accident or delay, the train arrived at the point from which it had first started, the head of the inclined plane at Albany. The passengers were pleased with the adventures of the day, and no rueful countenances were to be seen, excepting occasionally when one encountered in his walks in the city a former driver of the horse-cars, who saw that the grave had that day been dug, and the end of horse-power was at hand.

After the return to Albany, the author made a clean copy from his rough sketch of the engine "De Witt Clinton," and also the likeness of the engineer of

# THE FIRST LOCOMOTIVE AND TRAIN OF PASSEN

## The American Locomotive "DE WITT

The locomotive "De Witt Clinton" was ordered by John B. Jervis, chief engineer of the Mohawk and Hudson Railroad, and was the
taken to Albany in the latter part of June, 1831, and was put upon the road and run by David Matthew. The first experimental trial
from Albany to Schenectady on August 9, 1831, on which occasion the author of this History of the Early Locomotives in America rod
nounced a truthful representation of the locomotive, tender, and the first two of the number of cars in the train, and correct likenesses of
of black paper with a pair of scissors, a peculiar art with which the author was gifted from his earliest boyhood. The original picture
valued for its antiquity and truthfulness. The names of the engineer and passengers are as follows, commencing at the engine: D
Mr. Van Zant, Billy Winne, penny postman; second car, John Townsend, Esq., Major Meigs, old Hays, High-Constable of New York,
time they were taken—forty years ago. The outside seats were for the drivers when these cars had been drawn by horse-power, but on

omotive built in America for actual service upon a railroad. The machine was made at the West Point Foundery Works in New York, made on the 5th of July, and others at different times during that month. The first excursion-trip, with a train of passenger-cars, was made the cars (only the first two are represented above), and before the train started made the sketch as it appears above, which was pro- er and passengers represented in the cars. Some of them are yet living, as their letters in this work will show. The picture was cut out ted by the author to the Connecticut Historical Society; it was about six feet in length, and is yet preserved by the society and highly new, engineer; first car, Erastus Corning, Esq., Mr. Lansing, ex-Governor Yates, J. J. Boyd, Esq., Thurlow Weed, Esq., Mr. John Miller, , Jos. Alexander, of the Commercial Bank, Lewis Benedict, Esq., and J. J. Degraft. These likenesses were all readily recognized at the on were occupied by the excursionists.

the day, Mr. David Matthew, who controlled its movements on this memorable first occasion. As the tin horn sounded the signal for starting, just as the author had sketched the shape of the first of the passenger-cars in the train, he supplied the place of passengers with the likeness of several of the old citizens of Albany. Hence the appearance of Mr. Thurlow Weed, ex-Governor Yates, and others, as named in the article from the *Boston Advertiser*. This original picture, as we have before stated, was presented to the Connecticut Historical Society by the author. It has since been photographed by J. L. Howard & Company, of Hartford, and from this photograph the copy in lithograph by Sage & Son was taken; but the engine is there erroneously called an English machine, the " John Bull," and John Hampson, an Englishman, is said to have been the engineer. A second copy of this sketch, calculated to mislead the public, has just been circulated by a firm in Boston, called the Antique Publishing Company, 75 Haverhill Street, and copyrighted in 1870. This picture, like the one by Sage & Son, is taken from the same photograph of the author's original sketch in the Hartford Institute, and in its history, like the other, purports to be a likeness of the English locomotive " John Bull," and an Englishman, John Hampson, the engineer. In this volume we shall furnish the evidence to show that the original picture in the Connecticut Historical Society Rooms was a true representation of the American locomotive " De Witt Clinton," the third American locomotive built for actual service, and the first American-built locomotive run in the State of New York; Sage & Son, and the Boston Antique Publishing Company, to the contrary notwithstanding.

## CHAPTER XXXIV.

### FURTHER EVIDENCES.

THE following letter is from Mr. David Matthew. It is further evidence that the "De Witt Clinton," and not an English engine, was the first one to run on the road from Albany to Schenectady, in August, 1831:

"PHILADELPHIA, *February* 13, 1860.

"WILLIAM H. BROWN, ESQ.—

"DEAR SIR: Yours of January 17th is at hand. Having been absent, my reply has been delayed until this date. I will endeavor to answer your several questions as correctly as I possibly can, in the absence of records.

"*First.* I did run the 'De Witt Clinton,' on the 9th day of August, 1831, and every day that it run from the 2d day of July, when first put on the road, to December 1, 1831.

"*Second.* There was no English-built engine upon the road, until the 'Robert Fulton,' made by Stephenson, arrived, which was about the last of August. About the middle of September it was tried on the road, and commenced regular trips soon after. On the excursion-trip in September, the Fulton was assigned to haul the train, but something got wrong about the supply-pipe, and my engine, the 'De Witt Clinton,' was called out for that duty, and did it well.

"*Third.* I did know John Hampson and Adam Robinson. John Hampson was my assistant. He left West Point Foundery with me, and when the 'Robert Fulton' arrived and was placed on the road, he took her to run. Adam Robinson became my fireman on the 'De Witt Clinton' when we began to make regular trips.

"When the 'John Bull' came out, nearly a year afterward, John Hampson took her to run. Both of these men are now dead. John Hampson left the Mohawk and Hudson Railroad early in 1832. He brought the second engine from New York that was run on the Germantown and Philadelphia Railroad. He next took the 'Davy Crocket' to the Saratoga Railroad; then took charge of the Camden and Amboy Railroad machine-shops at Bordentown. Thence he went to the New Orleans and Carrollton Railroad, on a salary of five thousand dollars per year, where he remained several years.

"Adam Robinson was killed by accident on a railroad.

"Will you please procure and send to me one of the drawings, or photographs, from the original picture you took in Albany, of the old 'De Witt Clinton' and train of cars? I saw the original picture at your room in Albany, and was forcibly struck by the accuracy of your likeness to the old machine, the cars, and the passengers, several of whom I knew well.

"If I can give you any other information, write to me at once, and I will try to be more prompt in my reply.

"Respectfully yours,
"DAVID MATTHEW,
"205 Pear Street, Philadelphia."

From the freight-bills, custom-house charges, etc., etc., attached by Sage & Son to their lithograph copy of a photograph of the original picture in the Hartford Institute, the author is inclined to believe that these refer to those made upon the first English locomotive for the Mohawk and Hudson Railroad, which was the "Robert Fulton." This machine, as we see in the following articles from the *Albany Argus* of that period, arrived by the ship Mary Howland, from Liverpool, early in September, 1831. In several articles of the *Argus*, in which this engine is spoken of, it is called the "John Bull." This was done in allusion to the country where it was made, in the same manner as the *Argus* also uses the words "Brother Jonathan" when speaking of the "De Witt Clinton." These *sobriquets* are familiarly applied and understood by every one when speaking of the natives of either country.

A locomotive named the "John Bull" came from England, subsequently, but not for nearly a year after the events we are now recording.

Messrs. Sage & Son give the following as the costs

and charges as per invoice of locomotive-engine, per ship Mary Howland, from Liverpool, $3,763.67. Custom fees, $1,017.25. Freight-bills, September 18, 1831, $88.67.

The following extracts from the Albany *Argus.* will clearly show that the West Point Foundery engine was the first to run upon the Mohawk and Hudson Railroad, and that no English locomotive was in existence upon that road until the " Robert Fulton," built by Stephenson, arrived about the last of August, and was put on the road the 16th or 17th of September after:

(*From the Albany Argus, July 25, 1831.*)

"MOHAWK AND HUDSON RAILROAD.—We travelled over part of this road on Saturday, which is ready to receive the cars on Monday next, the 1st of August, if not earlier. The road will be open from the head of Lydius Street to the brow of the hill at Schenectady, a distance of about twelve miles and a half, and travelling upon it will be forthwith commenced. We learn that the company have decided on using steam-power alone. The company will begin their operations with an engine from the West Point Foundery, which we understand will be placed on the road for service on Wednesday, the 27th, being precisely twelve months from the day the ceremony of breaking ground was performed last year.

" In less than a month the company expect from England one of Mr. Stephenson's engines, similar to those now in use on the Liverpool and Manchester Railway.

" The work, we have no doubt, will do credit to the skill of the engineer, John B. Jervis, Esq."

"MOHAWK AND HUDSON RAILROAD.—On Saturday this work was completed and prepared for the passage of the cars. On that day an experiment was made with the locomotive 'De Witt Clinton,' from the West Point Foundery, but, owing to some defect in the ignition of the Lackawanna coal, the speed did not at any time exceed six or seven miles an hour. On Saturday next, if the weather is favorable, the company propose to celebrate the completion of the work, so far, by inviting our citizens to a ride through the entire line."

(*From the Albany Argus, August* 11, 1831.)

"MOHAWK AND HUDSON RAILROAD.—On Monday, August 9, 1831, the 'De Witt Clinton,' attached to a train of cars, passed over the road from plane to plane, to the delight of a large crowd assembled to witness the performance. The engine performed the entire route in less than one hour, including stoppages, and on a part of the road its speed was at the rate of thirty miles an hour."

(*From the Albany Argus, August* 27, 1831.)

MOHAWK AND HUDSON RAILROAD.—The company having received their locomotive from England by the Mary Howland, it will, we understand, be in operation on the road in the course of a few days. It is called the 'Robert Fulton.'"

(*From the Albany Argus, September* 3, 1831.)

"MOHAWK AND HUDSON RAILROAD.—Another trial was made on Thursday with the locomotive 'De Witt Clinton.' It performed the passage from Schenectady to this city in fifty minutes. Among the passengers was Brigadier-General Scott, of the United States Army."

(*From the Albany Argus, September* 9, 1831.)

"MOHAWK AND HUDSON RAILROAD.—The American locomotive 'De Witt Clinton' came down yesterday morning in forty-six minutes. The fuel was wood. A trial of the English locomotive will probably be made on Tuesday next. The power and weight of this engine are double those of the American engine."

(*From the Albany Argus, September* 19, 1831.)

"MOHAWK AND HUDSON RAILROAD.—Trials of the English locomotive were made on the 16th and 17th. They were, we understand, entirely successful, and particularly so with the use of anthracite coal. The engine was propelled with ease at the rate of from fifteen to twenty miles an hour, and will commence her regular trips this day."

The next we hear of the English locomotive, after the foregoing experiments, relates to transactions of the following week. The author was present, and remembers well every incident on that interesting occasion, as they are recorded in the *Argus*, and, had the English machine performed the duty which was assigned to her on that day, there is no doubt a sketch of her appearance would have found a place in our present volume. But the author did not " see it." The *Albany Argus*, September 26, 1831, says :

"RAILROAD EXCURSION.—On Saturday, September 24th, a numerous company, at the request of the president and directors of the Mohawk and Hudson Railroad Company, enjoyed a very gratifying ride upon the road. The company consisted of the Governor, Lieutenant-Governor, members of the Senate, now in session as a Court of Errors, our Senators in Congress, the Chancellor and Judges of the Supreme and District Courts, State officers, the president of the Board of Assistants and members of the Common Council of the city of New York, the Mayor, Recorder, and corporation of the city, and several citizens of New York, Albany, and Schenectady.

" Owing to a defect in one of the supply-pipes of the English locomotive, that powerful engine was not brought into service, and the party, having been delayed in consequence, did not leave the head of Lydius Street until nearly twelve o'clock. They then started with a train of ten cars, three drawn by the American locomotive 'De Witt Clinton,' and seven by a single horse each. The appearance of this fine cavalcade, if it may be so called, was highly imposing. The trip was performed by the locomotive in forty-six minutes, and by the cars drawn by horses in about an hour and a quarter. From the head of the plane, about a quarter of a mile from Schenectady, the company were conveyed in carriages to Davis's Hotel, where they were joined by several citizens of Schenectady, and partook of a dinner that reflected credit upon the proprietor of that well-known establishment. Among the toasts offered was one which has been verified to the letter, viz.: 'The Buffalo Railroad—may we soon breakfast in Utica, dine in Rochester, and sup with our friends on Lake Erie!' After dinner the company repaired to the head of the plane, and resumed their seats for the return to Albany. It was an imposing spectacle. It was a practical illustration of the great preference of this mode of travel and conveyance. The American locomotive started with a train of five cars, containing nineteen or twenty persons each, besides the tender, and never did 'Brother Jonathan,' as it was familiarly called, perform the trip in more beautiful style. It came down with its train in thirty-eight minutes, being at the rate of nineteen miles an hour, the last six miles were performed in fourteen minutes. The cavalcade with horses came down in sixty-eight minutes.

"'Brother Jonathan,' as it is familiarly called, is as yet decidedly in advance of 'John Bull.'"

We give the foregoing extracts from the *Argus* merely to prove more conclusively that the "De Witt Clinton" was the locomotive sketched by the author on the 9th day of August, and not an English engine, as some parties have represented. On neither of these excursions was the English locomotive in use. On the excursion of the 9th of August the English engine had not yet arrived, and on the excursion of the 24th of September her supply-pipe was not in order, and the American locomotive "De Witt Clinton" performed the duty successfully, as is recorded in the *Albany Argus* just quoted. It was on the occasion of the excursion on the 9th day of August, 1831, with the "De Witt Clinton," as mentioned in the article in the *Albany Argus* of August 11th, that the author made the sketch of the locomotive, the engineer, the tender, coaches, and passengers in the train, which was exhibited at his studio, and attracted great crowds for several weeks during his professional sojourn in Albany. This picture the author soon after presented to the Connecticut Historical Society, where it may be seen at the present time. In 1858 or '59 this original picture was photographed by J. L. Howard & Company, of Hartford, and a copy obtained by the author.

# CHAPTER XXXV.

## THE JUDGE'S FIRST RIDE.

SINCE this photograph has been in the possession of the author, he has been often asked why the engine and train are represented in the unique and sombre style in which they appear in profile, or black outline. To this inquiry he will reply by informing those who are not familiar with the facts, that, from his earliest recollection, he has been gifted with a rare and peculiar talent or faculty (entirely intuitive in him) of executing with wonderful facility and accuracy the outlines or form of any person or object from a single glance of the eye, and without any machinery whatever, but with a pair of common scissors and a piece of black paper.

This peculiar style of outline portraiture, or shaping exact resemblances of persons or objects with black paper, and commonly known as profiles, was invented, according to the elder Disraeli, in 1757, in Paris, and called by the French *silhouette*. In the author this faculty was not confined to shaping the mere outlines of persons or faces, but was extended to portraying entire family groups, military companies, fire companies with their engines and hose-carriages, sporting-scenes, race-courses, and marine views, representing a harbor and shipping. All were executed in black paper, and with a pair of scissors. Hence, in the same style he executed the above-mentioned likeness of the locomotive "De Witt Clinton," with the cars and passengers, and afterward presented the same to the Connecticut Historical Society. This rare and peculiar faculty or gift was so strongly developed in the author, that all objects, when once presented to the eye, are, as it were, photographed upon his brain, so much so, and with such indelibility, that it was not actually necessary for an individual to be present and stand for a likeness. A glance for a moment at an individual in some accustomed position or attitude only was necessary, and the likeness could be produced hours, days, weeks, and often years thereafter, entirely from memory alone.

The author, for several years, made a very lucrative business by the exercise of this peculiar faculty of taking likenesses, and during that time visited all the principal cities of the country. His first object on visiting a new field for the exercise of his art was to notice several prominent and well-known citizens as they walked upon the streets, and place their likenesses most accurately upon paper as evidences of his skill in this peculiar art and his wonderful memory of persons and forms.

It so happened that, on one of the author's professional visits to the city of Albany, that a trip, which was then supposed to be the first train of cars drawn by a locomotive in America, was run upon the Mohawk and Hudson Railroad. A graphic and particular description of this same first trip is given in a letter from a well-known and distinguished gentleman, now over eighty years of age, who is one of the few survivors. The letter is as follows:

"RIDGEWAY, PA., *June* 24, 1870.

"WILLIAM H. BROWN, ESQ.—

"DEAR SIR: Your note of the 21st inst., asking for my recollections of such incidents as impressed themselves on my mind in the ever-memorable first trip by locomotive-power from Albany to Schenectady in 1831, is before me. In the early part of the month of August of that year I left Philadelphia for Canandaigua,

New York, travelling by stages and steamboats by way of New York to Albany. Stopping at the latter place with my friend J. M. Hughes, now of Cleveland, Ohio, I learned that a locomotive had arrived there, and that it would make its first trip over the road to Schenectady the next day. I concluded to lie over and gratify my curiosity with a first ride after a locomotive.

"That locomotive, the train of cars, together with the incidents of the day, made a very vivid impression on my mind. I can now look back from one of Pullman's palace-cars, over a period of forty years, and see that train, together with all the improvements that have been made in railroad travel since that time, for I have been a constant traveller for over half a century, and have observed the steady and constant progression in motive-power and railroad facilities up to the present time. And now, taking 1870 as a standpoint, looking back and forward forty years, who can say that the next forty years will not exceed the past in railroad intercommunication, and that Dr. Krumer's theory of using compressed air as a motive power may not, ere that, be brought into general use, and that the engineer will manage his whole train with the same facility and ease that the Mexican *caballero* starts, runs, and stops his horse?

"I am not machinist enough to give a description of the locomotive that drew us over the road that day, but recollect distinctly the general 'make-up' of the train. The sketch you showed me when I was last at your place, taken by you in your peculiar style, is very correct, and brings to my mind, as vividly as though only seen yesterday, the engine and train as it appeared on that never-to-be-forgotten occasion.

"The train was composed of coach-bodies, mostly from Thorpe & Sprague's stage-coaches, placed upon trucks. The trucks were coupled together with chains or chain-links, leaving from two to three feet slack, and when the locomotive started it took up the slack by jerks, with sufficient force to jerk the passengers, who sat on seats across the top of the coaches, out from under their hats, and in stopping they came together with such force as to send them flying from their seats.

"They used dry pitch-pine for fuel, and, there being no smoke or spark-catcher to the chimney or smoke-stack, a volume of black smoke, strongly impregnated with sparks, coals, and cinders, came pouring back the whole length of the train. Each of the outside passengers who had an umbrella raised it as a protection against the smoke and fire. They were found to be but a momentary protection, for I think in the first mile the last one went overboard, all having their covers burnt off from the frames, when a general *mêlée* took place among the deck-passengers, each whipping his neighbor to put out the fire. They presented a very motley appearance on arriving at the first station. There rails were procured and lashed between the trucks, taking the slack out of the coupling-chains, thereby affording us a more steady run to the top of the inclined plane at Schenectady.

"The incidents off the train were quite as striking as those on the train. A general notice having been given of the contemplated trip, excited not only the curiosity of those living along the line of the road, but those living remote from it, causing a large collection of people at all the intersecting roads along the line of the route. Everybody, together with his wife and all his children, came from a distance with all kinds of conveyances, being as ignorant of what was coming as their horses, drove up to the road as near as they could get, only looking for the best position to get a view of the train. As it approached, the horses took fright and wheeled, upsetting buggies, carriages, and wagons, and leaving for parts unknown to the passenger, if not to their owners, and it is not now positively known if some of them have yet stopped. Such is a hasty sketch of my recollection of my first ride after a locomotive.

"Hoping that your contemplated history of early locomotives in America may be appreciated by the reading public, and a pecuniary success to yourself,

"I remain truly yours,

"J. L. GILLIS."

The writer of the foregoing letter, Judge Gillis, is a native of the State of New York, and is now eighty years of age. He served in the War of 1812, and was wounded at the battle of Lundy's Lane. He moved to Ridgeway, Pennsylvania, in 1822, then in Jefferson County, now the seat of justice of Elk County. He was an active member of the Masonic fraternity in the State of New York previous to his removal to Pennsylvania. Four years later, in 1826, when political anti-masonry took its rise in that State, in order to show the extent of the conspiracy for the abduction of one Morgan, a bill of indictment was procured against Judge Gillis and others at Canandaigua.  As soon as he heard of such indictment, he returned to the State of New York and surrendered himself to the court and was placed under bonds of ten thousand dollars for his appearance at the next term.  He visited that county nine terms of the court, the prosecutors putting the case off at each term. Finally, the trial came off in 1829, and he was acquitted, no evidence being found for conviction.*  Judge Gillis has served his district in the House and Senate of the State Legislature and in Congress.  He was an active and ardent supporter of internal improvement in the State of Pennsylvania, and one of the earliest advocates of the construction of the line of railroad from Phila-delphia to Erie, which he supported until completed. He was appointed Judge of the Court of Jefferson County in 1843, and reappointed in 1844 as one of the first Judges of Elk County.  In 1862 Judge Gillis re-moved to Mount Pleasant, Henry County, Iowa, where he now resides.

In 1859 the author, having quitted the profession of artist, was living in Huntingdon County, Pennsyl-vania, as an employé of the Huntingdon and Broad Top Railroad.  Many years had passed away since he had thought of the "De Witt Clinton," when he re-ceived from an unknown hand a newspaper containing a paragraph marked with a pen to attract his attention. It revived in his memory his old picture of the "De Witt Clinton" and his visit to Hartford very many years before.  The paragraph was as follows:

---

* It was some time during his trips to attend trial that Judge Gillis rode in the cars after a locomotive.

"A RARE CURIOSITY.—We were this day shown by Mr. Bradley, Secretary of the Fort Wayne and Chicago Railroad, at Pittsburg, a photograph copy of the first American locomotive ever
built in this country and run upon a railroad in the United
States. The photograph was made from the original picture
now in the Connecticut Historical Society, and was taken by a
Mr. Brown in his peculiar style of art. It was cut out of black
paper with a pair of common scissors. In the cars we recognize
the likenesses of several of the old citizens of Albany, Thurlow
Weed, Esq., ex-Governor Meigs, old Hays, of New York, the
celebrated thief-catcher, and several others. The picture is executed with great skill and fidelity, and is a rare curiosity when
compared with the locomotives and trains of the present day."

The author then determined to procure a copy of
his old work, and applied to Mr. Bradley for information, which he obtained, and also to J. L. Howard, Esq.,
of Hartford, from whom he received the following
letter:

"HARTFORD, CONN., *May* 26, 1859.

"WILLIAM H. BROWN, ESQ.—

"DEAR SIR: We have neglected to answer your very pleasant
letter of the 5th of March, not from any hesitation in complying
with your request, which we are happy to do, recognizing a right
in the *grandfather* to have one of his own children's children,
but, anticipating an opportunity of sending it as far as Altoona
free of cost, like the present, we have allowed time to pass.

"Have you any memorandum of the precise time this train
was run?—1832 is as near as we can locate the time. Please say
if you have any memorandum of the persons who are represented
in the cars. We personally remember you well, having had our
figure cut out by you when in this city.

"With respect, and very truly yours,
"JAMES L. HOWARD & Co."

A few days after receiving the above letter, the picture arrived by Adams's Express, free of cost and
charges. The author is at a loss how to describe his
pleasurable feelings of pride and satisfaction when, after

a lapse of twenty-eight years, he placed his eyes upon this specimen of his handiwork which he never expected to behold again, rescued as it was from almost absolute forgetfulness. Every curve and angle in the outline became as vivid as on the day when it was executed. The likenesses of the citizens represented in the cars were as fresh in his memory as if only seen the day before, and he was, as it were, transferred again to Albany and its associations.

## CHAPTER XXXVI.

### LETTERS FROM OFFICIALS.

DESIROUS of receiving some authentic statistics of this first locomotive, the author addressed a letter to Erastus Corning, Esq., who was president of the road at that time, and the following answer was received:

"NEW YORK CENTRAL RAILROAD, PRESIDENT'S OFFICE,
"ALBANY, *December* 9, 1859.

"MR. WILLIAM H. BROWN—

"DEAR SIR: Yours, respecting the introduction of the first locomotive on the Mohawk and Hudson Railroad, and asking information in relation thereto, was duly received.

"I referred your communication to John T. Clark, Esq., of Utica, who was at the time resident engineer and superintendent of transportation, requesting of him such information as he might be able to furnish. I send you herewith his reply, and by American and Adams's Express a photograph copy of the sketch in the Hartford Athenæum. I remember well your original cutting in black paper of the first locomotive, the 'De Witt Clinton,' and her train of cars. I was forcibly struck on viewing it by its accurate resemblance to the engine and train of cars attached.        Yours very respectfully,

"ERASTUS CORNING."

The following is Mr. Clark's reply to Mr. Corning's letter. It was forwarded to the author:

UTICA, N. Y., *November* 21, 1859.

"HON. ERASTUS CORNING, Albany—

"MY DEAR SIR: I received, on the 18th inst., your note, with Mr. Brown's letter to you, seeking for information as to the time when the first experiment was made, with a locomotive-engine, on the Mohawk and Hudson Railroad, and other particulars in relation to the early history of the road.

"Before answering your letter, I wished to consult Mr. John B. Jervis, of Rome, to procure from him some facts in relation to details in the construction of the first locomotive. I went to Rome on Saturday for that purpose alone, but, not finding him at home, I send you to day such facts as I can gather from memory, and some papers in my possession.

"The first experiment with steam upon the road was made with the locomotive 'De Witt Clinton,' in the latter part of July, 1831. This engine was built at the West Point Foundery Works, New York. A Mr. Matthew had charge of the hands fitting up the machine, and came with it in charge to Albany. This engine was contracted for by John B. Jervis, Esq., the chief engineer of the road. The estimated weight of the 'De Witt Clinton' was about six tons. It was mounted on four wheels, of about five feet diameter each, and had single drivers. The hubs and rims of the wheels were of cast-iron, with wrought-iron spokes and tires. I feel certain that the 'De Witt Clinton' had an iron tank or tender on four wheels. The first locomotive-engine which came from England, and was afterward put on the road, was made by Stephenson, and was called the 'Robert Fulton.' This engine was double the size and weight of the 'De Witt Clinton.' It arrived about the latter part of August, 1831, and was put on the road about the 10th to the 20th of September following. On the occasion of an excursion which was to take place the latter part of September, great preparations were made for a large crowd of passengers, as the Governor, judges of the courts, and members of the Legislature, were expected to participate in the ride, and consequently the most powerful engine, the 'Robert Fulton,' pull the train. But it did not so happen: something (I do not remember now) got wrong with 'Robert Fulton,' and 'De Witt Clinton' took his place at the head of the train, which being too heavy for

13

so small a machine, a part only was attached to the 'De Witt Clinton,' and the remainder were drawn each car by a horse, making a very amusing-looking cavalcade.  I think 'Fulton' would have done better and have been more at home upon the Hudson River than on the stand upon the Mohawk and Hudson Railroad. However, on that occasion the little 'De Witt' acquitted herself well, and got to the end of the road long before her companions by horse-power arrived, and did the same in returning.  Mr. Brown's sketch was taken on the first excursion with the 'De Witt Clinton,' before the time of this second excursion, and the arrival in this country of the first locomotive from England, the 'Fulton,' for our road.  The second locomotive which came from England arrived nearly a year after—perhaps not so long, but I remember it was late in the fall of the year.  This second engine came without a tank or a tender.  A temporary arrangement was made for supplying this English engine with water by means of a cask with the capacity of about three hundred gallons, made in the usual form and manner of a cask, and resting on saddles of wood fastened to a frame of the same material; and the whole, being mounted on four light cast-iron wheels, presented a very novel appearance.

" This English locomotive was called the 'John Bull,' and had four driving-wheels of four feet diameter.  The hubs and naves of the wheels were made of cast-iron, the spokes and rim or felloes were made of wood and secured by wrought-iron flanged tires.  It is, perhaps, needless to say that after this engine was put in use, those parts of the wheels made of wood gave audible complaint of hard service.  The 'shrieking' of the machine caused no little merriment among the knights of the whip, who were yet reluctant in believing that the beautiful tandem teams which they had the honor of driving formerly over the road, at the rate of twelve miles an hour, ' could ever be superseded by such a cursed-looking iron concern as that, as it was broken-winded already ! '

" The first regular trip for the public with a locomotive was on the 9th day of August, 1831, with the 'De Witt Clinton.'  A few experiments had been made with her previous to that date.

" Mr. John B. Jervis was chief engineer of the road, and the undersigned was resident engineer and superintendent of transportation; and he had the honor and satisfaction of receiving, with his own hands, the first fifty cents for regular established passenger-fare ever received on any railroad in the United States, as he believes.  The names of the first three engine-drivers employed by the company were David Matthew, who first run the 'De Witt Clinton,' John Hampson, and Adam Robinson.

"It has been said by some that the first locomotive-engine actually run in this country in the transportation of passengers on a railroad, was upon the Charleston Railroad, in South Carolina, drawn by an engine called the 'Best Friend,' but this I believe is a mistake. The fact can easily be obtained by Mr. Brown addressing a letter to Horatio Allen, Esq., now of the Novelty Works, New York. Mr. Allen was the chief engineer of the Charleston road in its commencement, and would know of this incident.

"I recollect seeing Mr. Brown's sketch of the 'De Witt Clinton' and her train of cars executed in black paper, in his peculiar style, when he was in Albany; and I could not but admire the wonderful correctness of his likenesses to the engine, engineer, and the old citizens of Albany, who are represented in the cars as passengers.

"I am very respectfully and truly yours,
"JOHN T. CLARK, *Utica.*"

We will now add the following letter from John B. Jervis, Esq., the chief engineer of the road, showing that the sketch of the engine and train of cars which appears in our work is the "De Witt Clinton," an American locomotive, the first ever run in the State of New York, and not, as has been represented in Sage & Son's lithograph, the "John Bull," an English engine and the first attached to a passenger-train in the United States, or as published since that time, by the Antique Publishing Company, of Boston, in 1870, as the "John Bull."

"ROME, N. Y., *April* 20, 1869.

"WILLIAM H. BROWN, ESQ.—

"DEAR SIR: Yours of the 15th inst. was duly received. I have no memoranda to refer to; but my memory serves me that you are correct in saying that the first engine or locomotive run upon the Mohawk and Hudson Railroad was named the 'De Witt Clinton,' and the date of the first trip correct, viz., the 9th day of August, 1831. The engine was built under a contract I made (as chief engineer of the road) with the West Point Association in

New-York City. Late in the same year, the English engine the 'John Bull,' was imported from England, for the same road. Mr. David Matthew was the machinist who put up the 'De Witt Clinton,' and run it, and no doubt his statements upon the subject are reliable. I do know, positively, that an American-built locomotive was put in successful use upon a railroad in this country prior to the 'De Witt Clinton;' my own impression is that there were two on the South Carolina Railroad.

"Respectfully, your obedient servant,

"JOHN B. JERVIS."

## CHAPTER XXXVII.

### ADDITIONAL LETTERS.

HAVING heard a short time since from an old citizen of Albany, who knew the individuals whose likenesses appear as passengers in the sketch of the "De Witt Clinton" and train, that, excepting Judge Gillis, whose letter we have already given, only two now survive that memorable event, namely, Erastus Corning, Esq., and Thurlow Weed, Esq., the author addressed them upon the subject, calling their recollections to his professional visit to Albany in 1831, and his original profile cutting of the first locomotive and train. He soon received the following interesting replies, which serve to prove the authenticity of his original in the Connecticut Historical Society:

"ALBANY, N. Y., *May* 30, 1870.

"WILLIAM H. BROWN, ESQ.—

"MY DEAR SIR: I have before me your letter of May 19th, 1870, referring to your proposed 'History of the Early Locomotives of America.'

"It gives me great pleasure to testify to the correctness of the photograph copy of your original cutting of the locomotive ' De Witt Clinton,' and the train of cars which passed over the Mohawk and Hudson Railroad, I think in August, 1831.

" I submitted a letter on the subject, written by you, in the year 1859, to Mr. John T. Clark, and sent you his reply, with a photograph copy of your picture.

" The likenesses of the passengers in the train are excellent, and probably the only collection of the kind in existence. Your forthcoming book will be a very interesting one and a valuable addition to railroad literature. I look for the appearance of it with the anticipation that it will be profitable and instructive.

" Yours very truly,

" ERASTUS CORNING."

The second letter was from Thurlow Weed, Esq., and was written by the veteran's daughter, Miss Harriet A. Weed, who acted as his amanuensis :

" NEW YORK, *February* 5, 1870.

" MR. WILLIAM H. BROWN—

" DEAR SIR : My father, who is not himself able to write, desires me to express his thanks for your interesting and welcome letter. He remembers you as temporarily residing at Albany. He also remembers your peculiar skill in fashioning paper pictures. Early in the day of photographs, a copy of your picture was sent to us from Hartford. My father has often been applied to for the names of the passengers, but could not remember them all. He does, however, remember Lewis Benedict, John Townsend, William Alexander, John J. Boyd, John Meigs (high constable of Albany), John J. De Graffs, and Hugh Robinson, of Schenectady. He thinks also that Billy Winne was one, and he remembers your being there looking at the engine.

" The best likeness we have of my deceased brother James is from your sketch of him as a member of the Burgess's Corps of Albany.

" The photograph copy of your Albany and Schenectady Railroad engine, copied from the original in the Connecticut Historical Society, now hangs in our library, looking precisely as my father remembers it while being fired-up for its first trip to Schenectady, thirty-eight or thirty-nine (nobody here can tell whether it was in 1831 or 1832) years ago.

"My father says that he shall look for your book with much interest. He, too, as fast as his impaired health permits, is putting his recollections together, with the material for history in his possession, on paper, with a view to publication.

"Truly yours,

"Harriet A. Weed."

Before we close this portion of our evidence, we cannot refrain from giving to our readers a second letter from John B. Jervis, Esq., who was chief engineer of the road, in reply to the author, who had transmitted to him some documents for his examination. This letter reads as follows:

"Rome, N. Y., *August* 24, 1870.

"William H. Brown, Esq.—

"My dear Sir: Yours of the 22d inst. came to hand this a. m. I have been quite interested in reading the letters and papers you sent me. The photograph picture of the first locomotive and passenger-train that certainly was the first run on the Mohawk and Hudson Railroad (Schenectady and Albany, now a portion of the New York Central Railroad) is a good representation.

"The engine was the 'De Witt Clinton' (and not the 'John Bull,' as the newspaper scrap from the *Boston Advertiser* gives it). There can be no doubt on this point—engine, tender, and cars, are an unequivocal delineation.

"I have had a copy of this picture for several years.

"I cannot speak as to exact date when the train was run, but it was about midsummer of 1831.

"I have no doubt Mr. Clark is correct as to the date trials were made, the latter part of July. The excursion-train was most probably made, as Mr. Clark states, on August 9, 1831. Mr. Clark's account of the building of the engine, at the shops of the West Point Foundery, in New York, is correct. I think, indeed I am certain, the English engine 'John Bull' did not arrive until the spring of 1832.

"I was quite interested in your biographical remarks, and hope the great labor you have given to prepare a correct history of the locomotive may prove amply remunerative. I shall be glad to see your book. It is a very important subject. Great progress has been made, and there is yet much to be done. I sometimes feel a desire to resume attention to this matter, but my age (seventy-five years) admonishes me that it is better to be quiet.

"Very truly your friend,

"John B. Jervis."

We will now add to our history of the early loco-motives built in America, by giving Mr. William Kem-ble's letter to the author upon the subject. Mr. Kem-ble was superintendent and manager of the West Point Foundery Works, in the city of New York, from 1829 to 1831, and for many years after.

"West Point Foundery Office,
"New York, *June* 12, 1871.

"Mr. William H. Brown—

"Dear Sir: Your letter informs me that you are about to publish a history of the early locomotives built in America, and ask me for some particulars respecting the first locomotives built at our shops.

"It gives me great pleasure, sir, to comply with your wishes on that subject; and I will commence by saying that the first locomotive ever run in this country was imported from England, and was called the 'Stourbridge Lion.' It came out in the spring of 1829; was in charge of Horatio Allen, Esq.; was landed from the ship John Jay at our wharf and put up at our works. This locomotive was for the Delaware and Hudson Canal and Railroad Company.

"The first locomotive ever constructed in this country and for actual service upon a railroad, was undoubtedly built at our works. It was contracted for by Colonel E. L. Miller, of Charleston, South Carolina, for the South Carolina Railroad. It was commenced early in the summer of 1830, and completed and sent to Charleston by the ship Niagara in the month of October of that year. This engine was called the 'Best Friend.'

"The second locomotive constructed in America was also built at our works, and for the South Carolina Railroad. This engine was contracted for by Horatio Allen, Esq., the chief engineer of the road, and was built from drawings sent out by him.

"This locomotive was called the 'West Point.' It was finished and sent to Charleston by the ship Lafayette, in February, 1831.

"A third locomotive was soon after constructed at our shops. This machine was contracted for by John B. Jervis, Esq., chief engineer of the Mohawk and Hudson Railroad, and was finished and forwarded to Albany in June or early in July, 1831. This engine was called the 'De Witt Clinton.' Mr. David Matthew, who had charge of the hands fitting up all these engines, went on to Albany with the 'Clinton' to put it on the road and to run it.

"There can be no doubt whatever but that these locomotives, the 'Best Friend,' the 'West Point,' and the 'De Witt Clinton,' were the first ever built in America for actual service on a railroad. Prior to and during that time, from 1829 to 1831, several small machines for experimental purposes were built and tried, but the three above named were the first ordered to be built in America for actual service upon a railroad.

"Hoping these facts may be of service to you in your forthcoming work, I remain, dear sir,

"Yours respectfully

"WILLIAM KEMBLE."

## CHAPTER XXXVIII.

### THE AUTHOR'S ART.

THE following are a few of over a thousand newspaper comments and letters upon the author's skill in the various departments of his art. They are given here merely as proofs that our readers may rely upon the accuracy of the representation of the "De Witt Clinton" engine, cars, and passengers which accompanies our work, and appears in simple black outline.

(*From the Albany Argus, August*, 1831.)

"Decidedly the best thing we have seen for many a day we met with yesterday in dropping into the rooms of Mr. William H.

Brown, the artist, on State Street. He has taken some of the best likenesses of a number of our citizens in his peculiar style, namely, cut out of black paper with a pair of common scissors. The one of our old and esteemed neighbor, Job Gould, is decidedly the most striking picture we have ever looked upon. The facility and correctness with which Mr. Brown takes these likenesses are really astonishing.

"We recognized also, at a single glance, others as natural as life itself. For instance, the venerable penny postman, Billy Winne, Jerry Jewell, Mr. Alexander, little Chapman, the dwarf, Mr. Carter, of the Clinton, John J. Quackenboss, ex-Governor Meigs, Thurlow Weed, General Root, Mr. Phelps, Mr. Van Zant, and a host of others, and, what is the most astonishing feature about them, they were all taken from memory. These individuals were pointed out to Mr. Brown upon the street as well-known characters in our city, and, after several hours, were transferred by his magic scissors upon paper, if not quite as large as life, at least twice as natural."

(*From the Albany Evening Journal.*)

"Our friend Mr. William H. Brown, the inimitable artist, has fairly taken the patronage of our citizens by storm. From morn to night his rooms are besieged by anxious applicants, awaiting their chance for the operation of his magic scissors. For every one accommodated, three stand ready as successors. We are gratified at the result of Mr. Brown's visit among us, not more for the encouragement extended to superlative skill than the satisfaction of witnessing individual worth so highly appreciated. He has recently taken in one large picture the entire Burgess's Corps, with staff and band in full parade, in which the likeness of each individual member is presented with an accuracy truly surprising, and stamps Mr. Brown as a perfect master of his profession. Those who have not seen his portraitures should embrace the earliest opportunity, as he remains, we regret to say, but one week longer, his departure for that time being deferred for the purpose of taking the likenesses of Engine Company No. 2. The courteous and cheerful deportment of Mr. Brown toward his visitors renders a visit to his rooms most agreeable and instructive."

(*From the St. Louis Bulletin.*)

"GREAT DOINGS AT BROWN'S.—This wonderful artist—yes, we will out with it—the immortal Brown—has just completed the most splendid thing in his line that was ever seen in this city. It is nothing less than a profile likeness of the St. Louis engine, the two hose-carriages, and sixty-five members of that valiant and invincible corps. The members are all in the uniform of the company, forty attached to the drag-ropes of the engine, thirteen to the ropes of one hose-carriage and twelve to the other. We will take the liberty of styling it a panoramic view of the St. Louis Fire Company, and we are compelled to say that in this kind of panorama all other artists must bow in humble submission before the scissors and the skill of the unequalled Brown. This method of styling it will not be deemed inappropriate when we tell you that the whole picture occupies a space of twenty-five feet in length. The representation of the engine is beautiful indeed, and true to the very letter, and is all the work of a pair of small scissors and black paper. On the opposite side of the artist's room may be seen another specimen of his skill in a second picture of the same kind, representing the Missouri Fire Company, with her engine, hose-carriage, and tender, with fifty-nine men in all. The company are represented in their winter costume as returning from a fire or drill, the whole picture presenting a fine and novel appearance, and are perfect and characteristic likenesses. The two pictures are intended as decorations for their several engine-houses."

"ARMORY NATCHEZ FENCIBLES.

"At a called meeting of the Natchez Fencibles, held at their armory on Thursday evening, June 13, 1844, the following resolutions were unanimously adopted:

"1. *Resolved*, That the thanks of this company be tendered to Mr. William H. Brown for the admirable picture of this corps, just completed by him, which, in all its details, fully sustains the high artistical reputation of Mr. Brown, and has won the undivided admiration of the members of the Natchez Fencibles.

"2. *Resolved*, That the foregoing resolution be published in the *Daily Courier*.

"LEVI S. HARRISON,
"*Secretary Natchez Fencibles*."

"WASHINGTON, *September* 20, 1843

"WILLIAM H. BROWN, ESQ.—

"MY DEAR SIR: Yours, postmarked Philadelphia, 1st September, addressed to me at Accomac Court-House, Virginia, I found on my arrival here last evening. I am under very many obligations to you for not publishing or printing the letter referred to by you without giving me the opportunity which you have so kindly done to correct its many imperfections. I do not desire it to-be published while it contains a single hard word or thought of any human being. I never have deliberately and wantonly wounded a fellow-being, though I have often done so, sometimes from a sense of duty and sometimes impetuously. Even if I were inclined to *lash* any one for 'lashing's' sake, I do not think your intended volume would be the proper place for it. I do not prize my fame for the faculty of saying severe things very highly; and he who is gifted with the power and constrained by the necessity of saying harsh things, or even of speaking out his mind and feelings strongly, however honestly, in this world, is not apt to be blessed with the mild judgments of men himself. I trust now that, having passed the profile stage of life, and got into the author's line, you can look at the world full-face. I have often seen and admired your productions and the wonderful faculty of fixing the resemblance of men on paper with the aid of your scissors and black paper only. I have never failed to recognize a striking likeness to the original in all I have seen even of the most casual acquaintance.

"With thanks for your kindness, and the flattering notice you propose to take of my humble self, I am,

"Gratefully yours,

"HENRY A. WISE."

"LINDENWALD, *September* 6, 1843.

"WILLIAM H. BROWN, ESQ.—

"DEAR SIR: It affords me much satisfaction to embrace the opportunity you have presented me, to express the very favorable opinion I entertain of your skill in your peculiar style of profile cutting; and with my best wishes for your success in your forthcoming work.*         Very truly yours,

"M. VAN BUREN."

"WASHINGTON, *January* 12, 1845.

"WILLIAM H. BROWN, ESQ.—

"DEAR SIR: I take pleasure in bearing testimony to your great aptitude in taking likenesses in your way, and the fidelity with which they are executed. I wish you great success in the

* "National Portrait Gallery."

work you are about to publish, and do not doubt but that you will make it worthy of public patronage.    With great respect,

"I am, etc.,

"J. C. CALHOUN."

"WASHINGTON CITY, *January* 13, 1843.

"WILLIAM H. BROWN, ESQ.—

"MY DEAR SIR: Your favor of the 3d instant is before me, and in reply I will say that the likenesses of the members of Congress and other public men of the times, taken by you in your peculiar and characteristic style, are remarkably correct, and easily recognized at a glance.

"My friends unite in saying that the one you took of myself is a striking likeness.    I cannot, however, see its resemblance to the original as I do in all the others.    It is an old and very true saying, 'that if we could see ourselves as others see us,' etc.

"I wish you great success in your contemplated work.    It cannot otherwise than prove acceptable to the public, who feel an interest in the records of men who have devoted their best faculties to their country's service, which your 'Portrait Gallery' will exhibit.    With great respect,

"Yours truly,

"DANIEL WEBSTER."

"LEXINGTON, KY., *October* 13, 1843.

"WILLIAM H. BROWN, ESQ.—

"DEAR SIR: Your favor of the 2d instant is received.    I well remember your collection of the likenesses of our public men, members of Congress, the Cabinet, and other officials in and about Washington City, and I will say that I was particularly struck with their truthfulness.    That of the Hon. John Randolph, of Roanoke, is the very perfection of your art.    I shall not soon forget the amusement you afforded the visitors at the Blue Lick Springs last summer, by your delineations of many of them in your peculiar and characteristic style of portraiture, unequalled by any other artist in that way I have ever seen.

"The work you propose to publish will, no doubt, be an interesting acquisition to the reading public, and I request you here to put my name down in the list of your subscribers for a copy as soon as it is ready for distribution.    With great respect, I remain,

"Yours truly,

"HENRY CLAY."

The foregoing letters are in allusion to a "Portrait-Gallery of Distinguished Public Men," published by the author a few years after. They are referred to in this work merely as further evidences of the author's skill in his peculiar art of sketching in black paper outline or profile, that our readers may rely upon the correctness of the representation of the "De Witt Clinton" and train, which we insert.

———◆◆◆———

# CHAPTER XXXIX.

### RECAPITULATION.

WE trust that we have now faithfully performed the task undertaken by us, when we commenced these pages; and we believe that our readers will not entertain a doubt, from the chain of authentic and reliable evidence we have brought before them, that the first locomotive ever run upon a railroad in this country was the "Stourbridge Lion," imported from England in 1829. We have shown that this machine was ordered by John B. Jervis, Esq., the chief engineer of the Delaware and Hudson Canal and Railroad Company, to be used upon their road, which connected with their canal; that Horatio Allen, Esq., the assistant engineer under Mr. Jervis, was on a visit to England, and witnessed the experiments then made in the contest for the prize of £500 offered by the Liverpool and Manchester Railroad for the locomotive that should perform certain requisitions; that Mr. Allen was instructed by Mr. Jervis to contract for three locomotives for the Delaware and Hudson Railroad; that the first of these engines, the "Stourbridge Lion," arrived in the city of New York by the ship John Jay on the 17th of May, 1829, and was set up by Mr. Allen in the yard of the West Point Foundery Works, then in the city, and, with steam from the shops, publicly exhibited for several weeks, and visited by thousands attracted by the novelty of the machine.

We have shown that the "Stourbridge Lion" was next shipped up the Hudson River to Rondout, where it arrived on the 4th of July, 1829, and thence forwarded by the Delaware and Hudson Canal to Honesdale, where it was landed on the 23d of July, was immediately placed upon the company's railroad, and made its first trial-trip under steam on Saturday, the 8th day of August, 1829, in the presence of several thousand spectators attracted from all parts of the country to witness the advent of the first locomotive in America. We have also shown that on that memorable occasion Mr. Allen stood alone upon the engine, and with his own hand opened the valve that gave the impulse to the driving-wheel that made the first revolution upon a railroad in America.

From the most reliable sources our readers have been informed that the first locomotive ever built in America was a "Liliputian" affair, made for experimental purposes alone. It was nevertheless a locomotive, and was built by Peter Cooper, Esq., of New York, well and most favorably known as the founder and patron of the Cooper Institute of that city. This little machine of Mr. Cooper's (we call it little because it weighed less than a ton) was expressly built to demonstrate a principle upon the Baltimore and Ohio Railroad with regard to the capability of a locomotive to sustain itself upon the track in running curves—a much and almost universally disputed point among engineers and scientific men of that early period in railroad experience.

From the evidences we have given, our readers must now be convinced that the very first locomotive built in America for actual service was ordered by and made for the South Carolina Railroad then just commenced, and but a few miles completed. This first locomotive was contracted for by E. L. Miller, Esq., an enterprising gentleman of Charleston, who had visited England and witnessed the contest for the £500 prize. Mr. Miller had his locomotive constructed at the West Point Foundery Works in the city of New York. Mr. David Matthew, then a foreman in the machine-shops, had charge of the hands fitting up this machine or locomotive. It was called by Mr. Miller the "Best Friend, of Charleston," and was forwarded by ship Niagara, and arrived in Charleston on the 23d of October, 1830. No person accompanied this locomotive from the works in New York to put it up and try its abilities upon a road. That duty was performed by Mr. Julius D. Petsch, foreman of Mr. Thomas Dotterer's machine-shops in Charleston, assisted by Nicholas W. Darrell, a young man just out of his time. The first experiments with a train, we have shown, took place on the 2d of November, and again on the 14th and 15th of December, 1830, on which last trial-trip before the public, as from the first, the machine was in charge of Mr. Darrell as engineer, who continued to act in that capacity until the June following, when, through the ignorance of the negro fireman, the "Best Friend" exploded, severely scalding Mr. Darrell, and resulting finally in the death of the negro from his injuries.

We have given evidence to show that the second locomotive built in America was likewise constructed at the West Point Foundery Works, and for the South Carolina Railroad. This machine was ordered by Horatio Allen, Esq., the chief engineer of the road, and made from plans and drawings sent out by him. The engine was completed and forwarded by the ship Lafayette, and arrived in Charleston on the 28th day of February, 1831, and made her first successful trial-trip over the road on the 5th of March, 1831. This locomotive was called the "West Point," and was in charge of Mr. Darrell, who meantime had recovered from the injuries received by the explosion of the "Best Friend." Mr. David Matthew also had charge of the hands fitting up the "West Point" as well as the "Best Friend" at the Foundery Works, New York.

We have produced satisfactory evidence to prove that the third successful locomotive constructed in America was the "De Witt Clinton," built also at the West Point Works for the Mohawk and Hudson Railroad. This engine was completed and taken to Albany the latter part of June, 1831, in charge of Mr. David Matthew, who put it upon the road, and, after several experimental trials in July, made the first excursion-trip with a train of cars on the 9th day of August, 1831, as represented in the author's sketch taken upon the spot just as the train was about to start.

We have shown that about this time (midsummer, 1831) the locomotive built by Mr. Davis at York, Pennsylvania, was put upon the Baltimore and Ohio Railroad, as the most effective of the number presented at the trial for the prize offered by that company. Of the doings of this engine, we have a further and more particular account in an extract we make from a work entitled a "History and Description of the Baltimore and Ohio Railroad," presented to us by B. H. Latrobe, Esq., of that road, thus:

"In pursuance of this call upon American genius, made by the directors, three locomotives were produced upon the road, only one of which, however, was made to answer any good purpose. This engine, called 'The York,' was built at York, Pennsylvania, by Phineas Davis (or rather Davis and Gartner), and, after undergoing certain modifications, was found capable of conveying fifteen tons at fifteen miles per hour on a level portion of the road. It was employed on that part of the road between Baltimore and Ellicott's Mills, and generally performed the trip to the Mills in one hour, with four cars, being a gross weight of about fourteen tons. This engine was mounted on wheels, like those of the common cars, of thirty inches diameter, and the velocity was obtained by means of gearing with a spur-wheel and pinion on one of the axles of the road-wheels.

"The curvatures were all travelled with great facility by this engine, its greatest velocity, for a short time, on straight parts of the road, having been at the rate of thirty miles per hour, while it frequently attained that of twenty miles, and often travelled in curvatures of four hundred feet radius, at the rate of fifteen miles per hour. The fuel used was anthracite coal, and answered well; but the engine, weighing but three and a half tons, was found too light for advantageous use in ascending grades. The performance of this engine fully confirmed the board and its engineer corps that locomotives might be successfully used on a railway having curves of four hundred feet radius, and from that time forward every encouragement was given by the company to the inventive genius of the country to improve on the partially successful experimental engine that had been produced by Mr. Davis.

"In September, 1835, Mr. Davis met with a sudden and unexpected death. He was riding upon the tender of a new locomotive, on its trial-trip upon the Washington branch, accompanied by a large number of his employés on an excursion to the capital. The engine struck the end of a broken rail and was thrown off the track. Mr. Davis was hurled with great force against the engine, causing his instantaneous death. This melancholy event produced a deep gloom over the excursionists and the whole community where Mr. Davis was known. In his death the Baltimore and

14

Ohio Railroad met with a great loss.   He was an able and ingenious mechanic, and one of the most indefatigable assistants to the
company, in its experimental and mechanical department."

But to resume our history.   We have shown that, as
early as 1831, the first eight-wheeled locomotive ever
built, either in England or America, was constructed from plans by Horatio Allen, Esq., and put upon the
South Carolina Railroad.   This machine was made at
the West Point Foundery Works, and forwarded to
Charleston in charge of Mr. John Degnon, who run it
for a short time until accepted by the road, and then it
was placed in charge of Mr. Darrell.

We have, in the course of our narrative, shown that
the South Carolina Railroad was the first railroad in
the world built expressly for locomotive-power; that
when Mr. Bennett's famous resolution to that effect was
unanimously adopted by its board of directors, the
directors of the road from Liverpool to Manchester in
England, just completed, had not yet determined what
kind of power should be used upon the road.   A
majority of the committee of engineers, appointed to
examine and report upon that important matter, were
in favor of stationary engines with long chains or ropes
to draw the trains over the road.   George Stephenson,
being one of their number, was alone in favor of the
locomotive.   Again we show that the first one hundred
consecutive miles of iron rails upon a road was laid
upon the South Carolina Railroad.   These statements,
though startling to the minds of many, are nevertheless
true, and can be sustained by the best authority, and
without a shadow of doubt.

Mr. William Kemble, who was in charge of the
West Point Works during the year 1829, and afterward while these machines were built, in his letter to

the author fully sustains all the facts connected with the early history of the English engine "Stourbridge Lion," and the first three American engines built in the United States, viz., the "Best Friend," the "West Point," and the "De Witt Clinton;" and no further evidence is required to establish these facts.

## CHAPTER XL.

### FIRST TRUCK-ENGINE.

THESE experiments on the South Carolina Railroad paved the way for several others which soon after followed, and at this day they are looked upon as more remarkable, from the early date in locomotive enterprise in which they were attempted, and with such surprising results. One of the most important of these early efforts was the introduction of the truck under the front part of the machine, to assist in sustaining the weight of the boiler, and to give direction to the machine in running upon curves.

As this truck attachment has now become so universally adopted, and has never been patented, we will give a description of the first machine ever built which used it. We take it from a letter received by the author from Mr. David Matthew, who superintended the hands while constructing the machine. Mr. Matthew thus writes:

"American locomotive No. 1, second series, was built at the West Point Foundery Works, for the Mohawk and Hudson Railroad, from plans sent by John B. Jervis, Esq., chief engineer of that road. I left New York in August, 1832, with the engine in charge to place on the road and run it.   This was the first bogie engine or truck used under the front part, ever built in this country or any other.   The engine had nine and a half inch cylinders, sixteen-inch stroke, and had two pairs of driving-wheels five feet in diameter, and set aft the furnace; had four wheels, thirty-three inches' diameter, in the truck.   This truck was placed under the front end of the boiler for support, attached by a strong pin, and worked upon friction-rollers so as easily to follow the curves of the road, as the fore-wheels of a carriage upon common roads.

"The boiler-furnace was five feet long, by thirty-four inches wide, with three-inch tubes, and made to burn anthracite coal. With this engine I have crossed the Mohawk and Hudson Railroad from plane to plane, fourteen miles, in thirteen minutes, making one stop for water.   I have tried her speed upon a level, straight line, and have made one mile in forty-five seconds by the watch. She was the fastest and steadiest engine I have ever run or seen, and she worked with the greatest ease.

" The first of this kind of engine, with the truck in front, ever built in England, was the ' Davy Crocket,' constructed by Robert Stephenson, for the Saratoga Railroad Company, from drawings and plans sent out to him by John B. Jervis, Esq., who was the inventor of this attachment.   I never tried this engine at her speed, but all her movements were with similar ease, and it did not work us all over to take eighteen to twenty cars over the road. This machine was placed on the road in 1833, and run for many years.   She had two driving-wheels aft and four truck-wheels. The driving-wheels were aft the furnace, which plan was adopted by M. W. Baldwin, who claims this as the general arrangement. But the original plans and drawings, from the inventor, John B. Jervis, Esq., are yet in my possession."

Of this engine Mr. Jervis thus speaks in a letter addressed to the author, April 20, 1869:

"Not satisfied with the working of four-wheel engines, in the fall of 1831 I made a plan with a set of trucks as leading-wheels, which was executed by the West Point Foundery Association, New-York City.

" This engine gave rise to the plan of truck-leading, or rather this engine was made on the plan which is now in general use on American railways.

"Mr. David Matthew was the machinist who put up this truck-machine. I regard it as the greatest point that an American engineer, in the face of English practice, should have devised a plan, which at the time was considered very radical, of introducing a truck to support the end of the frame and guide the motion of the engine, and which, after thirty-seven years of experience, is now adopted on every engine of nearly fifty thousand miles of railroad in America."

During the past forty years, while railroads were stretching forth their iron arms over vast sections of our country, and indeed of the civilized world, and even through the wild and thinly-populated domains of the savage, where exist vast forests and hitherto pathless deserts of sand, locomotives, those absolute essentials to the economy and success of these enterprises, were in like manner making giant strides in the way of improvement, from the "Rocket" of Stephenson in England, and the "Best Friend, of Charleston," in this country, to the perfection which characterizes the first-class locomotive of the present day. When we compare the performances of these and their readiness at all hours, and under all circumstances, to brave the torrents, the winds, and the snows of the most terrific tempest, we cannot but call to mind an advertisement in a Philadelphia paper in 1832. This we will extract just as it appeared. It will, no doubt, draw a smile upon the faces of our present locomotive engineers. It reads thus:

"NOTICE TO THE PUBLIC.—The engine, with a train of cars, will be run daily, commencing this day, when the weather is fair; when the weather is not fair, the horses will draw the cars. Passengers are requested to be punctual at the hour of starting."

When we contemplate the rapid march made, upon this continent alone, in railroad and locomotive improvement, it seems like the work of enchantment. The mind is bewildered and almost carried away in its efforts to keep pace with or follow its giant strides.

Let us (by way of illustration) conduct our reader for a few moments to some imaginary eminence, from which his eye could command in one sweep the entire surface of our country. Let him turn his gaze toward the north, the south, the east, or the west, even across the Rocky Mountains to the shores of the broad Pacific, and he will behold a scene of life and industry which few could be prepared to believe had been developed in less than half a century. And then let him predict the future—if he can. Lead his mind back to the period just forty years ago, when, on the 15th day of December, 1830, the first locomotive built in America for actual service upon a railroad, and known as the " Best Friend, of Charleston," started out upon its solitary journey, a few miles only in extent, upon the unfinished track of the South Carolina Railroad—the second railroad commenced in this country for commercial purposes, and the first railroad in the world built expressly for locomotive-power. Let him contemplate this scene for a moment, then turn his mind to the one presented to him at the present day; all over the wide expanse of our Union, behold the countless railroads extending for thousands of miles in every direction, bearing upon their rails their droves of iron horses, of every imaginary form and pattern, dashing with lightning-speed from city to city, with their long and heavy trains of living, breathing human creatures, or with their lengthened trains of freight-cars, loaded with thousands of tons of the products of the industry of the people, adding millions to the trade and commerce of the nation, rushing on, overcoming all obstacles, crossing wide, deep, and rapid rivers, ascending the steepest grades, or driving headlong through lengthened tunnels—then ask the beholder if we have yet reached the summit, the consummation, the ultimatum of this great instrumentality in the advancement of the trade and commerce of our prosperous republic. He will answer, " No ! No one can tell—no one can predict—no mind can conceive—no figures can compute the sum of what will be the progress in the next forty years of this great achievement of the present century, in the railroad and its iron steed."

Forty years ago an imported locomotive (weighing scarcely a half-dozen tons) made the first experimental trip, of a few miles only, upon a coal-road belonging to the Delaware and Hudson Canal Company. This machine proved to be too heavy for the structure, and its innumerable trestles and bridges, and it was abandoned, and the road soon after remodelled into a graded one with stationary engines, as was recommended about the same time (1829) by the most prominent English engineers to the directors of the Liverpool and Manchester Railroad, in preference to the locomotive system, which they looked upon as impracticable.

Not the least daunted or discouraged by the failure of this first experiment at home, and the opinions and examples before them in England, the directors of the South Carolina Railroad, at their first regular meeting, only five days after their organization, passed unanimously that memorable resolution in these very words : " that their railroad should be built for locomotive-power alone; that in selecting that power in its application to railroads, the maturity of which will be reached within the time of constructing their road, and render the application of animal power a great abuse of the gifts of genius and science." Their example was fol-

lowed in quick succession on several railroads soon after
in the progress of construction, and continued to spread
with unprecedented rapidity to the present day.

We cannot quit the subject without again drawing
before our readers a comparison between the locomotive passenger-trains of the present day and those of
forty years ago, when the old-fashioned stage-coach-
body pattern was the model for the first-class passenger-
cars, as represented in the author's sketch, in this volume, of the "De Witt Clinton" and train.    When we
compare these vehicles with the splendid drawing-room,
sleeping, and dining-room cars now coming into use
upon some of the principal railroad thoroughfares and
soon to become universal; and when the old and familiar voice of the conductor, announcing "Twenty minutes for dinner," will no longer be heard, but, instead
thereof, the hungry traveller will be ushered into a
splendid dining-saloon (attached to the train) and
vying in elegance with the most sumptuous apartment,
furnished and provided with all the concomitants of a
well-appointed hotel, a table groaning under the weight
of well cooked and prepared provisions, followed by
all the luxuries of the various seasons through which
they travel, served by polite and attentive waiters;
and, at length, at the end of a well-enjoyed meal, the
traveller will find himself some twenty-five or thirty
miles farther advanced upon his journey than when he
took his seat at the summons to dinner—all, all seems
like the work of enchantment!    In no other language,
perhaps, can we better illustrate the wonderful strides
made in the march of improvement, and the facilities
of intercommunication within less than a quarter of a
century, than by quoting here the words of John H. B.
Latrobe, Esq., the eminent counsellor of the Baltimore

and Ohio Railroad, at a banquet given in Wheeling in 1853, on the successful completion of that great enterprise :

"With your permission, Mr. President, I will read, as my text for what I propose to say, the following extract from the *Virginia Gazette*, published in 1836 : 'The Baltimore and Ohio Wagon Company, with a capital of two hundred thousand dollars (one-fourth of which is paid in), transport goods and produce between Wheeling and Baltimore. One wagon departs and arrives daily from each of these places, with a load weighing from two and a quarter to two and a half tons, and occupying eight days upon the road, and arrangements are in progress to increase the number of daily arrivals and departures, from one to three wagons, and eventually to five.'

"Were a new edition to be prepared for the *Virginia Gazette*, and the paragraph relating to the intercourse of the two cities, Wheeling and Baltimore, to be placed side by side, how modest would appear to have been the conception of its author, only sixteen years ago!

"The arrangements to which we refer, carried out by a different company it is true, but still the arrangements, uniting Wheeling and Baltimore, have resulted in the existence of a company with a capital of twelve million dollars, all of which has been paid in; having in charge a work which, when completed and stocked, as it is intended that it shall be, will represent a capital of about twenty million dollars, and whose preparations, so soon as the delays attending the first use of all good public works shall have been surmounted, will insure the daily transportation, between the Ohio and Baltimore, of a thousand tons of goods and produce in the space of thirty-six hours now, and who can tell how much faster ere a few years have been added to the less than the quarter of a century just referred to.

"Why, Mr. President, the weight of the tonnage-engine alone used by this railroad company almost equals the weight of the five loads that limited the hopes of the wagon company, teams, wagons, and all; and behind this engine there rolls at the uniform speed of twelve miles an hour three hundred tons of gross weight, one-half of which is the exchange which the Western valleys send to the cities of the Atlantic border. We talk of the course of empire. Its type is the locomotive and its train, whose tread is the tread of a giant, from hill-top to hill-top. We speak of the array of a conqueror: where is there a conqueror like steam? Its panoply, too, is of iron; man has made it not less than mortal, as it performs the work of one hundred thousand of men's hands, and, as it is impatient of delay, it rushes through and through the bosom of the hills, its white and feathery plume is the ensign of a daring, a courage that treads its way through the forest, or climbs the side of the mountain, and a power which, while it may find its comparison in the crest of Henry IV. at Ivry, is the precursor of the triumphs, not of war, but of peace, as they build up the fame, not of heroes, but of the people. . . . That the fruition of these hopes will disappoint no reasonable expectations, but surpass them all, who of us can doubt? The West built up Baltimore—first with the pack-saddle, then with the county road, then with the turnpike—as it is now about to employ the greatest agent of modern times to realize for us the destiny appointed by Providence, when the waters of the fountains of the Potomac are made to flow from the same hills that sent their tribute to the Ohio."

In what language would Mr. Latrobe (who still lives to see it) express the wonderful results of the sixteen years which have succeeded the events we have just recorded? What comparison now would he draw of the daily transit over the Baltimore and Ohio Railroad with that daily wagon-load of from two and one-fourth to two and a half tons, and the ultimate prospect of it reaching five wagon-loads per day?

Again, on this memorable occasion, the completion of the Baltimore and Ohio Railroad, and the arrival of the first locomotive and train from Baltimore at Wheeling, a guest from Cleveland, James A. Briggs, Esq., made these appropriate remarks in allusion to the march of internal improvements in railways and locomotives:

"This is an occasion of no common interest. The men of Maryland, and Virginia, and Ohio, and Pennsylvania, have met here to commemorate the completion of one of the great lines of trade and travel between the Atlantic Ocean and the Ohio River. This line of railroad is a great work. It was originated by men who had the capacity to conceive great designs and the courage to execute them. The work is finished. The iron horse has travelled on his iron pathway from the 'Monumental City' over the Alleghanies to this not long since frontier settlement, but now the flourishing city of Wheeling. Here, in this room, are men who have heard the warwhoop of the Indian on this very spot, and to-day they have heard the shrill whistle of the locomotive. How wonderful that such changes have come within the memory of those who still live! And this is a change which tells not of war and carnage—not of cities desolated, and villages ruined, and fields laid waste—but of the progress of the arts of peace, of the advancement of a high order of civilization, and of the onward course of the car of Christianity, freighted with innumerable blessings for the whole world-wide family of man. . . . I do most cordially congratulate the people of Maryland and Virginia upon the completion of the Baltimore and Ohio Railroad. It is one link in the chain which binds us together as a nation. While I am now speaking, the locomotive that drinks and smokes, and is a 'fast fellow,' is thundering along on his iron track from the 'Queen City' of Ohio, and from the far-off prairies of Illinois, heading long trains freighted with men and the products of the rich fields of the West to Eastern markets.

"As I stood last evening on the bank of the Ohio, looking at the beautiful and magnificent iron bridge which spans the river like a bow, and gemmed and sparkling as it was with a thousand lights, I could but believe that the tall pipes of the majestic steamers would, in all coming time, bow as they passed to this grand work of the genius of man. Last March, a goodly number of the people of Cleveland and the Reserve were here to celebrate the completion of the railroad from the Lake to Wellsville. We are here to-night to rejoice over the advent of the iron horse from Baltimore to Wheeling, and, before this year shall have passed away, to be numbered with the years that have gone, we hope the last link in the line of railroad between Baltimore and Cleveland will be finished; and then, in return for your energies and enterprise and hospitality, we trust you may be invited to partake of true and genuine Yankee hospitality in the 'Forest City,' 'the City upon the Lake-shore,' and although the season may make it winter without, we can assure you that the warmth of the heart shall make it summer within."

All this has been verified, and how much more will be accomplished within the next forty years to come no man can predict; for even now the author has noticed advertisements announcing through-tickets for sale for the round-trip from New York to San Francisco, passing through all the intermediate cities on the plains and returning, with beautiful and comfortable parlor, dining-room, dressing-room, and sleeping cars throughout the entire route. Price ninety dollars for the round-trip. N. B.—Excursionists have the privilege of going by any train or at any time, without restriction.

Another announcement on a much more extensive scale may now be seen posted up at all the hotels and railroad offices in the city of New York, and no doubt by this time in all other cities, which reads as follows:

" GREAT EXCURSION TO EUROPE AND THE EAST.

" Visiting London, the seat of the last war in France, Switzerland, Rome, Naples, Pompeii, Vesuvius, Greece, the pyramids of Gizeh; returning to Venice and Vienna to spend the carnival there, and over Paris to New York.

" Prices $1,500, $1,200, $1,000, gold.

" Concerning the participation for four or five months, including excellent board, with wine, free entrance to all sights, partly to theatres and concerts, all drives in carriages, on horses, and in boats or gondolas; free guiding all during the voyage, free luggage, the use of tents, saddles, jars, and the escort of Bedouins, on the land-tour through Palestine.

" A courier, a physician, a lady companion for the ladies, and a servant speaking all forecoming languages, accompanying the party.

" Only first-class steamers and hotels will be frequented; the undertaking provides for every thing, and the greatest attention paid to ladies. Apply to

" Messrs. KUNHARDT & COMPANY,
          " 61 Broad Street, New York,
" Or at the Universal Excursion Company,
          " Prescott House, 531 Broadway, New York."

This company (well known in Europe) was present with two parties at the inauguration of the Suez Canal in Egypt, November, 1869. Excursions under their charge are made every year to Spain and Portugal; Norway, Sweden, and Russia; Italy, Greece, Turkey, Palestine, and Egypt, a trip up the Nile included; and special excursions twice a year to London, Paris, Vienna, and Venice, staying over the carnival. Doubtless in a few years these prices above will be regarded as fabulous. Competition has already commenced in the routes to the Pacific coast, as appears by the following:

"UNION PACIFIC RAILROAD.—Two hundred and twenty-six miles saved for Chicago by the Union Pacific Railroad, *via* Omaha. One hundred and thirty-five miles saved from Indianapolis. One hundred and seventeen miles saved from Cincinnati. Twenty-five miles saved from St. Louis to Salt Lake City, Sacramento, San Francisco, Sandwich Islands, New Zealand, Australia, China, Japan, and India. The best route to Denver, Colorado, New Mexico, and Arizona.

"Remember that only those tickets *via* Omaha are sure of places in the through Pullman palace cars. For sale at all the principal ticket-offices in the United States and Canada."

All this is the work of the locomotive, under the impulse of that powerful yet invisible offspring from two of the most conflicting elements brought within control, by the ingenuity of man, in the invention of the steam-engine, advanced as it now is to a stage of perfection in less than a century.

In the present improved state of this machine, it seems to be a thing almost endowed with human intelligence. It regulates with perfect accuracy and uniformity the number of its revolutions in a given time; it regulates the quantity of steam required to do its work; it opens and shuts its valves with absolute precision as to time and manner; it helps itself to all the water it wants; it oils its own joints, and, when any thing goes wrong which it cannot itself rectify, it gives timely warning to its attendant.  Yet, with all these talents and qualities, and even when fully capable of exerting the power of six hundred or a thousand horses, it is obedient to the hand of a child.  Its food is coal or wood, or any thing combustible; it consumes nothing when idle; it never tires or wants to rest or sleep; it is not subject to malady when originally made well, and only refuses to work when worn out with age; it is equally active in all climates, and will do work of any kind; it is a water-pumper, a miner, a sawyer, a tanner, a stone-cutter, a turner, a carpenter, a blacksmith, a cotton-spinner, a weaver, a sailor; in short, it is a mechanic in every branch of art.  It has revolutionized the whole domain of human industry, and almost every year is adding to its power and its conquests.  In our manufactures, arts, commerce, and our social accommodations, it is constantly achieving what, less than fifty years ago, would have been accounted marvellous or an impossibility; it can engrave a seal, and crush masses of the hardest metal like wax before it; draw out, without breaking, a thread as fine as gossamer, and lift a ship like a feather in the air!  It can embroider muslin, and forge huge anchors; cut steel into ribbons, and impel loaded vessels against the fury of the wind and waves; and in the shape of a locomotive, or iron horse, it can now be seen daily and hourly dragging after it, on a railroad, hundreds of tons of merchandise and crowds of living freight, in the shape of men or animals, or an army of soldiers with all their munitions of war, at the rate of thirty miles or more an hour.

The locomotive, the most potent and at the same time the most perfectly controllable of all our mechanical agencies, has already been impelled at the flying speed of thirty, forty, and even sixty miles an hour; and if so much has been done already, it would be rash to say or conclude that this is to be its ultimatum. After the results of the last few years, we ask, has it yet reached its limits? No. Only as late as 1837 or '38, twenty-three years ago, the editor of a well-known and popular magazine in New York, the *Knickerbocker*, in noticing in its columns Parker's " Journal of an Exploring Tour beyond the Rocky Mountains," predicted the ultimate building of a railroad to the Pacific. After briefly extracting some of the scenes and interesting objects, together with the adventures described by the explorers, before and after crossing the " Black Hills," he thus writes:

"There would seem to be no insurmountable barrier to the construction of a railroad from the Atlantic to the Pacific. No greater elevations would need to be overcome, than have been surmounted on the Portage and Ohio Railroad. And the work will be accomplished. Let this prediction be marked. This great chain of communication will be made with links of iron. The treasures of the earth in that wide region are not destined to be lost. The mountains of coal, the vast meadow seas, the fields of salt, the mighty forests, with their trees two hundred and fifty feet in height, the stores of magnesia, the crystallized lakes of valuable salts—these were not formed to be unemployed and wasted. The reader is now living who will make a railroad trip across the vast continent.

" The granite mountain will melt before the hand of enterprise; valleys will be raised, and the unwearying fire-steed will spout his hot, white breath where silence has reigned since the morning hymn of young Creation was pealed over mountain, flood, and field. The mammoth's bone and the bison's horn, buried for centuries, and long since turned to stone, will be bared to the day by the laborers of the Atlantic and Pacific Railroad Company; rocks which stand now as on the night when Noah's deluge first dried, will heave beneath the action of ' villanous saltpetre;' and when the prairie stretches away 'like the round ocean,' girded with the sky, with its wood-fringed streams, its flower-enamelled turf, and its herds of startled buffaloes, shall sweep the long, hissing train of cars, crowded with passengers for the Pacific sea-board.   The very realms of Chaos and old Night will be invaded; while in place of the roar of wild beasts, or howl of wild Indians, will be heard the lowing of herds, the bleating of flocks; the plough will cleave the sods of many a rich valley and fruitful hill, while from many a dark bosom shall go up the pure prayer to the Great Spirit."

The foregoing passage was copied at the time of its publication into one or two metropolitan daily journals, and, while its manner was courteously commended, it was pronounced visionary and absurd in its speculations; and yet, ere a dozen years had passed, such were the manifest improvements in railroads and locomotives, that the very ablest and most influential of these journals expressed its convictions that the time was close at hand when the nation would put forth its strength and commence the greatest and most important work ever devised or contemplated by man.   A national railroad, designed to connect the inhabitants on our Atlantic border with our colonists lying on the coast of the Pacific; a national railroad traversing a vast continent, and passing over two thousand miles of wilderness still in the undisputed possession of the red-man, the buffalo, and the bear; a national railroad that shall become the highway of nations for the commerce of the Eastern world, and make New York its great depot; a national railroad, the cost of which will not fall much short of a hundred million dollars, and which will not really cost the nation one dollar, but increase its natural revenues more than five times its cost, by reason of the value it will impart to our public domain—such an enterprise is indeed a project worthy of the age in

which we live.    The subject was soon before the country ;  and our readers will admire with us the eloquence
of Thomas H. Benton, the Missouri Senator, in his
speech before the Pacific Railroad Convention held in
St. Louis:

"We live in extraordinary times, and are called upon to ele-
vate ourselves to the grandeur of the occasion.    Three and a half
centuries ago the great Columbus—the man who was afterward
carried home in chains from the New World which he had discovered—this great Columbus, in the year 1492, departed from
Europe to arrive in the East by going to the West.    It was a sub-
lime conception.    He was in the line of success, when the inter-
vention of two continents, not dreamed of before, arrested his
progress.    Now, in the nineteeth century, mechanical genius
enables the great design to be fulfilled.    In the beginning, and in
barbarous ages, the sea was a barrier to the intercourse of nations :
it separated nations.    Mechanical genius, in inventing the ship,
converted that barrier into a facility.    Then land and continents
became the obstruction.    The two Americas intervening have
prevented Europe and Asia from communicating in the straight
line.    For three centuries and a half this obstacle has frustrated
the grand design of Columbus.    Now, in our day, mechanical
genius has again triumphed over the obstacles of Nature, and converted into a facility that which had so long been an impassable
obstacle.    The steam-car has worked upon the land, and among
enlightened nations, and to a degree far transcending it, the
miracle which the ship, in barbarous ages, worked upon the ocean.
The land has now become the facility for the most distant communications, the conveyance being invented which annihilates both
time and space.    We hold the intervening land ; we hold the obstacle which stopped Columbus ; we are in the line between Europe
and Asia.

"We have it in our power to remove that obstacle, to convert
it into a facility, and to carry him on to his land of promise and
of hope with a rapidity, a precision, and a safety, unknown to all
ocean navigation.    A king and a queen started him upon his great
enterprise ; it lies in the hands of a republic to complete it.    It is
in our hands—we, the people of the United States, of this first half
of the nineteenth century.    Let us rise to the grandeur of the

15

occasion. Let us complete the grand design of Columbus by putting Europe and Asia into communication, and that to our advantage, through the heart of our own country. Let us give to his ships, converted into cars, a continuous course unknown to all former times. Let us make the iron road, and make it from sea to sea; States and individuals making it east of the Mississippi, the nation making it west. Let us now, in this convention, rise above every thing sectional, personal, local; let us beseech the national legislature to build the great road upon the great national line which unites Europe and Asia—the line which will find on our continent the bay of San Francisco at one end, St. Louis in the middle, the national metropolis and great commercial emporiums at the other; and which shall be adorned with its crowning honor, the colossal statue of the great Columbus, whose design it accomplishes, hewn from the granite mass of a peak of the Rocky Mountains, overlooking the road, the mountain itself the pedestal and the statue a part of the mountain, pointing, with outstretched arm, to the western horizon, and saying to the flying passenger, 'There is the East; there is India!' "

This has been consummated; and is it all that is to be? We answer, No! Almost every daily revolution of the earth upon its axis develops some new idea, some improvement upon what has already been accomplished in bringing the railroad and its auxiliary, the locomotive, nearer and nearer to a state of perfection. Within the last few years the construction of the narrow gauge has, as we may almost say, been conceived and sprung into existence, and, from experiments made, it has been demonstrated to a certainty to possess all the advantages that could have been conceived, even exceeding the most sanguine expectations of its projectors, and deciding its ultimate success.

The future improvement in the locomotive, when fully consummated, before another half century shall pass away, will confer upon man nearly as much new power and new enjoyment as if he were actually endowed with wings.

SCHENECTADY LOCOMOTIVE WORKS.

The locomotive is truly the king of machines and a permanent realization of the genii of the Eastern fable, whose supernatural powers were at the command of man. When the next fifty years have rolled around, how little will men think of what we now call distance! The term will be obsolete in our vocabulary, and become entirely forgotten.

## CHAPTER XLI.

### LOCOMOTIVE-WORKS.

WHEN we contemplate the progress made in loco-motives within the last forty years, how forcibly comes to our mind the old but often the very truthful saying, "From small beginnings great results sometimes turn out!"

Let us look back to the year 1830, to Mr. Peter Cooper's experimental locomotive, the "Tom Thumb," and in the same year to Colonel Miller's contract to construct, for the South Carolina Railroad, a locomotive to perform at the rate of ten miles an hour, and draw fifteen tons' weight. This required, for construction, several months at the West Point Foundery Works. None of the beautiful machinery of the present day, for every department of mechanical labor, was then dreamed of, and the only tools at command were the rasp, the anvil, and sledge. Compare that work with the magnificent system which characterizes the locomotive works of the present day. Compare that with what we witnessed a few days ago in a visit and examination of one of the principal works devoted to the manufacture of that powerful machine. We allude to the locomotive-works in the ancient city of Schenectady, with a representation of which we present our readers. Schenectady is one of the oldest cities in the State of New York, and one of the points of termination of the first railroad ever built in the State—that very same road over which the first passenger train drawn by a locomotive in the State was run in 1831, which event we have fully described in a former chapter, and Schenectady can now point with pride to having in its limits one of the largest and most perfect works for the construction of the locomotive to be found in America or in the world.

How few individuals who journey thousands of miles upon a railroad ever give a passing thought to the origin and history of that most powerful machine by which they are spirited along, as it were, annihilating both time and distance! We are often surprised at the want of interest displayed by them in the contemplation of the iron horse, if we may so call it, who draws them along as on the wings of the wind to their destination. We, ourselves, always like to stare at the giant locomotive. For us it possesses any amount of school-boy fascination. If we, when travelling, have a few moments to spare at the depot, we are sure to find ourselves strolling in the direction of the engine and contemplating, in silent admiration and wonder, its immense size, its strength, and its marvellous power and construction. We look back and think of the old-fashioned four-horse coach of former times, and contrast the sound of the tin horn with the steam-whistle, the old chain skid with the Creamer brake; the compliments of the passengers to the heavy-coated coachman on his making twelve miles an hour, and the coolness with which we now travel thirty, thirty-five, and even fifty miles an hour with the locomotive. Our forefathers did not believe at first in the locomotive. The wise men of fifty years ago regarded railroads by steam beyond the reach of practical science. We gave our readers in a former portion of our work Chancellor Livingston's letter to Colonel Stevens, of Hoboken, as a specimen of public opinion of that time. What would Chancellor Livingston say now about the locomotive crossing the American Continent on its railroad in six days and a half, when he doubted Stevens's project of loads of five tons carried on proposed railroads at five miles an hour! What would the chancellor say now to our present freight-engines, weighing, as they frequently do, over forty tons each, and drawing a train of a hundred cars, each with a load of eight tons of merchandise, in all one thousand tons; and what would he say, if now alive, and he were to be told that the Schenectady Locomotive Works here in his own State, and the works we visited a few days ago, turned out one of such engines every three days throughout the year! These locomotives, too, are not like the playthings of forty years ago—Peter Cooper's Tom Thumb, for instance, which we have described in a former chapter, which, on August 28, 1830, performed the astonishing feat of outrunning a horse-car on the Baltimore & Ohio Railroad, in a contest for the trial of speed; or the first locomotive built for actual service on a railroad in America, The Best Friend, of Charleston, the contract for which was that it should run ten miles an hour and draw three times its weight, and from the president's report after its trials, that "it had exceeded their most sanguine expectations, drawing fifty passengers at fifteen miles an hour on the straight and level parts of their road." Not such locomotives as these, but we alluded to the first-class locomotives of the present day. Schenectady can point with pride to her locomotive-works, established now over twenty-one years. These works are situated about a quarter of a mile from the depot, between the Central and Saratoga Railroad tracks.

The building devoted to the machine and erecting shops is of two stories, most substantially built, and is 350 feet long by 80 wide. The machine-shops are perfectly bewildering. Looking down their length, the various machines used for the work look like groves of trees, from which all the branches have been cut, leaving only the trunks. Here in the two shops is a respectable list of these machines, and it must be borne in mind that each and every one of them is most elaborate and costly. Sixty turning-lathes. A turning-lathe for iron with its cold chisel gives a forcible expression of the scriptural idea, "iron entering the soul." It grinds its sharp edge mercilessly into the metal, and turns out shavings too hot to handle. There are fifty iron planes, thirty drill-presses, fifteen bolt-cutters, seven slotting and five shearing machines, and all these of the newest and most approved patents. In the erecting shops we saw the locomotive in every stage of construction, from the boiler-sheet until its name has been painted on the tender, before it starts out on its rushing journey through locomotive life. When we visited these works on our tour of investigation a few weeks since, we saw eleven locomotives in course of erection, besides several in the repair and painting shops, and two ready to go out. About sixty days are occupied in building an engine from the time the flat iron plates go into the boiler-shops until the entire machine is completed in all its various parts and ready for firing up in active service. An engine varies in weight from 40,000 to 80,000 pounds, and, if it be a large one, with its tender will not weigh less than 125,000 pounds. The weight of a single driving-wheel is 1,800 pounds, and the machine will cost from $10,000 to $18,000.

The progress of engine-building may, to a certain extent, be judged of from their progressive cost. Of the cost of the earlier locomotives it would be idle to

make a comparison; but thirty years ago the building of locomotives had come to years of discretion, though far from maturity. In 1842 the average cost of a locomotive was $6,500; in 1852, $7,500; in 1862, $8,500, and in 1872, about $11,500. An engine, with fair wear and tear, will last ten or eleven years.

There are some interesting points with regard to the construction of engines at the Schenectady works. The framework of the tenders is all made of iron, which, in addition to giving greatly increased strength, considerably decreases the weight of the tender; the wooden beams, formerly in use, requiring to be very massive and cumbrous in order to stand the jar and strain on them.  Some of the drills are marvellous; we saw on our visit steam-drills drilling the great cast-steel plates, through which all the boiler flues open into the furnace.  The plates are half an inch in thickness, and the holes two and one-sixteenth inches in diameter.  But this operation of drilling so large a hole in solid cast-steel (it is done in less than five minutes) must be seen to be fully appreciated.  In the blacksmith's shop it is most interesting to watch the forging together of the huge iron beams which form the pedestals of the engine; not the least astonishing part of it, the precision with which the smiths wield their ponderous sledge-hammers, often weighing twenty-nine or thirty pounds, and strike the exact spot pointed out to them by the foreman.

In the boiler-shop there is a new and most powerful machine for riveting the seams of the boiler.  The old method was for a man inside the boiler to pass a red-hot bolt with one hand through the punched holes, and for two men to pound the protruding part into an outside head with hammers.  The new method is carried out by machinery.  The boiler is hoisted, end upward, over a side anvil, in which is a die fitting the existing head of the red-hot bolt.  When the man inside the boiler has put the bolt through the hole, he turns the boiler so that the bolt-head fits into the die. A powerful steam hammer, with a corresponding die, is driven with immense force against the outside end of the bolt, in a moment pressing it into shape.  This has the additional advantage of pressing the two plates tightly together, at the very moment the second bolt-head on the outside is formed.

Besides the erecting and machine shops, there are the blacksmith-shop, 225 by 70 feet; boiler-shop, 150 by 95 feet; iron and brass founderies, pattern and carpenter shops. There is also a building where there are "stalls" for ten engines. We suppose the iron horse is entitled to its stall the same as any other horse. Increased facilities for engine-building have lately been introduced into the works, and it is anticipated that the works will turn out at least 120 locomotives during the current year. As it is, the company keep constantly employed from 700 to 800 men, and have supplied engines to and have orders now from every section of the United States and South America.

In the brief space allotted to us in our present work, we are unable to describe and follow out more fully the great facilities brought into successful use by this company in the construction of the locomotive, this wonderful invention of the present century. A week could be pleasantly and profitably occupied in a ramble through the various departments of these extensive works, and a quire of paper would be needed to chronicle all that would be seen to interest and instruct.

These works furnish with promptness and dispatch the best and most improved coal and wood burning locomotives, and all railroad machinery, tires, etc., etc., and also do repairs and rebuild locomotives; and their works, being located on the New York Central Railroad, near the centre of the State, possess superior facilities for forwarding their work to any part of the country. John C. Ellis is president, Walter McQueen is superintendent, and Charles G. Ellis is treasurer.

# CHAPTER XLII.

## CAR-WORKS.

Following close upon the footsteps of the locomotive in its progress toward that perfection it has attained at the present day, comes that necessary appendage in all the various uses to which it is applied, from the plain and substantial freight-car, capable of transporting with ease and safety its tons of valuable merchandise, the products of the industry of the millions of our people, up to the magnificent passenger palace-cars of the present day, vying with each other in every thing that could contribute to the pleasures and comfort of the travelling occupant. The introduction of the railroad and its concomitants has developed and given employment to thousands in those branches of mechanical industry unknown and not dreamed of half a century gone by. In one particular we allude to the extensive railroad-car works of the present day. Most prominent among these branches of industry and enterprise stand the complete and well-appointed carworks of Messrs. Gilbert, Bush & Co., at Troy, New York.

Being in Troy a few weeks since, the author paid a visit of observation to these extensive works, and, with a friend, well posted in the ramifications of the establishment, as a guide, made a minute examination of every department of the extensive and well-arranged premises, from which we gather the following facts :

The Green Island Car Works, as they are familiarly known, being situated on that island between East and West Troy, date their origin from the early history of

TROY CAR-WORKS, GILBERT, BUSH & CO.

manufacturing in this section. About sixty years ago an unpretending manufactory for building carriages and stages was started on Sixth Street, in Troy, on the present site of the Union Depot. In a very few years this manufactory became extensively known to the different stage companies throughout the country, as one of the most reliable existing sources of supply for the vehicles which formed an important part of their equipments for facilitating travel. The term "Troy stages" became a synonyme for strength, elegance, and durability, and the work of the concern was to be found running in all parts of the nation—even in the extreme Southern States. In the early beginning of the street-car introduction into our principal cities, that new branch of business was added to the stage and carriage works, Sixth Street, the firm of Eaton & Gilbert furnishing the new instrument of conveyance used in the city of Boston for many years after their introduction, and nearly monopolized the patronage of the leading lines in New York City.

In February, 1853, the erection of the Green Island car-shops was commenced; but previous to this the firm of Eaton & Gilbert had become thoroughly identified with the inauguration and progress of steam railroading in this country.

One of the senior members of the present firm of Gilbert, Bush & Co. assisted Mr. James Goold in the construction of the pioneer train of cars, the primitive apparatus that had the honor of conveying, with others, the renowned Thurlow Weed over the Mohawk & Hudson Railroad, on the occasion of the memorable experimental trip between Albany and Schenectady, a sketch of which locomotive, cars, and passengers was made upon the spot at the time by the author of this history, and afterward presented to the Connecticut Historical Society, at Hartford.

At the time Eaton & Gilbert transferred their base of operations from Troy to Green Island, the latter place was comparatively little better off as regards population than the legendary habitation of one Robinson Crusoe is reported to have been. But the erection of the Green Island car-shops inaugurated a new era. The employés of the company required homes convenient to the scene of their labors, and building improvements became the order of the day; and at present it is safe to assert that Green Island is one of the most flourishing suburbs of the city of Troy, a result largely due to the fact that the Green Island Car Works have there established "a local habitation and a name."

In August, 1864, the car-works were almost entirely destroyed by fire; but the proprietors, nothing daunted by the calamity, immediately proceeded to rebuild the establishment upon a new and improved plan. It now covers an area of ground measuring over eight acres, and is one of the most complete manufactories the author has ever seen, and he has seen many in his day throughout the country.

The facilities for transportation and for the receipt of the immense quantities of coal, iron, and lumber used, are unsurpassed. A dock frontage of six hundred feet on the Mohawk Basin furnishes easy communication with the Hudson River and Erie Canal. The Rensselaer & Saratoga Railroad, running close to the works, supplies accommodations for running cars on their own wheels to all parts of the United States and the Canadas accessible by rail.

The reputation of this firm for manufacturing su-

perior work is not confined to the United States or
Canada, but has long since penetrated into South
America, Mexico, and other distant countries. In the
early days of steam railroading in South America,
English manufacturers nearly monopolized the patronage in this line of that country; but, since that time,
foreign competition has been placed at defiance by
Gilbert, Bush & Co., and now the arrival of an English
car is a rarity in the southern portion of our hemisphere.

In passing through the works a few weeks since,
our attention was attracted to a very peculiar style of
car, intended for shipment to Chili. Although in some
respects similar to our regular passenger-car, this is
furnished with state-rooms like those of a drawing-
room car. It is elaborately finished in mahogany, and
presents a handsome appearance.

The cars intended to be shipped to distant parts,
unlike those used in this region, are made in sections,
for the purpose of allowing them to be packed in a
very small compass for transportation. We saw on
our visit, ready for shipment, the sides, ends, tops, and
floors, of fifteen cars all packed in less space than one
car would occupy when put together. Each of these
cars, preparatory to shipment, is put together in the
works. Each hole and mortice is made according to
standard scales, so that, in case of the loss of any part
of the car in the process of transportation, a duplicate
can be immediately forwarded, on application of the
purchaser. Each piece, as well as the boxes, containing the small iron-work, such as screws, bolts, etc., is
numbered and registered at the office. As many as
forty cars have been shipped in an ordinary canal
freight-barge, and on arriving at New York the con-

tents of these barges are transferred to ships bound for such countries as Mexico and South America. The cars from this concern are extensively ordered from Chili and Peru, and no car-factory in the world is better known to projectors of railroads in South America than that of Gilbert, Bush & Co.

There is a wonderful difference between the first steam-cars in early times and the rolling palaces now turned out by this establishment. They are continually turning out for Mr. Wagner the finest sleeping-cars ever run upon a road, with all the approved novelties yet developed, and vast improvements upon the first sleeping-cars. To be " rocked in the cradle of the deep " is all very nice, and extremely poetic; but the idea of seeking "tired Nature's sweet restorer" through that lulling influence, the gentle motion of a palatial, comfortable Wagner sleeping-car, as it skims along like a streak of lightning on wheels, suits much better, in these days of fast travelling, the practical fancy of your American business-man. The construction of sleeping-cars forms a prominent feature in the operations of Gilbert, Bush & Co.; but all other vehicles are manufactured by them. They make all sizes, to suit the different gauges, and their prices range from $500 to $18,000 per car. The immense buildings of the concern are substantial two-story brick structures. If placed end to end, these would reach a distance of over two miles. The railroad-tracks connecting the different buildings have turn-tables for handling the cars as they progress toward completion, and will aggregate one mile in length. When necessary, the firm find room for manufacturing eighty cars at a time. All the iron used is either cast in the foundery of the firm or forged in their own blacksmith-shop.

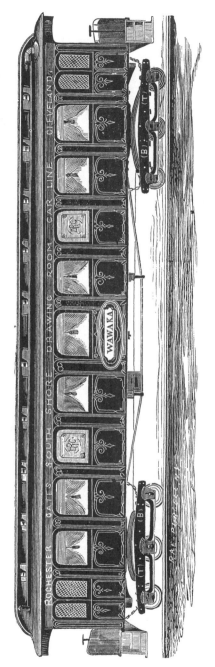

DRAWING-ROOM CAR, MANUFACTURED BY GILBERT, BUSH & CO.

The multifarious mechanical operations of the concern are particularly suggestive. Here are different departments for cabinet-makers, wood-workers, moulders, blacksmiths, machinists, plumbers, silver-platers, upholsterers, painters, lantern-makers — ten distinct kinds of business, and each department larger than many a respectable manufactory in the country.

Among the patrons of this firm are numbered a large majority of the most substantial railroad companies in the United States—those who prefer to pay and are able to pay a fair price for a first-class car. One secret of the reputation of the firm is, that no inferior or careless workmen are ever retained in their employ.

The force of hands employed ranges from 350 to 400. Of iron, over 3,600 tons are yearly worked up; and of lumber, 2,500,000 feet. Only the most perfectly seasoned lumber is allowed to enter into the composition of the cars. They use extensively black walnut, Georgia pine, white-wood, oak, and many other costly varieties of lumber. One of the equipments of their thoroughly appointed lumber-yard is worthy of notice. It is used for drying the lumber by steam, and consists of an immense horizontal cylinder of iron. The lumber submitted to the action of this apparatus becomes as dry in fifteen minutes as if exposed to the open air for two or three years.

The firm of Gilbert, Bush & Co. consists of Uri Gilbert, Walter R. Bush, Wm. E. Gilbert, Walter R. Bush, Jr., and Edward G. Gilbert. Mr. Uri Gilbert, the senior partner, has been connected with the concern for over fifty years. He has seen American steam railroading grow up from a mere experiment to its present wonderful proportions, and has also enjoyed the gratification of knowing that the establishment of which he is the head was keeping pace with that marvellous growth.

———————•◦•———————

# CHAPTER XLIII.

### STREET-CAR WORKS.

The facility presented for the transportation of passengers from one city to another by the introduction of this great achievement of the present half-century, the railroad, became so soon apparent that from its earliest beginnings, and even before it had emerged from its infancy or attained its present stage of perfection, the public became clamorous for its introduction into the streets and thoroughfares of our principal cities. They soon became dissatisfied with the old-fashioned stage and omnibus and all the other primitive means of conveyance, such as our forefathers indulged in, and regarded as luxuries in transportation. These (to the present generation) were considered as too far behind the times, and should be immediately dispensed with, to make way for the railroad and street cars. This change was soon accomplished. The experiment was tried, and has now become an indispensable necessity. When we now experience how comparatively close together the most distant parts of our extensive cities are brought by this great instrumentality, the railroad and street car, the wonder is how our forefathers were content so long without them. Forty or fifty passengers sometimes ride upon a single car, when heretofore a dozen was the ultimatum of an omnibus or old-fashioned lumbering stage-coach, the only means of cheap transportation from place to place throughout our cities.

The first charter for what are termed city passenger or horse railroads was obtained in the city of New York and known as the New York & Harlem, and this was the first road of the kind ever constructed, and was opened in 1832. A portion of it within the city limits, that portion below Twenty-seventh Street in the city of New York, was always worked by horse-power. No other road of the kind was completed till 1852, when the Sixth Avenue was opened to the public. This was followed in 1853 by the Second and Third Avenues, in 1854 by the Eighth, and in 1859 by the Ninth Avenue.

The success of these roads is a remarkable illustration of their adaptedness to the wants of large cities,

and they have since been adopted and introduced in every city of any size in the United States, and, indeed, throughout the civilized world.

The saving effected by city passenger roads over the cost of transportation of passengers in cities in coaches and omnibus is as great as that effected by the railroad over the ordinary highway.

The first passenger-car for street railroad purposes was built by Mr. John Stephenson, the senior partner of the now extensive and enterprising firm of John Ste-

16

phenson & Co., organized in 1867, and located at No. 47 Twenty-seventh Street, New York. This first street-car was named, in compliment to the president of the company, the "John Mason." To Mr. Stephenson we are indebted for the beautiful cut representing this pioneer in street railroad cars. The driver of this car was a well-known knight of the whip, Lank O'Dell, who always drove a pair of gray horses.

The first trial or experimental trip was a most important affair in New York. The road commenced about Prince Street and the Bowery, and extended to Harlem Bridge. On this occasion the streets along the route were crowded with spectators. Two cars were ready for the occasion, Lank and his grays taking the lead with the beautiful pioneer, John Mason, and occupied by the mayor and members of the City Council; while the second car, driven by a hackman (his name not now remembered), and filled with some of the city officials and invited guests, brought up the rear.

Great apprehensions were expressed by some of the passengers and many of the spectators that the trouble would be in bringing these cars to a stand-still at any desired point to avoid any accident that might occur in the crowded thoroughfares of the city.

An old citizen, who witnessed this first experiment trip, related an incident that occurred on the occasion, which, though it resulted in nothing serious or fatal in its consequences, must have been ludicrous in the extreme. The vice-president of the road, Mr. John Lozier, being very desirous of removing all apprehensions from the minds of the doubtful, and anxious to exhibit the great facility with which the cars could be brought to a dead halt in an instant when running at full speed, and all danger of collision with vehicles in the street rendered impossible, determined on an experiment.

He posted O'Dell and the hack-driver of the second car to watch him, and look out for the signal, and, inviting a number of the spectators to witness the ex-

periment, he placed himself somewhere about the corner of the Bowery and Bond Street. As the first car approached, he raised his arm and gave the signal to stop.   O'Dell, who, with his grays, had some previous practice, while hauling materials in the construction of the road, performed to the admiration of the specta-tors, and had just come to a halt, when the second car approached rapidly.   The vice-president gave the sig-nal to stop; but the hackman, unpractised in the duty, forgot the lever, but drew hard his lines, and shouted " Whoa!" but too late—the tongue of his car went crash-ing through the rear of the John Mason, and the mayor and City Council beat a retreat in double-quick time and in disorder from the dilapidated car, amid the

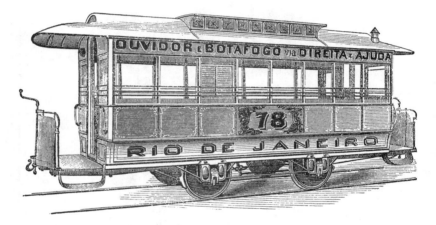

laughter of the surrounding spectators.   The danger over, and nobody hurt, the excursionists resumed their seats and the cavalcade proceeded on the way toward Harlem Bridge, where it arrived without any other accident, in an incredibly short time.

  This is the first street-car collision on record, and was the subject of amusement to the citizens for several weeks, and a source of great annoyance to the vice-president, especially when some wag among his ac-quaintance, on seeing him afterward approaching in the street, would assume his position, and personate his action by giving the signal for him to stop.

No just appreciation can be formed of the extent of these car-works without a personal visit through every department. The author called at the establishment a few days ago, and his attention was arrested immediately on entering the great gate-way, by seeing a huge packing-box being elevated upon a strong truck drawn by a powerful team of horses and ready for its transit to some one of the shipping-points of the river. On looking at the address, the author was surprised to find its destination Montevideo, South America. On alluding to the subject, to one of the clerks of the establishment, the author was shown the order-book, and there saw orders for street-cars of all imaginable patterns destined for Buenos Ayres, Rio de Janeiro, Valparaiso, Santiago, Pisco, Maranham, Para, Porto Alegre, Montevideo, Concordia, Rosario, Guayaquil, London, Liverpool, Birkenhead, Leeds, Glasgow, Lisbon, Brussels, Copenhagen, Vienna, Java, and the last order and work in hand on our visit destined for Bombay; and all this accomplished so quietly, and with such systematic regularity in every department, that no one could believe that over three hundred mechanics were daily employed in the works.

We give our readers a sketch of one of the numerous car-patterns for the South American market.

The latest improvement, and one which is rapidly coming into use, is the one-horse street-car manufactured by this company. The great economy in this car has become so apparent that since its introduction, only a dozen years since, over three hundred and fifty railroads have had them built and forwarded by this company. We give below a cut of one of these useful vehicles, which will strike the eye at once by its utility and fitness for a particular service, where the large two-horse car would be burdensome and expensive.

The manufacture of the omnibus is another branch of this extensive establishment. The greatest variety and the most beautiful specimens of that useful vehicle the "omnibus" are daily turned out from their premises. Orders for every variety of street-cars are continually coming in, and it is wonderful with what facility and promptness they are executed and forwarded to every quarter of the globe. We sincerely regret that our limits here will not permit us to extend our description further in speaking of all we saw and learned

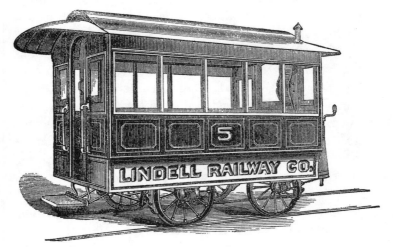

on our visits to the establishment. The courteous and gentlemanly deportment exhibited toward visitors renders the occasion both pleasant and instructive.

GRAND CENTRAL DEPOT, NEW YORK.

# CHAPTER XLIV.

## GRAND CENTRAL DEPOT, NEW YORK.

Within the last quarter of a century, while improvements have been marching on with giant strides in every department of the railroad and its concomitants, by bringing nearer and nearer to perfection that powerful and indispensable auxiliary the locomotive and its train of cars, there has been a march of advancement onward in the costly and splendid depots to be seen in every section of our wide-extended domain, vying with each other in all the conveniences and facilities which contribute so much to the comfort of the vast crowds assembled by day and night awaiting the hours of arrival and departure of the numerous trains. Prominent among these magnificent edifices stands the Grand Central Depot, in the city of New York. To Commodore Vanderbilt, its founder and builder, we are indebted for the accompanying engraving representing that noble structure, and to the *New-York Herald* for the following full description of all its various departments and their uses. In describing this beautiful and massive specimen of architecture, the *Herald* justly says:

"The Grand Central Depot of New York eclipses any thing of the kind that the world has ever seen.

"The Grand Central Depot is located fronting on East Forty-second Street. It is designed for the permanent use of the Harlem, New York & New Haven and the New York Central & Hudson River Railroads.

"This vast edifice covers nearly five acres within its

walls. The size of the roof, the intricate gorgeousness of the richly-worked trusswork, the brilliant effect of the two acres of glass set in the iron sashes of the roof, and the thousand other details combined, put the structure on a level, for vastness and grandeur, with any Old-World cathedral. In this depot, which is five feet longer and many feet wider than the Great Midland Depot in London, the most perfect system yet seen in America will be perfected under the care of depot-masters, who will have charge of all the details of passenger transportation and all terminus-work. Every improvement that the human mind could suggest, and that could be procured by the lavish outlay of money, has been made available in the new Union Depot.

"The building covers the area from Forty-second Street to Forty-fifth Street, and from Fourth Avenue to a new street intervening between the depot and Madison Avenue.

"In it there are about one hundred rooms for different purposes, all of which are handsomely fitted up and heated by steam, with gas and water. Each of the rooms contains from 35 to 112 feet of vertical tube-heating radiators. The offices are fitted up with black-walnut, oak, and ash wood-work, and upholstered furniture. The depot contains ladies' and gentlemen's restaurants and dining-rooms, in which food of the best quality is served in a style as good as at Delmonico's. The floors below the sidewalk have a number of stores, which are rented out, with first-class barber-shops and hair-dressing saloons, bath-rooms, bar and lunch rooms, restaurants for ladies, toilets for ladies and gentlemen, and every accommodation for the thousands of people who get off trains while waiting for transmission to other roads, or while waiting to leave the city by any of the three roads above named.

"There are also large waiting and drawing rooms fitted up in the best fashion. The New York & New Haven Railroad Company have their offices on the Forty-second Street or south front of the building. The New York & Harlem Railroad Company have their offices on the west side of the building fronting on the new street, which is 60 feet in width.

"These last offices, which extend 200 feet north from Forty-second Street, and 495 feet of the north end of the building, are devoted to the offices of the New York Central Railroad and the Hudson River division of the Central road. Part of this end is used as a baggage department for the Central Railroad.

"The car-house proper, into which all the trains run and from which they all depart, 102 trains a day in number, is 650 feet long by 200 feet wide. It is brilliantly lighted by twenty-four immense sunlights hanging from the ceiling, all of which are lighted by electricity. The roof of the structure is supported by sixty-two heavy wrought-iron trusses, that add not only to the solidity, but also to the beauty of the interior of the depot. No mortar is used in the building, which is entirely fire-proof, constructed of iron, glass, granite, and brick; cement and concrete are used instead of mortar. There are two acres of glass in the roof alone. The building is three stories high above the ground, making four stories with the basement, and cost about three million dollars. The exterior view is one of great beauty, the material being red brick with iron trimmings, painted white to give them the appearance of marble. The structure is topped off by four small towers, and one larger tower on the Forty-second Street front that can be seen down Fourth Avenue as far as Union Square, rising up gradually above the pile of iron, granite, and brick, that supports it. All the employés of the four roads are uniformed, and every thing done that would perfect the system as far as possible.

"At this magnificent depot, unlike almost every stopping-place or public landing, passengers are not annoyed by the impetuous importunities of porters, cab, hack, or omnibus drivers. The most perfect system in this department is observed. A strong body of police, detailed expressly for this depot, are always at their post day and night. No Jehu is permitted to quit his seat, but, as soon as the passenger, escorted by the police, selects the coach, the driver is compelled to hand his card, with the number. This card the passenger will hand to the porter of the company, who transports the luggage from the baggage-room free of charge. The most perfect system is to be seen in every department. This edifice is a monument of Commodore Vanderbilt's wealth, and a building in which all New-Yorkers take pride."

# NATIONAL WIRE AND LANTERN WORKS,

*Warehouse, 45 Fulton Street, New York.*

## HOWARD & MORSE,

MANUFACTURERS OF

# BRASS, COPPER, AND IRON WIRE CLOTH,

RIDDLES, SIEVES, COAL AND SAND SCREENS,

IRON and STEEL Locomotive

## SPARK WIRE CLOTH,

Plain and Ornamental Wire Work,

### WIRE FENCE & RAILING,

DOOR AND WINDOW

# GUARDS.

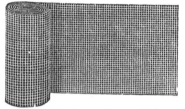

Wire Cloth, partly unrolled.

Roof Crestings.

ALSO,

Ship and Railroad

ADJUSTABLE GLOBE

# LANTERNS.

Star Lantern.

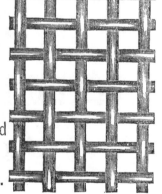

No. 3, Mesh, No. 10½ Wire.

Bank and Counter Railing, No. 12.

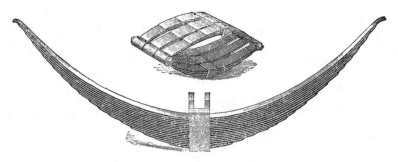

T. S. RAY.                                                                C. A. MARVIN.

# BUFFALO STEAM GAUGE COMPANY,

MANUFACTURERS OF THE

## BUFFALO PRESSURE AND VACUUM GAUGES,

LOCOMOTIVE HEAD LIGHTS, TAIL LAMPS,

# REVOLVING SIGNALS,

**PORTER HAND LAMPS,**

TARGET AND GAUGE LAMPS, ETC.

*DEALERS IN*

# HEAD-LIGHT GLASS AND CHIMNEYS.

Manufactory and Office, corner Washington and Perry Streets,

## BUFFALO, N. Y.

*Reflectors Replated, Gauges of all Kinds and Locomotive Balances Repaired at Short Notice.*

Screw the Cup on the top of the Steam Chest or on the Steam Pipe
Fill it with Oil or melted Tallow up to the side hole of the inside tube, then open the
ready for use.

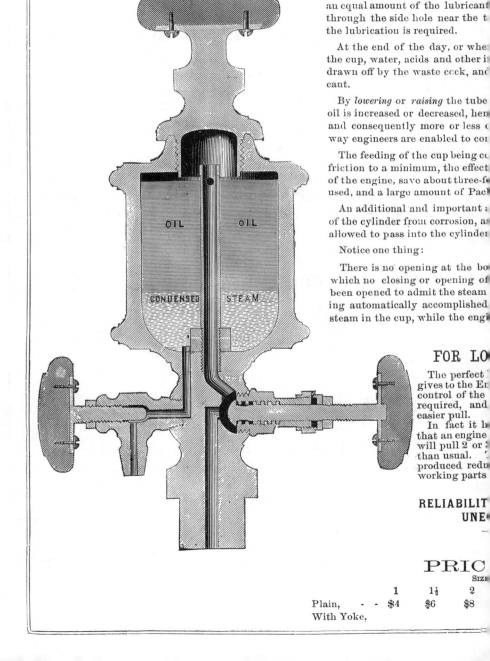

While the engine is in motio
to the upper part of the Cup wl
produced, being heavier than th
an equal amount of the lubricant
through the side hole near the t
the lubrication is required.

At the end of the day, or whe
the cup, water, acids and other i
drawn off by the waste cock, and
cant.

By *lowering* or *raising* the tube
oil is increased or decreased, her
and consequently more or less c
way engineers are enabled to con

The feeding of the cup being cc
friction to a minimum, the effect
of the engine, save about three-fc
used, and a large amount of Pacl

An additional and important a
of the cylinder from corrosion, as
allowed to pass into the cylinder

Notice one thing:

There is no opening at the bo
which no closing or opening of
been opened to admit the steam
ing automatically accomplished
steam in the cup, while the engi

## FOR LO

The perfect
gives to the En
control of the
required, and
easier pull.

In fact it b
that an engine
will pull 2 or
than usual.
produced redu
working parts

### RELIABILIT
### UNE

## PRIC
Si

| | 1 | 1½ | 2 |
|---|---|---|---|
| Plain, - - | $4 | $6 | $8 |
| With Yoke, | | | |

**FOR USE.**

bout one quarter and it is

team passes up the Tube
ondenses, and the water so
ks to the bottom and lifts
top, causing it to overflow
e Tube to the parts where

l or tallow is exhausted in
es remain, which should be
p be refilled with the lubri-

ndensing space above the
e or less water is produced,
d to the cylinder. In this
e feeding of the cup.

and regular reduces internal
ch is to improve the power
f the oil or tallow generally

ge gained is the prevention
nd other impurities are not

the cup, in consequence of
lve is required, after it has
up the tube, the feeding be-
condensing action of the
motion.

**TIVES.**

ion obtained
n immediate
valve when
command an

ascertained
d with them
reight) more
action thus
wear of the
nsiderable.

**ECONOMY**
**ED I**

**LIST.**

| | 3 | 4 | 5 | 6 | 7 |
|---|---|---|---|---|---|
| | $12 | $16 | | | |
| | $20 | $27 | $36 | $45 | $60 |

# Dreyfus' Patent Locomotive Cups.

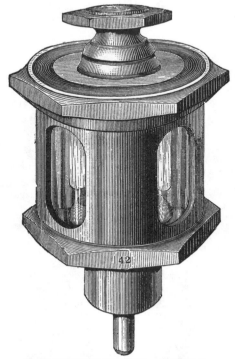

## LOCOMOTIVE CUPS.
### Design Patented March 30, 1869.

Are shell-cased, made very ornamental, constantly exposing the oil to view, and are generally considered the best ever used.

|  | | CAPACITY. | DIAMETER. | HEIGHT. | PRICE PER DOZ. |
|---|---|---|---|---|---|
| No. 28—Shell Case, for small connections, . | | $\frac{1}{4}$ oz. | 1$\frac{1}{2}$ in. | 2$\frac{1}{2}$ in. | $36 00 |
| " 36— " Eccentrics, . . . | 1 " | 2 " | 3$\frac{1}{2}$ " | | 48 00 |
| " 42— " Connecting Rods, . | 1$\frac{1}{4}$ " | 2 " | 4 " | | 48 00 |
| " 42— " Guides with Steel Spindle and Spring, . . . . . . | 1$\frac{1}{4}$ " | 2 " | 4 " | | 48 00 |
| No. 43—Shell Case, Regulators with Valve and Set Screw, to feed as required, . | 1$\frac{1}{4}$ " | 2 " | 4 " | | 56 00 |

The rod Cups will run from fifteen to eighteen hundred miles with one filling, and the Guide Cups seven hundred miles with one filling.

[For Locomotive Guides, without Regulating Valve.]

Permit the spindle to extend below the Guide far enough to allow the Cross-Head to strike it, and round the end so that the Cross-Head will strike it in the centre.

After properly adjusting the Guide Spindle (as above directed), have them taken out and hardened to a degree that will prevent them from wearing.